CONGREGATIONAL MISSIONS
AND THE MAKING
OF AN IMPERIAL CULTURE
IN NINETEENTH-CENTURY
ENGLAND

Acknowledgments

I have accumulated an enormous debt during the very long time it has taken me to finish this book, and I will begin by apologizing to anyone I neglect to mention among the many friends and colleagues who have helped me along the way. I want first to thank the teachers—especially Carl Pletsch, Lee Schlesinger, Joan Scott, Beverly Grier, Nell Painter, and Thomas Reefe—who guided me to and through the beginnings of this project during my undergraduate sojourn at the University of North Carolina. The enthusiastic and respectful manner in which they responded to my naive and undereducated efforts to grapple with the past taught me to value what I had to say enough to imagine that I could be a historian too. I found at the University of Michigan the ideal faculty ensemble with whom to pursue my developing interests in the intersection of race, class, and empire. For their extraordinary intellectual insight and many personal kindnesses, I want to thank Frederick Cooper, Thomas Holt, Jacob Price, Ann Stoler, Louise Tilly, and especially Geoff Eley. Geoff Eley's warmth, good humor, and keen intellect made him the perfect supervisor. I was also extremely fortunate in my graduate student cohort. For their inspiration, encouragement, and friendship I thank Rich Bodek, Joel Harrington, Young-Sun Hong, Sue Juster, Kären Mason, David Mayfield, Becky Reed, Matt Shaeffer, and Elizabeth Wood.

While in England, I benefited enormously from the helpful advice and friendly hospitality of Kelly King Boyd, P. J. Corfield, Anna Davin, David

Feldman, Rohan McWilliam, Clare Midgley, John Seed, John Styles, Amanda Vickery, and Julie Wheelwright. Since leaving graduate school, I have also been fortunate in good colleagues, both at Worcester Polytechnic Institute and at Duke University. I offer special thanks to the senior women in Worcester and the Triangle, whose thoughtful overtures both large and small have done so much to smooth my way. I would particularly like to mention Judith Bennett, Jan Ewald, Jacquelyn Hall, Cynthia Herrup, Nancy Hewitt, Claudia Koonz, Joanne Manfra, Kristen Neuschel, and Ruth Smith. I hope that my generation will be as generous with our privilege. I could not have survived without the comradely encouragement of those who shared the trenches of junior facultydom with me, especially Joel Bratton, Catherine Peyroux, Julius Scott, Jennifer Thorn, and Kären Wigen. I want also to acknowledge the inspiring example of politically engaged and intellectually rigorous scholarship set by the graduate students alongside whom I've worked at Duke. My admiring best wishes go to Michael McQuarrie, who helped me learn from my many mistakes.

I could not have completed this project without the generous financial support of the Social Science Research Council, the Woodrow Wilson Fellowship Foundation, the American Council of Learned Societies, the University of Michigan, and Duke University. Nor could I have found my way to many of the sources consulted without the expert guidance of many helpful librarians and archivists at the Harlan Hatcher Library at the University of Michigan, the Perkins Library and the Divinity School Library at Duke University, the Divinity School Library at Yale University, Dr. Williams's Library, the Library at the School for Oriental and African Studies, the British Library, Colindale Newspaper Library, the Greater London Record Office, the Cornwall Record Office, the Leicestershire Record Office, the Leeds Archives Department, the West Yorkshire Archive Service, Bradford Central Library, Leeds Central Library, the East Sussex Record Office, and the Essex Record Office.

The suggestions and concerns raised by seminar and conference audiences have been extremely useful to me. I want to thank Jacquelyn Hall for inviting me to speak to the Feminist Women in History Group in Chapel Hill; Richard Price for the opportunity to address the British Studies seminar at the University of Maryland; Rachel Weill for the opportunity to address the European History seminar at Cornell University; David Feldman, Peter Mandler, and Martin Daunton for the opportunity to address the Social History Seminar at the Institute of Historical Research at the University of London; and Hugh McLeod for the opportunity to participate in the Decline of Christendom Colloquium sponsored by the Missiology of Western Culture.

My greatest debt is to all those who read some or all of this manuscript in its various incarnations. John Cell, Fred Cooper, Arif Dirlik, Laura Downs, Geoff Eley, Jan Ewald, Cynthia Herrup, Susan Juster, Hugh McLeod, Clare Midgley, Jacob Price, and Ann Stoler read the dissertation through in its entirety and gave me helpful comments about its possibilities as well as its problems. Further down the road, Anna Clark, Geoff Eley, Fred Cooper, Catherine Hall, David Mayfield, Nathan Quandt, Russell Richey, Tim Schrand, John Seed, Ruth Smith, Richard Soloway, Ann Stoler, Jennifer Thorn, Rachel Weill, and Kären Wigen provided meaningful comments on various sections of the book manuscript that emerged. That it did emerge is thanks in no small part to the always encouraging admonitions of my local mentors, Judith Bennett and Nancy Hewitt. Nancy Hewitt also undertook the Herculean task of reading the resulting manuscript in its entirety, as did Antoinette Burton, John Cell, David Feldman, Cynthia Herrup, Danny James, Philippa Levine, Catherine Peyroux, Norris Pope, Andrew Porter, Matthew Price, and Laura Tabili, all of whom lent to the sometimes painful process of revising yet again a dialogic pleasure. I want also to thank my editors at Stanford University Press: Norris Pope, Peter Kahn, Kate Warne, and Ruth Barzel. The book would be better had I been able to execute more of my readers' many insightful suggestions, and it owes most of what virtue it claims to those I was able to take on board. Unfortunately, I am responsible for its shortcomings.

I want finally to thank my family—the Schrands, Thornes, Brzorads, and DeMumbrums—for putting up with my often grumpy self-absorption and for providing much needed perspective. Michelle and Jennifer, you're my loves; the next one is for you. I am dedicating this book to your father, a small recompense for making everything possible, and to the memory of your great-grandmother, whose commitment to the Ladies Missionary Auxiliary of the First United Methodist Church in Hamlet, North Carolina, was my introduction to the ties by which foreign missions have bound the most local of worlds to global arenas.

S.T.

CHAPTER I

Introduction

British historians have largely failed to ask what empire has done to "us."
—Shula Marks, "History, the Nation and Empire:
Sniping from the Periphery"

The problem is to devise a route that offers a plausible way of connecting the history of Britain to the history of the empire.
—P. J. Cain and A. G. Hopkins, *British Imperialism:
Innovation and Expansion 1688–1914*

When the Rev. George Greatbatch arrived in North Meols, a small village in western Lancashire, his "heart sank" at the condition of the native population.[1] Greatbatch was one of the first home missionaries deployed by the Lancashire Itinerant Society shortly after its founding in 1801, and the area to which he was sent was described by his successor as "probably one of the most unenlightened and uncivilized parts of the kingdom."[2] Greatbatch decided to submit to an arduous fifteen-mile commute from Newburgh rather than bring his family to live among such a people. "I recollect the awkward gaze wherewith the people looked upon me, and the painful feelings of my heart when I retired to a little hovel from among them," he wrote. "The thought of living among them would have overwhelmed me." Greatbatch explained his recoil from the people to whom he was to minister by saying that "I had little thought there was a station for me at home which so much resembled the ideas I had formed of an uncivilised heathen land."[3]

That Britain's laboring poor resembled the inhabitants of the purportedly uncivilized heathen lands in which Greatbatch's foreign missionary counterparts operated was a commonplace in the social discourse of Victorian England. Foreign analogies were among the first to spring to mind when contemporaries struggled to describe and in describing to direct, contest, and contain the social, cultural, and political transformations of the age of revolution. The very selection of North Meols as a home mission field was likened to the process by which foreign mission fields were chosen. "As the founders of the London Missionary Society selected the South Sea Islands as their first sphere of labour, than which none was more distant, dark, unpromising and perilous, so acted the promoters of the Lancashire Itinerant Society," argued Benjamin Nightingale, a Lancashire Congregationalist, in 1906. "No part of the county could have been more remote from the center of operations, and certainly none was more hopelessly heathen and lost than Western Lancashire."[4] Such comparisons were not limited to the circles of missionaries and their supporters; indeed, they pervade the language of social class taking shape during the decades that bracketed the nineteenth century's turn. E. P. Thompson's classic work, *The Making of the English Working Class*, is littered with such allusions. "The instant we get near the borders of the manufacturing parts of Lancashire," he quotes a commercial traveler writing in 1808, "we meet a fresh race of beings."[5] Contemporaries seem to have found in racial and imperial referents the only words adequate to describe the social changes being wrought by industrialization.

The countryside was the initial subject of such comparisons. It was a veritable breeding ground for barbarians, according to early industrialism's observers. But the darkness at the heart of urban civilization quickly displaced its agrarian progenitor. As middle-class anxieties became increasingly focused on the industrial city—and especially London—over the course of the nineteenth century, the deployment of foreign analogies if anything intensified in ever more elaborate efforts to distinguish the respectable working classes from the unrespectable "residuum."[6] As Henry Mayhew argued in 1851, "In passing from the skilled operative of the West End to the unskilled workman of the eastern quarter of London, the moral and intellectual change is so great that it seems as if we were in a new land and among another race."[7] By the 1890s, literary depictions of the urban "jungle" explicitly invoke its colonial counterpart, as in William Booth's *In Darkest England and the Way Out* (1890), the title and the text of which allude to Henry Morton Stanley's popular travelogue, *In Darkest Africa*, published only a few months before. It was in the surprised recognition of the conditions chronicled by Stanley that the founder of the Salvation Army claims to have found his inspiration.

> While brooding over the awful presentation of life as it exists in the vast African forest, it seemed only too vivid a picture of many parts of our own land. As there is a darkest Africa is there not also a darkest England? . . . May we not find a parallel at our own doors, and discover within a stone's throw of our cathedrals and palaces similar horrors to those which Stanley has found existing in the great Equatorial forest?[8]

British historians have yet to explore in a systematic way colonialism's imprint on metropolitan language, institutions, and practices.[9] Here, if not in other regards, we appear to have acquiesced in the conventional wisdom that influence flows down the hills of power, that imperialism was a one-way street on which the traffic in people, practices, institutions, and ideas moved always out from all-determining European centers to appropriating if not supine peripheries.[10] Social historians have been particularly remiss in this regard. Until very recently most social histories of Britain in this period were written without significant reference to the empire's existence. Despite his subjects' frequent reference to the colonized and soon-to-be-colonized world, E. P. Thompson, for example, confines his analysis of *The Making of the English Working Class* to the geographical space of the British Isles, with the single and important exception of the influence accorded to developments on the continent. Yet Thompson, who was born in India to a Methodist missionary, was, like many intellectuals of his generation, himself a product of the colonial encounter.[11] The factors that led Thompson's subjects to their consciousness of class were certainly numerous and complex: the radical religious legacies of the seventeenth century, on the one hand, combined with the innovative political and intellectual currents generated in the course of the French Revolution on the other. These provided the culturally specific framework that informed working people's apprehension of early industrialization and of the counterrevolutionary reprisals of the political establishment alike. Imperialism, however, does not appear to have mattered in Thompson's assessment, either to the course of industrialization or to the making and remaking of popular identities in its wake.[12]

Thompson's many followers have continued to conceive of class in ways that effectively and often explicitly preclude consideration of imperialism's influence on social relations in the metropole.[13] History from the bottom up has been preeminently a history of everyday lives whose horizons are invariably local. National—much less international or imperial—developments are marginalized in the main as superstructural ephemera, bread and circuses that sometimes deflect metropolitan social developments from their purportedly natural course but that are seldom conceived of as prominent among their constitutive forces. Those numerous occasions on which working-class crowds went a-mafficking or to jingo music halls are typically explained away, when acknowledged at all, as chimerical distractions from the immediate and material realities that ultimately determine working-class life chances.[14] Imperial historians have similarly assumed without basis that the empire's appeal was limited to the nation's governing elite.[15]

This study will argue, in contrast, that the empire enjoyed a much broader social catchment than is often assumed, one that encompassed the influential fraction of the provincial middle class as well as a substantial minority within the working-class population. Important conceptual space for understanding such ostensibly supraclass involvement has been opened in recent revisionist interventions, including but not limited to postmodernism and the "linguistic turn." The "narrow and impoverishing force" of scholarly portrayals of ordinary people as "concerned with nothing but their material circumstances and that set of social relationships in which they were most immediately involved" has been effectively called into question.[16] Revisionists across the political and methodological spectrum have insisted—and quite rightly, I think—that working-class people, like any other, have a complex subjectivity and that they find "dignity and meaning in their relation to things they did not create— their religion, their country, their rulers."[17] I will argue that they similarly find "dignity and meaning" in relation to their nation's far-flung empire.

Revisionist histories of nineteenth-century Britain have yet, however, to locate changes in social discourse or trends in social relations in the context of the rapid imperial expansion with which Britain's economic and political modernization coincided.[18] Widespread doubts about some of social history's other underlying precepts—such as the existence of social classes as historical subjects, the revolutionary character of industrialization, and even social causality itself—have not extended to the geographical boundaries of the British historical subject in ways that would bring the empire into consideration.[19] The conventional wisdom of the British historical establishment, at least as far as the nineteenth century is concerned, remains, as Linda Colley has recently put it, that, "for most of the time . . . empire simply did not loom all that large in the minds of most men and women back in Europe."[20]

This book will argue that in fact the empire did "loom large" in the minds of many Britons. While it may at some future point be important to remind ourselves that imperial ambitions were not pursued or imperial identifications embraced at the expense of all else, we have a long way to go before we have adequately attended to the many and profound ways that Britons were affected by their encounters,[21] whether real or represented, with the colonies. And these encounters occurred more frequently than we may realize. British men and women from all walks of life were connected by many and powerful ties to their nation's rapidly expanding empire. Institutions and individuals, cultural practices and capital, political philosophies, and supplies of labor, as well as commodities, capital, and raw materials flowed in large quantities and in both directions between colonized periphery and metropolitan core.[22] To be sure, the absolute numbers of Britons who experienced the empire firsthand as soldiers, sailors, commercial travelers, tourists, the means of communication. Missionary propagandists were among the first to use magic lanterns to illustrate their lectures. The arrival of a traveling missionary caravan, filled with material artifacts from the colonies and free missionary pamphlets and magazines, was a signal event in isolated rural communities as late as the turn of this century. Among the more ubiquitous methods of missionary communication was the missionary collecting box. These small wooden boxes were illustrated with pictures of missionaries and converts as well as of heathens and their idols; the graphic messages about the degraded status of heathendom, the abject gratitude of converts, and the superiority of Christian civilization with which they were imbued were displayed in the very heart of the Victorian home.[35] Missionary organization throughout the British countryside was so effective that by midcentury contemporaries could claim that "many a small tradesman or rustic knows more of African or Polynesian life than London journalists."[36]

This book explores the terms on which ordinary Britons used this knowledge to imagine themselves in relation to their nation's empire. It has as its larger aim to model how we, that is British historians and especially social historians, might go about rethinking our subject from the imperial bottom up. I am here appropriating the mantra of an earlier generation of social historians. Just as they were concerned about rethinking political history in ways that took popular agency, and elite concerns to contest it, into account, I am endeavoring to excavate the imperial dynamics that informed and were informed by social relations and political culture on the British Empire's home front. For in the process of mobilizing popular support for missionary and imperial projects, which was in itself of considerable significance, the missionary movement also helped to position the empire as a determining context of the language or languages in which social relations of power in nineteenth-century Britain were described and contested. The imaginative relationship to the empire encouraged by missions contributed, I will argue, to some of the central developments of British social history in this period: class formation, gender relations, the rise and demise of English liberalism, and the role of organized religion therein. I will spend the remainder of this introduction locating my argument in relation to this wide-ranging albeit overlapping set of historiographical concerns.

✧

I want to begin by locating this study in the politically charged debate about the missionary perspective on imperialism. Mission historians have generally insisted that theological motivations were the primary determinants of missionary practice; imperial considerations or attachments are dismissed

in this line of argument as a diversion from the real concerns of the missionary lobby.[37] The fact that most missionaries identified themselves as enthusiastic imperialists is typically explained away with the platitude that missionaries were simply children of their time, an explanation that removes the
problem of the politics of imperialism from the domain of mission studies.[38]

Imperialism is certainly not the only frame of reference in which mission
history should be located; nor did the missionary embrace of an imperial
ideal preclude vociferous criticism of colonial practice. Theological concerns,
not personal profit, were the preeminent influence on missionary society policy.[39] Most missionaries were genuinely committed to advancing the welfare,
at least as they understood it, of the indigenous peoples to whom they ministered. Missionaries led the protests against slavery in the West Indies, against
land expropriation in Africa, against coerced labor in the South Pacific.[40] And
the sacrifice popularly associated with missionary service was very real. Death
rates among foreign missionaries remained extraordinarily high throughout
the nineteenth century. Travel was difficult and dangerous, and the rewards
were frustratingly limited in many mission fields. Many missionaries lived to
see their children and wives die of illness, or, to prevent this eventuality, were
separated from them for years at a time.[41]

Moreover, British missionaries were not confined to areas of British imperial influence; they were posted all over the world.[42] And when they were
posted in the empire, they were often thorns in the side of British colonial
administration. Missionaries were often critical of British colonial practice
and individual agents of the British colonial state. Generalizations about the
missionary perspective on colonial policy are difficult to come by; there was
little consensus within a missionary field force divided by denomination, foreign location, and individual personality.[43] The missionaries on which this
study focuses appear to have oscillated rather radically over the course of the
nineteenth century from being generally hostile to the British colonial establishment to being on the vanguard of expansionist sentiment, and back to
being vocal critics of colonialism once again.

And even when they were supportive of imperial principle or colonial
practice, missionaries sought to preserve order, authority, and property by using means very different from the methods favored by those whose imperial
visions were predicated upon slavery, as in the West Indies, or migrant labor,
as in Africa. These differences mattered to a degree belied by simplistic attacks on missionaries as simply the thin end of the imperial wedge, their religion but a ruse behind which the European imperial monolith advanced.
Not only did missionaries sometimes pay with their lives for their principled
opposition to alternative modes of power, but colonized peoples themselves

found opportunities for resistance as well as for accommodation in what were very real divisions within European colonialists' ranks.[44]

✣

How then can I justify the connection I make between missions and imperialism—the connection on which this study is predicated? In answer to this question, I will say first that, however critical they were of colonial practice, missionaries were never able to sever altogether their connection to British imperial power. Their access as Europeans to its coercive force, whether it was activated or not, shaped the terms of the missionary encounter, even for those stationed outside the British Empire's rapidly expanding boundaries. Missionaries operated on the front line of the colonial encounter, engaging in face-to-face contact with indigenous peoples on a large scale and a daily basis to a degree that few other European functionaries could claim. Their location rendered missionaries the advance column of imperialism's cultural assault on indigenous subjectivities, and missionaries were often the first to claim that they were "colonizers of consciousness" itself. And even those missionaries opposed to imperialism in principle contributed to the destabilization of indigenous cultural and political structures in ways that facilitated European encroachments.[45]

Second, religious motivations and humanitarian concerns were explicitly championed by many missionaries, not as an alternative to imperial control but as the best means of securing it. As the Church Missionary Society instructed its missionaries in 1878, "The chief secret of power is sympathy and nothing so conduces to this as an intelligent and appreciative knowledge of the people whose hearts you want to win."[46] Missionary praxis advertised itself as "moral conquest," a way of obtaining consent to European rule through humanitarian intervention.[47] David Livingstone personified this missionary prescription for hegemony. Livingstone was lauded by his eulogists as a "conqueror of men, by loving-kindness," "loved and feared, not as a magician or a spectre, but as a just and kind benefactor."[48] For the British public, to whom his name was a household word,[49] Livingstone's purported influence over Africans demonstrated to his countrymen "that open and aboveboard dealing has its effect even upon the barbarous tribes of Central Africa." And the effect desired was power: "Black men, who had never seen the white man before, now exhibited themselves ready and willing to accord him the supremacy belonging to his race."[50] "Kindness, brotherliness and the Gospel of God's Love . . . all the world knows how Livingstone succeeded with these weapons where another would have required an army," or so claimed Livingstone's fellow missionary, J. A. Ross, almost a half century after Livingstone's

death. Ross, like Livingstone, served with the LMS in central Africa, and in
the article from which this quotation is taken he goes on to recall that missionaries "did much to pacify the tribes, whose chief occupation in the past
had been war" and thereby "prepared the people for the advent of civilised
government, making the task of the latter much simpler. The necessity for
fighting was obviated, and not even a display of force was necessary to bring
this promising country under British dominion." Ross concludes that "with
proper treatment the native is exceedingly respectful and even deferential to
the European."[51]

We must not forget, however, that missionary prescriptions of kindness in
dealings with indigenous peoples did not preclude cruelty, coercion, and other
forms of violence. Accounts of corporal punishment (floggings) on mission
stations recur in the private correspondence between parent societies and
their operatives in the field, and there were occasional scandals involving missionaries securing forced labor.[52] Short of these extremes, hierarchy was produced in the missionary community on a day-to-day basis through wage and
status differentials between European missionaries and "native agents" and
through the rules that regulated converts' deportment. These latter were subjected to strict controls on mission stations, and "conceit" ranked highest on
European missionaries' list of their converts' unacceptable behaviors.[53]

Nor must we forget the limits of missionaries' influence, as opposed to
their intentions. In mission fields such as India, the proportion of converts to
total indigenous population was always quite small. Even in places where
missionaries were more successful in converting their targets to Christianity, they were not always, if ever, able to control the terms of their religion's
appropriation. Converts were capable, in other words, of separating the
word of God from the actions and attitudes of its all-too-human carriers.
However close the association between European missionaries and the colonial state, the native church in the colonies often went in its own direction,
leaving missionaries to follow if they chose.[54] Nationalist leaders were frequently Christian converts or at the very least had been educated in mission
schools.[55]

Missionaries were considerably more successful in securing imperialism's
hegemony in Britain than in their foreign fields of operation, and it is their
influence on social relations and political identifications in Britain that concerns me here.[56] Developments in the colonies play an important role in the
narrative I will relate; however, British historical developments occupy center stage. This is, obviously, not the only perspective from which the history
of British missions or imperialism can be viewed. And I wish in no way to
minimize the urgency of engaging imperialism's impact on colonized peoples

the world over or of giving voice to the experience of the colonized. But these are, as Gauri Viswanathan reminds us, essentially separate stories.

> How the native *actually* responds is so removed from the colonizer's representational system, his understanding of the meaning of events, that it enters into the realm of another history of which the latter has no comprehension or even awareness. That history can, and perhaps must, be told separately for its immensely rich and complex quality to be fully revealed.[57]

Fortunately, the activities and influence of British missionaries in their foreign fields of operation are the subject of a very rich and sophisticated historiography, whose apologist origins have long been subject to challenge from nationalist and other anti-imperial perspectives.[58] We know less about the missionary movement's influence on the making of an imperial culture in Britain, the primary studies of their home organization having eschewed questions of this kind.[59] On their home front, missionaries' ambivalence about particular colonial policies and their apparent empathy with the empire's colonized subjects lent their nearly universal identification with the British nation's imperial destiny considerable ideological potency. In this important regard, missionaries were not simply products of their times but were agents in its making. The missionary movement disseminated an ethical language in which authoritarian colonial practices could be defended or simply obscured by the missionary emphasis on service. The missionary defense of the imperial ideal constituted one of the most powerful rationales imaginable in Victorian political culture, given the intense religiosity by which the latter was characterized.[60]

✝

British historians have only recently begun to acknowledge that the empire mattered to their metropolitan subjects or that it should figure in our histories of this period. The combined influence of World War II, decolonization, and postwar immigration precipitated a scholarly revulsion for Britain's former imperial attachments. This revulsion manifested itself in an erasure of their existence.[61] The victorious Allied powers attributed racial identifications discredited by Nazi atrocities to the peculiarities of German culture, the obverse of which was the comforting assertion that Anglo-Saxons had somehow been ethnically inoculated.[62] Discrediting imperialism in the aftermath of decolonization was similarly projected into the past by historians' largely unexamined assumption that the empire lost to the present had somehow never really mattered, that it had been foisted upon an innocent British public by the machinations of duplicitous elites. This line of argument originated in the anti-imperial Left at the turn of the twentieth century, as in, for example, the work of J. A. Hobson. However, it has been wielded more recently to the racially conservative political end of denying the historical basis of the claims to citizenship of postwar immigrants from the (former) British Commonwealth. The most notable example of this is Enoch Powell's argument that immigrants' imperial ties to Britain were established during an aberrant episode in British history in which the British state had been hijacked by foreign (and especially Jewish) influence.[63]

Literary critics and cultural historians have joined Third World scholars in questioning the "little island" conventions that continue to inform the writing of modern British history.[64] Numerous "snipings" from the geographic, chronological, and disciplinary peripheries of British history have presented persuasive evidence that imperial imagery pervaded the visual and performing arts, literature, theology, and philosophy. Or, as African historian Shula Marks has recently put it, the empire left its imprint on everything "from diet to industrial discipline, from sexual mores to notions of governance" throughout colonizing Europe and from the age of discovery down through the present.[65] Thanks to these pathbreaking studies, we are now at the point at which our attention can shift from the larger question of whether the British public was mobilized behind its nation's imperial project to more nuanced inquiries about how this was accomplished, to specifying with greater precision its domestic repercussions, and to attending to variations over political and social space and to change over time.

This study departs from the predominantly cultural thrust of recent studies of imperialism's popularization in its social-historical perspective. Its methodological assertion is that we can only understand *how* imperialism acquired its "enormous hold over the British imagination" and, even more important, the consequences of such influence, if we read missionary and other texts in relation to the essentially local and everyday social and institutional contexts in which they were disseminated, consumed, and politically (re-)deployed.[66] It was, in other words, not simply the consumption of missionary (or any other form of imperialist) propaganda, but its appropriation in dynamic social contexts that determined the influence of missionary visions of empire on British political culture. Who was reading missionary texts or paying to have them read, as well as when and where they were read, will be shown to have influenced their metropolitan reception at least as much as what was said.

In order to locate missionary texts in specific local contexts, I have had to forage well beyond the correspondence, committee minutes, and official publications of the national missionary organizations on which previous historians of missions and their metropolitan organization have focused. I have had to delve into that wealth of archival material pertaining to the local culture of organized religion, that lived terrain, so to speak, into which the missionary movement interjected its colonial narratives. Most evangelical chapels and churches, for example, joined one another in town, city, and sometimes countywide auxiliaries, which raised support in their locale for their denomination's missionary operations at home as well as abroad. These institutions generated records that illuminate more clearly than usual the organizational techniques and discursive strategies used to convey the missionary agenda to local sensibilities; they also highlight the local obstacles that stood in the way of this agenda.

Over the course of the nineteenth century, British Protestants alone sponsored more than 20 foreign missionary organizations, each of which generated and preserved a wealth of propaganda. In the interest of attaining the kind of social specificity necessary to read missionary texts in relation to the local contexts from which they drew their meaning and to attend to change over time,[67] I have focused on the missionary outreach of a single denomination, the Independent, or Congregational, churches, and I have limited my inquiries almost entirely to England.[68]

Nonconformists (that is, members of those Protestant sects that included Congregationalism and who worshipped outside the Established Church of England) were the most enthusiastic supporters of missions in Britain. Although Congregationalists comprised the largest denomination within Victorian Dissent, they have been neglected in the scholarly literature in comparison to Quakers, Unitarians, and especially Methodists.[69] But Congregationalists not only included some of the most economically successful and politically active Victorian Nonconformists (Titus Salt, Samuel Morley, Edward Baines Jr., John Crossley, J. Wycliffe Wilson, Albert Spicer, Edward and James G. Miall, and so forth); they also enjoyed a sizable popular base. The majority of the people who attended Congregational services were from working-class backgrounds. And in many urban areas, the number of Congregational chapel-goers approached and even exceeded those attending Methodist and Anglican services.[70]

The LMS was the principal institutional beneficiary of Congregational support for foreign missionary operations, and, in the words of one of its Leicestershire supporters, "may be taken as a type of all the rest."[71] The LMS was founded in 1795 by a cohort of Anglican, Methodist, Presbyterian, and Independent ministers, who continued to channel support its way for many years to come. Referred to for many years as, simply, *the* Missionary Society, it remained officially nondenominational throughout the period under study, but the founding of separate denominational missionary organizations meant that the LMS would be effectively dependent on British Congregationalists for most of the nineteenth century. The society's income (a fairly accurate indicator of the extent of both its home support and its foreign operations) ranks it just below the Church Missionary Society and the Wesleyan Methodist Missionary Society.[72] Certainly, the propaganda disseminated on LMS podiums was likely to reach a denominationally diverse audience. Most evangelicals attended missionary meetings and read missionary publications regardless of their denominational origin. Ministers and missionaries also spoke with ecumenical generosity on platforms not their own.[73]

The immediate and material concerns of the Congregational supporters of the LMS played a crucial role, I will argue, in the metropolitan reception of the missionary message. The essentially local logic of the power relations between the propertied and the poor, between husband and wife, and between adults and children exerted a powerful influence on the meanings attributed to missionary texts as well as on the missionary movement's ability to mobilize funds, volunteers, and other forms of public support. Hence the attention paid to these local conditions by the organizing agents the society employed to seek its fortune in the provinces, whose reports comprise an important source for this study.

Social context was not all-determining, to be sure. Indeed, I will suggest, to the contrary, that the British public's engagement with missionary intelligence about the empire helped to shape social relations and political identities every bit as much as social relations and political identities influenced the reading of missionary texts. This was a mutually constitutive dynamic. As a result, the affects of missionary propaganda were not felt at the expense of more domestically inclined social identities, including those of class, as revisionists across the disciplinary spectrum would have it, but as their very precondition. Here my argument contests the retreat from class analysis that informs colonial cultural studies and revisionist social history alike.[74] The martial dramas and material superprofits that cultural historians and literary critics have associated primarily with the new imperial expansion of the nineteenth century are often presumed to have worked on popular identity in ways that precluded—or at least sharply limited—social divisions along class lines.[75] Feminist historians have been more sophisticated in this regard, approaching colonialism not as an alternative to but as constitutive of Victorian gender identities. Here too, though, colonialism has been incorporated, in practice if not in theory, as an alternative to the emphasis on "class" that has until recently distinguished, and favorably I might add, British feminist accounts of gender formation from those of their more liberal and pluralist counterparts in the United States.[76]

We owe most of what we know about the connections between colonialism and class formation to scholars whose primary research interests are in the geographical space of the colonies.[77] In order to apprehend more clearly the disparate and divisive visions of empire battling for hegemony on the colonial ground, literary critics, historians, and historically minded anthropologists have increasingly looked over their colonized subjects' shoulders, so to speak, to the European origins of the colonial encounter.[78] Class-based tensions are shown in these studies to have intruded into the colonial social process in complex and often contradictory ways. On the most obvious level, capitalism's penetration into the colonized world set in motion processes of class formation within indigenous societies that complicated the racial divide on which the colonial power structure was predicated. But European colonizers as well as the colonized were affected by class divides in ways that incited as well as disrupted racial thinking. The racialist rationales on the basis of which Europeans justified their imperial supremacy were continually being undermined, for example, by a consciousness of class that Europeans brought with them on their voyage from Europe to the colonies.[79] Class struggles within the European colonial community proved dangerously divisive in colonial contexts where European unity was at a premium, and it was to counteract the disruptive and everpresent consequences of class that colonial regimes undertook deliberate campaigns to foster racial identifications designed to unify an otherwise divided European community. Such efforts to substitute race for class were rendered more plausible by the degree to which these emergent racial discourses borrowed from the moral and rhetorical taxonomies of European languages of class.[80]

Scholarly discussions of the intersections of class and race in colonial social discourse have emphasized the ways in which metropolitan ideas about class were transformed in the colonies into a discourse about race. Or, to put it another way, the primary concern has been to illuminate the ways in which the language of race spoken in the empire—as well as at home—was "classed." But if the Rev. Greatbatch was typical, and I intend to show that he was, the ideas about class that British colonizers brought with them to the empire were already "raced," having been constructed on the basis of a social nomenclature whose primary referent was the colonial encounter. And the missionary movement played a central role in the process. The extraordinary scale of British imperial expansion at the end of the nineteenth century has obscured the magnitude of Britain's colonial involvement at the eighteenth century's turn, which is when historians generally agree that the word *class* first entered the English social lexicon.[81] The rapid accumulation of such geographically immense and culturally diverse territories was brought home to British men and women through a vast array of institutional and cultural channels. But, among them, foreign missions played a critical role in helping to bring into contact these geographically dispersed fronts of European bourgeois power.[82]

For missions were not only an effective conduit of information about the empire; they were also a primary source of information about the poor and laboring classes in Britain. Home missions will, as a consequence, figure large in this story. Congregational home missions were more institutionally diffuse than were their foreign missionary counterparts. Rather than being administered through a single central denominational agency in the manner of foreign missions, home missionary outreach was conducted by a number of different and competing local, regional, and national organizations. From the 1780s on, Sunday schools were established in connection with most Congregational chapels to educate the children of the poor.[83] Itinerant societies were established and supported by Congregational chapels on a countywide basis; indeed, it was out of these institutions that the County Unions of Congregational Churches emerged, and from them, the denomination's central umbrella institution, the Congregational Union of England and Wales.[84] Interestingly, ecumenical missionary organizations proved more viable on the home than on the foreign front. The London City Mission and the British and Foreign Bible Society (BFBS) were among the nondenominational missionary institutions to attract significant Congregational support.[85]

The missionaries deployed by organizations such as the Lancashire Itinerant Society were arguably the most visible bourgeois presence in the working-class community during the first half of the nineteenth century, when police, social welfare, and public educational provisions were minimal. These organizations were also very effective at broadcasting their findings about the poor to curious middle-class audiences. Like their foreign missionary counterparts, home missionary institutions involved a large cross section of the evangelical community in their activities. They did this through fund-raising campaigns, sermons, printed propaganda, and the numerous opportunities available for voluntary service in the home mission field itself. These involvements constituted what were arguably the principal occasions on which the propertied classes in Britain came into contact with the poor.[86]

Historians have generally approached home and foreign missions as separate undertakings that were functionally and ideologically independent, the assumption being, presumably, that their targets were too different to make direct comparison viable (except for occasional rhetorical gestures).[87] But the very perception that a cultural and social chasm separated subaltern races in the colonies from the laboring classes of industrializing Europe is itself, I will argue, an outcome of the historical processes that are the subject of this study.

For at least their first half century, home and foreign missions were viewed by most evangelicals as two fronts of the same war, separated by geographical happenstance and little more. As contemporaries proudly noted, although institutionally distinct, home and foreign missions were invariably promoted by the same individuals. Greatbatch himself had originally intended to become a foreign missionary. And in this he was far from alone. Indeed, the two causes were so closely associated in the evangelical psyche that many chapels took up a single missionary collection each month and divided the proceeds between the home and foreign fields.[88]

The missionary comparison of "heathen" groupings in Britain with those in the colonies and the soon-to-be colonized world is discussed in chapters 2 and 3. The institutional proximity of home and foreign missions also facilitated the use of the exotic attractions of foreign missions to lure the laboring poor in Britain back into the fold of the institutional church. The Rev. William Alexander, Greatbatch's successor in North Meols, wrote a letter to his son that contained a revealing account of the ways that home and foreign missionary outreach converged on the British Empire's home front. Alexander recounted his conversion of a local woman at a cottage meeting, a prototypical home missionary setting. The woman's husband reacted angrily to her change of heart, threatening violence if she persisted. Yet, even someone as hostile to organized religion as this found himself shortly thereafter compelled by curiosity to attend a missionary prayer meeting, where he was so impressed "by the missionary facts which were narrated, that he determined to attend the service on the Sabbath." In due course, this former enemy of religion was converted "and became a holy and useful member of the church."[89]

Both these impulses—the disciplinary propensity to compare purportedly heathen people across the colonial divide and the incorporationist use of foreign missions to attach working-class Britons to organized religion—are present throughout the period under study. Over the course of the nineteenth century, however, the balance between them shifted. During the second half of the century, the propensity to compare was gradually displaced by a "social imperial" project predicated on racial contrasts; its emergence and operation are described in chapter 5.[90]

This shift, I will argue, was mediated by the simultaneous feminization of foreign missionary philanthropy. During the same period (that is to say the second half of the nineteenth century) that race was being reshaped in opposition to class, missions were becoming an increasingly gendered institutional practice. Establishing the connections between these two contemporaneous processes—the gradual process whereby colonized races were increasingly juxtaposed to the British working classes *and* the feminization of missionary philanthropy—is the work of chapter 4. That gender was to be a fulcrum on which this missionary story turned will not surprise those familiar with post-colonial cultural studies: by far the most innovative of the recent efforts to incorporate imperialism into metropolitan historical accounts have been undertaken by feminist literary critics, feminist anthropologists, and feminist historians.[91] Women's historians have been the exception to the insular rule in British social history as well. Anna Davin, Catherine Hall, Clare Midgley, Vron Ware, and Antoinette Burton, among others, have established that the empire—from the abolitionist crusades at the turn of the nineteenth century through the social and moral reform and feminist campaigns at the turn of the twentieth—was a prominent concern of British women as well as a pre-eminent influence upon their lives.[92]

Women's historians have long acknowledged the significance of the opportunities afforded by organized religion for British women's political as well as professional emancipation.[93] My primary interest here, however, is in the connection between missionary philanthropy's feminization and the separation of race and class with which it coincided. British women's embrace of the mission cause, at home as well as abroad, transformed missionary praxis in ways that were more conducive to racial distinction. In order for women to participate, missionary practice had to shift away from an exclusively spiritual emphasis on preaching to hardened heathen hearts (a role only men were entitled to play) to a more social gospel designed to improve the health, education, and welfare of colonized bodies. This social gospel was the religious counterpart if not the precipitant of political progressivism. Yet, as will be discussed more fully in chapters 4 and 5, it was accompanied by if not predicated upon a hardening of racial attitudes. By deflecting evangelical attention away from the earlier emphasis on the equality of souls and toward the realm of culture, society, and the body, the social gospel rendered difference more readily inscribed in terms of those racial taxonomies in which our own social discourse continues to be mired.

✦

Congregationalists were not unique in their simultaneous involvement in home and foreign missionary outreach nor in the feminization of their institutions and ideology. However, I do not wish to suggest that my findings will be uniformly applicable across the denominational board. To the contrary, the distinctive features of my Congregational subjects play an important role in my argument. The peculiarities of the Congregational church order, for example, exerted a determining influence on social relations within the Congregational community through which foreign missionary intelligence was

refracted. Also, as a primarily urban, provincial, and liberal middle-class constituency, the Congregational supporters of the LMS present a very different
social and especially political profile than that typically associated with imperialism's metropolitan base of support. The latter has been conventionally
limited to the gentlemanly capitalist establishment, the public school and
Oxbridge-educated outfitters of the colonial civil and military services. That
Anglican missionary supporters found colonialism congenial would not be especially surprising, given the Established Church's traditional ties to this social grouping. Even the Methodist hierarchy's colonial complicity might be
linked to its aping of the muscular Christianity of the religious establishment
from which it sprang.[94] Congregationalists, by contrast, were on the left wing
of the evangelical spectrum. They were, ostensibly, radical liberals opposed to
state intervention, archetypal little Englanders within a Liberal Party self-
identified with fiscal retrenchment and, subsequently, with domestic social
reform. They were also ostensibly opposed to colonial expansion on both
counts, in principle if not in practice.[95]

It is precisely the convergence of imperialism and domestic social reform
within this preeminently liberal fraction of English Nonconformity that calls
into question the historiographical convention by which these are construed
as antithetical pursuits—namely that liberals' (much less socialists') progressive engagement with poverty could not have produced positive assessments
of imperialism as well.[96] There was, to be sure, a version of imperialism associated with the Conservative Party to which most social reformers (including
the vast majority of Congregationalists) were congenitally opposed, and Richard Price is correct to complain that historians have paid too much attention
to the relatively small number of progressives who crossed this divide for
largely opportunistic reasons.[97] These Fabians, Coefficients, and Liberal Imperialists were not, however, the only imperialists at the progressive end of the
British political spectrum, however avidly they tried to claim the empire as
their exclusive preserve. There were many other sites at which imperialism
and reform intersected in less antithetical ways.

Indeed, well into the twentieth century most British liberals and socialists were generally supportive of their nation's imperial project, which they
viewed as an extension of their progressive political principles.[98] Labour MP
and then Lord Henry Snell, for example, was well within the accepted ideological norms of his party when he defended Britain's obligation and right to
"develop the colonial possessions on lines which would enrich and ennoble
their native peoples, and prepare them gradually to take their place in the
British Commonwealth of Nations," an argument that encountered virtually
no opposition in British politics throughout the interwar period.[99] Even those

most critical of British colonial policy did not question the basic principle of Britain's right to rule over non-European populations. Communist Party member and noted literary figure John Strachey, for example, likened the British Empire to the soviet system, in which "advanced" regions of Russia "co-operated" with the "former subject races of the Tsarist empire."[100]

More to the point at hand is the interdependence between imperialism and reform assumed in F. H. Stead's *How Old Age Pensions Began To Be* (1909). In addition to being secretary of the National Pensions Committee, Stead was the warden of Browning Hall, a Congregational settlement house in South London that was a "center of London Progressivism," whereas Stead himself "was a thoroughgoing 'New Liberal.'"[101] Far from viewing social reform as "an act of repentance for the sins of imperialism," as has been suggested,[102] Stead argues that the suffering of the poor disgraced an imperial nation's honor, thereby promoting a war on poverty as an imperial responsibility:

> More than a million of the aged left destitute, degraded, unfriended, in a land of overflowing plenty, under the shadow of a Christian civilization: and beyond them a huge host, well nigh ten times their number, hungry and ill-clad and ill-housed, struggling in poverty and worthlessness, or sinking into sodden despair: all this mass of misery at the Home of an Empire the like of which His world has never seen, which includes one-fourth of His human family, which could and might lead mankind along the paths of social justice and of universal peace: was it not "time for Him to work?" Was not intervention in such an "extremity" and at such an "opportunity", with consequences and influences reaching right round the earth and extending to far-off ages, worthy of a Divine interposition?[103]

According to Stead, Britain would not have its new pension plan were it not for the empire, which provided a useful laboratory for "social experiments."

Stead was eager for this sort of imperialism to become more, not less, widespread. For him, the crucial distinction was not between imperialism and social reform but between what he referred to as "intensive" and "extensive" imperialisms, distinguished, to be sure, by their position on domestic social reform. The Parliament of 1900 displayed a merely extensive imperialism in its opposition to domestic reform. Stead contrasts this imperialism of geographical expansion only to the intensive imperialism advocated by Will Crooks, Poplar's socialist mayor and eventual Labour member of Parliament, who was, like Stead, a Congregationalist. In a speech before the National Pensions Committee in 1902, Crooks urged his audience to remember always that

> You created this great Empire; you have all got a bit in it. You are proud of it. . . . We are a wonderfully patriotic nation. I have seen you Mafficking, and if you only "mafficked" for Old Age Pensions, Chamberlain would give them to

you to-morrow. . . . Now, we've got to be pals to the aged poor, and see that they get something, because they've helped to make a great Empire for us.[104]

The religious, philanthropic, and political milieu that inspired Stead's commitment to social reform occupied a pivotal place in the evolution of class relations and state formation throughout the nineteenth century, but increasingly so in the period between 1880 and 1914.[105] While this book does not engage the history of this social reform impulse in its own right,[106] it does suggest that Liberal as well as socialist Congregationalists such as Stead and Crooks were encouraged to identify with the empire by the missionary involvement incumbent upon their religious practice. This was especially true at the local level, where the home missionary outreach to the poor, from which social reform impulses drew much of their inspiration, was repeatedly and intimately associated with the imperial work of foreign missions. This institutional nexus thus represents a convergence of one kind of imperialism with a dominant strand of social reform, a convergence that occurred primarily within the Nonconformist mainstream of the British Liberal party.

The prevalence of imperialist assumptions about the legitimacy of European rule over non-European populations among one of British liberalism's most socially progressive factions (indeed, the empire's patent sacralization as a precondition of world salvation and the second coming) suggests that few if any Victorians could have been inured to the temptation of imperial identifications. This is not to say that the missionary influence on popular perceptions of the empire was always that intended. Powerful attachments to the empire were generated in reaction against as well as in support of the imperial vision that missionaries were concerned about promoting. As is discussed more fully in chapter 5, many of those who rejected the missionary imperial ideal did so in terms that favored more conservative alternatives to missionary imperialism rather than an outright rejection of imperialism itself.

This study, then, will describe the ways in which the LMS helped to position the colonies and their inhabitants in that quotidian space where, as Thomas Holt has recently reminded us, popular racial (like any other) identities are primarily forged.[107] It will also (and more originally, I think) explore the influence of missionary ties to the colonies on social relations within the Congregational community and beyond. For just as the missionary encounter enabled and disabled particular strategies of rule and resistance in the colonial setting, so too did it contribute in equally profound albeit qualitatively different ways to the constitution and contestation of power, to the making and remaking of social relations in metropolitan Britain itself. Missionary imperial identities were not alternatives to but were the medium through which domestic identities of class as well as gender were forged. And it was from

this social grounding that the British Empire derived much of its considerable domestic purchase. Just as local concerns contributed to the resonance of
imperial dreams, so did imperial and racial allusions permeate the languages
through which Victorians imagined their place and took charge of their space
in communities both intimate and remote. Imperialism was thereby made to
matter in the most immediate of ways to the larger British public in whose
name it was perpetrated.

CHAPTER 2

The Birth of Modern Missions

For after all, what are the heathen, but men, like ourselves, partakers of
the same corrupt nature, needing the same salvation, and, though perhaps environed with prejudices which it has been our happier lot never
to encounter, yet by no means beyond the reach of religious suasion.
—Rev. S. C. Wilks, "Christian Missions,
an Enlightened Species of Charity"

For most of the nineteenth century, British evangelicals and many of
their non-evangelical counterparts found intolerable the prospect that "the
large majority of the overwhelming number of immortal souls, each of which
in value outweighs the world, will . . . be irrevocably lost." How, given our
"tremendous convictions, can we sit still?" asked the evangelical author,
Jemima Thompson, in 1841.[1] Her forebears, however, were not as troubled by
heathenism's extent or as convinced of the efficacy of missionary solutions. It
was not until the closing decades of the eighteenth century that British Protestants began to show much of an interest in missions at all. The massive missionary expansion of early modern Europe was financed and directed almost
entirely by the expanding Catholic powers on the continent—Portugal, Spain,
and France. Protestant Britons remained indifferent to the cause.[2] Although
missionary expeditions included the occasional Englishman, Anglican and
Dissenting theologians actively discounted missionary claims to the nation's
attention, arguing that biblical imperatives to proselytize had been incumbent
upon the early Christians alone.[3]

There was no dearth of philanthropy in England during the Stuart and
Hanoverian periods, but it was neither global in its scope nor missionary in its
orientation, by which I mean it was not primarily concerned with securing
the religious conversion of its targets. Health, education, and welfare, rather
than spiritual salvation, were its aims, and Britons were its primary targets.

The colonies were almost entirely neglected, save for the "sporadic and hap-hazard" exertions of the Anglican philanthropic agencies founded at the eigh-teenth century's turn: the Society for Promoting Christian Knowledge, which was founded in 1699, and the Society for the Propagation of the Gospel in Foreign Parts, which was founded in 1701. Their colonial ministry was con-fined to European settlers for the most part, although individual clergymen sometimes took it upon themselves to minister to the indigenous people who lived in their immediate vicinity.

The first intimations of that more ambitious and self-propelling mission-ary program for which the Victorians were renowned came from the Methodists. In 1783, Wesley's close associate Thomas Coke published a *Plan of the Society for the Establishment of Missions Among the Heathen*, which resulted four years later in the dispatch of Methodist missionaries to the West Indies.[4] In 1784, Melvill Horne, a chaplain of the Sierra Leone Company, published a collection of *Letters on Missions*, in which he appealed to evangelicals across the denominational spectrum to unite in support of foreign missionary ad-vance. In 1787, David Brown and Charles Grant, who were in the employ of the East India Company, issued a similar *Proposal for Establishing a Protestant Mission in Bengal and Bihar* to Evangelical Anglicans. The response to these calls to missionary arms was electric. Missionary organizations were quickly established by every major denominational grouping in Great Britain, with the single and predictable exception of the Unitarians. The first evangelical organization devoted explicitly to foreign missions was established by a group of Northamptonshire Baptists in 1792. William Carey, a former shoemaker and minister at Harvey Lane chapel in Leicester, published *An Enquiry into the Obligations of Christians to Use Means for the Conversion of the Heathens* in May 1792; a few months later the Particular-Baptist Society for Propagating the Gospel Among the Heathen came into being. Carey himself left for India in June 1793 to set up the Society's first mission. This provincial initiative was duplicated in the capital three years later with the founding of the LMS. Un-like the Baptist Missionary Society, the LMS initially enjoyed the interde-nominational support of Anglicans, Wesleyans, Presbyterians, and Indepen-dents (as Congregationalists were then known). Denominational suspicions proved insurmountable, however. In 1799, Evangelical Anglicans broke away to form their own Church Missionary Society; interestingly, a separate orga-nization for foreign missionary outreach was not established by the Wesleyan Methodists until 1818. And with the establishment of a missionary society in connection with the Church of Scotland in 1825, the LMS was left effectively dependent on the support of Britain's Congregational churches.

Scholarly explanations of this sudden expansion of British Protestantism's missionary horizons can be grouped in two opposing camps. Historians of colonized or formerly colonized societies have typically viewed foreign missions as an expression of the exigencies of colonial rule, a theologically and politically undifferentiated agency of the British colonial state. The coincidence of the birth of modern missions with British imperial expansion has encouraged their analytical conflation. In this way, missions have been seen as little more than the spiritual reflection of Western cultural arrogance, an expression of the will to power of an increasingly expansionist imperial nation. The religious pretensions of Victorian missionaries and their evangelical supporters have thus been discounted as the veneer behind which exploitation and expropriation in the colonies proceeded.[5]

Metropolitan historians of missions have countered by emphasizing the metropolitan sources of missionary inspiration, among which theological developments figure prominently. Citing missionaries themselves on the subject of their motives, these studies give the Evangelical Revival center stage in their accounts of the origins of British Protestantism's missionary ambitions. That missionaries were sincerely devoted to bringing all the world to Christ is presumed, moreover, to exonerate the missionary project from its present state of postcolonial disgrace. As Brian Stanley has most recently put it, "the only adequate explanation of the origins of the missionary societies is in terms of theological changes which were quite autonomous of developments in imperial history."[6]

This study concedes that religion must be taken more seriously than it often is, that the birth of modern missions cannot be understood without reference to the revival of British Protestantism during the eighteenth and early nineteenth centuries. However, theological developments are not sufficient in themselves to explain the timing or account for the geographical emphasis of the missionary project that did not emerge until relatively late in the eighteenth century. The Evangelical Revival had been underway for at least two generations before its missionary potential was realized. Furthermore, theological imperatives to evangelize do not explain why foreign missions achieved their extraordinary pride of place in evangelicalism's "movement culture."[7] Foreign missionary expansion was accompanied by considerable missionary outreach to Britain's own ostensibly heathen working classes. Growing up alongside and often at the instigation of the same activists who founded foreign missionary organizations were Sunday schools, itinerant societies, bible societies, and the like. Despite its equal claims to theological validity, however, the home missionary movement lacked the support—in terms of funds raised, volunteers recruited, and propaganda produced and disseminated—enjoyed by its hugely popular foreign counterpart. Neither evangelical theology nor colonial social control can alone account for the missionary movement's geographic farsightedness, or "telescopic philanthropy," as its critic Charles Dickens would later describe it in *Bleak House*.

This chapter will suggest a more contingent explanation for the outpouring of interest in foreign missions among British Protestants and for the institutional and geographic forms in which this interest found expression. The origins of the foreign missionary preoccupation for which the Victorians are renowned are located in the multiple transformations and crises that constituted the "age of revolution" in Britain as well as in the colonized and soon-to-be colonized world.[8] Following the historical processes that gave rise to the missionary obsessions of the Victorians requires our moving back and forth and back again across the geographical, social, and political space between metropole and colony, rulers and the ruled. We must complicate if not dissolve altogether these complex social, political, and spatial boundaries. We should remember that as their missionary zeal was developing, our subjects were also experiencing the multiplicity of pressures that are considered separately here in the interest of narrative clarity. By following our subjects' lead, this chapter will begin its account of the birth of modern missions with the theological determinations around which all other forces converged and to which they were in this sense subordinate.

"I went to America to convert the Indians, but oh, who shall convert me?"[9]

One of the primary obstacles in the way of Hanoverian missionary expansion was the widespread aversion to the kind of religious "enthusiasms" that had embroiled the nation in civil war during the previous century. Religious fanaticism was viewed by most eighteenth-century Britons with far more fear and loathing than was the purportedly "noble savagery" of the heathen world.[10] This anxiety took different forms across the denominational spectrum, but in none of its forms did it encourage a missionary praxis. Old Dissent (members of the churches that formed around the Puritan ministers who were ejected from the Church of England after the Stuart Restoration in 1662) took advantage of the Act of Toleration (extended in return for Dissenters' support of William and Mary's accession to the throne in the Glorious Revolution of 1688) to withdraw into their "gardens walled round."[11] In retreat from if not in repudiation of the political activism of their Puritan forefathers, eighteenth-century Congregationalists, Baptists, Quakers, and Presbyterians effectively turned their backs on the world outside their closely knit communities. They found solace in their Calvinistic doctrine of predestination, which if anything hardened in response to the discrimination under which Dissenters continued to live and labor. Shrinking numbers could be brushed away or even embraced with pride, as evidence of the election of those who remained. But their continued belief in predestination did little to encourage missionary outreach to those beyond the community of the saved.[12]

The Unitarian alternative that attracted a small but influential grouping of Presbyterians and Baptists did not do much in this vein, either. Rational Christians rejected predestination and all forms of theological controversy in favor of a "view of Christianity as a way of life," an "appeal to reason as illuminated by the Spirit." They emphasized a benevolent God over an atoning Christ whose divinity was called into question. And with Christ decentered, Unitarianism could easily tolerate alternative articulations of the divine.[13] Deists went even further in rejecting the revelatory foundations of piety laid down in the Middle Ages in favor of a belief that true religion was encoded in human nature. Individuals could look within their own hearts to discern the will of the divine, which was only obscured by the priestly interposition in organized religion. The new worlds brought to view in this age of exploration were not condemned for their heathenism but embraced as evidence that "unspoiled man" was "far superior to the decadent, priest-ridden faith of the Christians."[14]

Anglicans were also suspicious in the aftermath of the Restoration of any and all intense or enthusiastic professions of faith on which efforts to proselytize depended. The increasingly dominant latitudinarian strain within Anglican theology emphasized the ostensibly uncontroversial practice of "good works" as the primary means to salvation. This perspective produced extensive philanthropy; for philanthropic generosity the Hanoverians would not be surpassed for many generations to come.[15] However, eighteenth-century philanthropy differed from its nineteenth-century successor in at least two connected regards. The religious goals toward which it was directed had more to do with the philanthropists' salvation than with their beneficiaries'. Good works were performed, in other words, to secure the philanthropists' entry into heaven. The spiritual well-being of philanthropy's target populations was simply not at issue, as is reflected in the emphasis of Hanoverian philanthropy on the relief of physical suffering—on building hospitals, foundling homes, Magdalene societies, insane asylums, and so forth—rather than, as would later be the case, on religious indoctrination for its own sake.[16]

It was in opposition to these prevailing tendencies that foreign missionary ambitions first surfaced in Britain. There were those, especially within the Anglican High Church Party, who were disturbed by the doctrinal tolerance of those for whom works were the uppermost concern. During the opening decades of the eighteenth century, their alarm mounted at what they perceived to be a growing problem of moral laxness and heterodoxy. It was the church itself, rather than any "heathen" external world, that was in need, they felt, of purification. And it was to these ends that this cohort directed its intensely spiritual energies, establishing religious societies to promote holiness and morality within the Church of England itself.

These religious societies included the Society for Promoting Christian Knowledge (SPCK) and the Society for the Propagation of the Gospel (SPG), which were founded in 1699 and 1701, respectively. Although important and inspirational precursors to the modern missionary movement, these societies differed from their evangelical successors in a number of important ways. Their efforts to export the Christian faith were "sporadic and haphazard."[17] Their outreach abroad, moreover, was confined, at least for the most part, to European settlers. Their missionaries were, in effect, chaplains to the European functionaries of the joint stock companies through which British colonization was pursued in this period. Individual chaplains occasionally took it upon themselves to minister to the indigenous people who lived in their proximity, but even these efforts were "entirely subordinate" to their "conception of the colony." As the Rev. William Fleming Stevenson explained a century later, the eighteenth-century mission was "a kind of spiritual clearing round the settlement. As far as the heathen came within its range, were settlers on its land, or fringed its log-houses, they were under Christian care."[18]

Among the missionaries sent out to the colonies by the SPG was one John Wesley, who went on to become a leading figure in Britain's Evangelical Revival. Wesley's father, the Rev. Samuel Wesley, was a High Churchman and a staunch supporter of spiritual reform, and John Wesley was in many ways simply following in his father's footsteps when he organized prayer groups at Oxford to support his efforts to lead a more godly and spiritual existence. The intensely spiritual self-scrutiny to which Wesley's High Church cohort were prone took place in addition to rather than in place of the good works of their latitudinarian peers. Like so many of his contemporaries, Wesley was an active philanthropist: he visited prisons, he taught orphaned children to read, he cared for the poor and the elderly, and so forth. And with similar motivations he embarked for Georgia in 1737 under the auspices of the SPG.

Wesley went to Georgia for the express purpose of doing missionary work among the Indians. But like most of his missionary counterparts in the colonies, Wesley's ministry was effectively confined to Europeans. The reasons Wesley abandoned his ministry to the Indians are not entirely clear. He was certainly discouraged from ministering to the Indians by the governor of the colony, James Oglethorpe. And Wesley's ability to resist Oglethorpe's directive was weakened by the difficulties of ministering to scattered European settlements in the frontier conditions of the day; there simply was not sufficient time for him to do both. But Wesley was tellingly quick to place the blame for the failure of his mission to Georgia's native inhabitants squarely on the shoulders of the Indians themselves, complaining repeatedly in his journal that they had not "the least desire of being instructed." For Wesley, this was sufficient justification for ceasing his efforts on their behalf.[19]

Wesley's impatience with the Indian beneficiaries of his ministry reflects a very different structure of feeling than that which would characterize his nineteenth-century successors. The latter typically spent the better part of their adult lives at mission stations where they were often ridiculed when not ignored, and where they might see decades or more go by without a convert to show for their labors. But Victorian missionaries were far more likely than were those of Wesley's day to remain at their posts. Their willingness to minister did not depend on the desire or virtue of their target audience. Indeed, quite the opposite was the case; it was the latter's vices and resistance that called and kept the missionary in the mission field and that sacralized his sacrifice.

Wesley's inability to persevere at his post was, perhaps, a function of the very theology of works that brought him to the colonial mission field in the first place. Wesley himself made it clear that anxieties about his own spiritual salvation, rather than that of his audience, directed his steps in the foreign field, as they had at home. As Wesley insisted in a letter to John Burton in 1735, "My chief motive is the hope of saving my own soul. I hope to learn the true sense of the Gospel of Christ by preaching it to the Heathen . . . to know what it is to love my neighbor as myself."[20] The emotions stirred up by his few contacts with Indians, however, were far from the loving peace of mind he sought. Wesley refers to Indians repeatedly in his journal as "gluttons, drunkards, thieves, dissemblers, liars"—no loving sentiments these. But even worse, their alleged limitations rendered missionary outreach futile: "they show no inclination to learn anything, but least of all Christianity, being full as opinionated of their own parts and wisdom as either modern Chinese or ancient Roman."[21]

Nineteenth-century missionaries often drew similarly disparaging conclusions about the communities to whom they ministered, openly delighting in the thought that their missionary presence would secure the eternal damnation of those audiences who dared to reject their message.[22] Their targets' resistance, however, did not call into question the missionary's own spiritual prospects; these latter were secured elsewhere. Wesley had no such theological defense to hand when he went into the mission field in 1737. The failure of those to whom he preached to tolerate much less seek his counsel deprived Wesley of the opportunity to perform those good works on which his own salvation depended. Wesley's desperation reached new depths in the resistant colonial setting, which he fled in disgrace in December 1737, less than two years after his arrival. "I went to America to convert the Indians," he confided miserably to his journal on the eve of his humiliating retreat back to England, "but oh, who shall convert me?"[23]

Wesley's encounters with Indians in the colonies contributed to the spiritual crisis that culminated in Wesley's personal awakening and, through his subsequent evangelical ministry, in that of the British nation at large.[24] Within only a few months after his return to London, Wesley would find peace and power in the assurance that salvation was his by faith. On May 24, 1738, Wesley reluctantly attended a small Sunday evening gathering of fellow travelers in the pietistic way (who were already being called Methodists for their regular habits of meeting, prayer, and daily routine) on Aldersgate Street in London. While listening to a reading of Luther's Preface to the Epistle to the Romans, Wesley's heart was "strangely warmed." It was then that he knew for the first time with certainty that in dying on the cross, Christ "had taken away *my* sins, even *mine*, and saved *me* from the law of sin and death."[25]

The importance of this theological shift is signaled by the fact that it was shortly thereafter that Wesley began finding himself barred from Anglican pulpits to which he had been welcomed years or even months before. His attempts to awaken others to the fact that eternal salvation was theirs through faith and faith alone was socially as well as theologically offensive, forming as it did a direct challenge to the more exclusive pathways being advertised by the Anglican establishment and its Dissenting critics alike. The Anglican theology of works was limited in practice if not in theory to those who could afford them, whereas Dissent's theology of predestination reserved hope for the narrow band of the elect. Wesley's Arminian doctrine of salvation through faith offered hope to all who chose to embrace it. It was on this choice that the urgency, the optimism, and the capacity to persevere that made Victorian missions possible would depend.

Wesley was not singly responsible, of course, for Britain's Evangelical Revival. This was international in inspiration as well as in consequences, and it connected Britain to Europe as well as to its own colonies. The first recorded conversions attributed to the Revival's influence took place not in Europe but in the colonies, under the revivalist ministry of Theodorus Frelinghuysen, a Dutch Reformed minister in New Jersey, as early as 1719.[26] The Moravian pietist community based at the estate of Count Nicholas von Zinzendorf in Berthelsdorf, Saxony, began sending missionaries out during the 1730s to the West Indies, Greenland, Surinam, South Africa, the Gold

Coast, and Ceylon. Wales was yet another apparently autonomous site of evangelical revelation. The Welsh revival began with the conversion of Howell Harris, a 21-year-old Anglican layman, and of Daniel Jones, an Anglican curate, in 1735.[27]

But it was Wesley's Oxford cohort that brought these separate developments into productive contact. George Whitefield was the first member of the Holy Club, a student prayer and study group that assembled around Wesley, to experience conversion, and he became the most popular preacher of the revival on both sides of the Atlantic. But it was the organizational genius of John Wesley himself that gave revived religion its historic purchase. His tightly centralized structure of bands, classes, and societies secured his Arminian branch of Methodism its prominent place in the Anglo-American religious spectrum. Wesley's influence was also felt outside Anglican and Methodist circles. In reaction to his authoritarian disposition, many of his converts made the decision to embrace Old Dissent, ensuring in the process the revival of the moribund and shrinking bands of Baptists, Independents, and Presbyterians as well.[28]

Although Congregationalists, including most notably Jonathan Edwards of Massachusetts, played a prominent role in the American Great Awakening, their English counterparts are notable for their absence from the roll call of the Revival's leaders. The latter were almost all connected with the Established Church, to which most remained loyal to the end of their career. By contrast, leading Congregationalists expressed considerable hostility toward evangelical zealots who were accused of disturbing the order and diverting the membership of Independent chapels throughout the nation. A century and more of persecution had encouraged English Congregationalists to withdraw from the world at large into what Isaac Watts described as "a garden wall'd around," a sensibility far removed from that insatiable desire to secure others' salvation that drove evangelicalism's missionary offshoots.[29]

These early fears were quickly put to rest by the dramatic gains in membership experienced by the heretofore stagnant congregations of Old Dissent in the Revival's aftermath. Wesley's insistent loyalty to the Church of England coupled with his personal authoritarianism made evergrowing numbers of his converts available to Independent, Baptist, Presbyterian, and Quaker congregations. Dissent benefited even more from the evangelical labors of yet another Anglican, George Whitefield, whose inattention to organizational matters left his numerous followers, many of whom drifted into Calvinist Dissent, bereft of institutional moorings.[30]

No Dissenting group gained more from this process than did Congregationalism, which was transformed in the second half of the eighteenth century from an inward-looking sect experiencing serious numerical decline into the third-largest denomination in the nation.[31] The Revival's impact on Congregationalism was gradual and uneven: "a minister here or a minister there" coming under its influence, "chapels filling with people eager to listen to the[ir] sermons . . . all happening quietly, unobtrusively, efficiently over a period of a half a century."[32] As a result, Congregationalism's relation to larger British society and to the world as a whole was radically transformed. Evangelicalism provided the missionary motive to "go forth" into the world as well as the means, in the form of an everexpanding rank and file, to finance missionary operations.

The Collectivization of Sin

As we can see from the narrative above, theological and colonial developments are not antithetical explanations of the birth of modern missions. To the contrary, the theological underpinning of modern missionary outreach, namely the certainty that salvation was achieved by faith, was brought home to John Wesley, at least in part, as a result of encounters in the colonies. His failure to convert the Indians underscored for Wesley the limitations of his High Church faith. However, while it was a necessary and preeminent feature, the evangelical assurance of salvation through faith was not sufficient to bring the missionary consciousness of the Victorians to life, at least not in its historically specific form.

The early missionary outreach of eighteenth-century evangelicals differed in important ways from the missionary project of the Victorians. Chief among these differences was the fact that their newfound interest in their beneficiaries' souls and their confidence in their own ability to secure another's salvation did not yet manifest the spatial boundedness of sin and salvation on which the institutional form of Victorian missions depended. Sin and salvation were for Wesley and his cohort the attributes of individuals; they did not yet mark the boundaries that separated discrete communities from one another.

For almost half a century after Wesley's conversion, evangelicals continued to locate their target (Satan, sin, heathenism) *within* the social worlds to which they imagined themselves to belong. Saved and sinners trembled together before Wesley's message, just as they lived and worked alongside one another in the communities through which Wesley moved. Depravity was as elusive as it was ubiquitous; the very fact that it existed was often unknown even to its host until he or she could be moved by evangelical eloquence and divine intervention into the revelatory throes of abject repentance.[33]

Travel the early Methodists certainly did, but from community to community in which sinners and saved were on the surface indistinguishable. Colonized peoples were sometimes their targets, though to a markedly lesser degree than were Europeans. Indeed, like their non-evangelical counterparts in the Establishment and Dissent, the early Methodists put home before foreign needs. Wesley himself never went back to the colonies, effectively handing the North American ministry over to his colleague, George Whitefield. Whitefield's efforts were almost entirely devoted, in turn, to saving the souls of European colonists. Wesley refused Whitefield's request for help with the work in America for decades on the grounds that he had no one to spare from the work at home.

Notwithstanding their pronounced theological differences (Whitefield embraced the Calvinist doctrine of predestination, in contrast to Wesley's Arminianism), Wesley and Whitefield proceeded from a similar conception of their heathen enemy, one that was markedly different from the conception underlying the practice of their Victorian missionary successors. Proselytism was the point of *every* ceremony that Wesley and his cohort performed in the belief that heathenism was ever present and that Satan must first be rooted out from within our midst, which extended right down to the individual evangelical. Victorian missionary practice, by contrast, was predicated on the assumption that heathenism resided outside the individual, that it was a characteristic feature of entire communities.

The institutionalization of the missionary impulse—the formation of organizations and the appointment of functionaries explicitly devoted to missions—depended upon there being identifiable boundaries between the missionary and his target population. For missionary work to be institutionalized, its proponents had to have a priori knowledge of where to recruit as well as where to station their missionaries. Missionary institutions depended, in other words, on sinners and the saved living in geographically separate worlds, whose connection missionaries could be sent out to effect.

The perception of heathenism as spatially confined was, to an even greater extent than was the missionary presumption that salvation derived from faith, a consequence of imperial developments. It was the product, more specifically, of that seismic shift in British colonial policy in the decades bracketing the nineteenth century's turn. The British colonial project was recast in this period from its former emphasis on promoting European settlement to the conquering and governance of large indigenous populations. I do not mean to suggest here that British settlement in North America had not required violence; I simply mean that the British were less concerned about governing indigenous American peoples than they were about removing them from their land. By contrast, Britain's primary concern in India and later Africa would be to establish and maintain political sovereignty over the indigenous majority of the colonial population.[34]

This fundamental transformation in the British colonial project had enormous implications for how colonized peoples would be regarded by those who governed them. As we shall see, the imperatives of rule even more than the privileges of pillage helped to produce ever more derogatory views of the colonized, including an increasing emphasis on their heathen status. Less heralded but equally important insofar as the birth of a missionary consciousness is concerned are the consequences of the imperial developments of this period for the empire's British home front. For heathenism's recasting during the 1780s and 1790s included a narrowing of its frame of reference at home, where it was increasingly viewed as a characteristic condition of the poor.

The social construction of the poor as characteristically heathen required not only a transformation in the religious public's understanding of sin and salvation but a transformation in philanthropic constructions of poverty as well. As we have seen, eighteenth-century philanthropy was not designed, at least primarily, to enhance its targets' spiritual well-being.[35] The poor, in other words, were not construed in this period as distinctively heathen at all. In fact, poor people were generally believed to be protected by their simplicity (as poverty was often euphemistically described) from the temptations to which their betters succumbed. Salvation in the life to come would be their reward simply for accepting as God's will their station in this world.

Such humanitarian forms of charity were gradually displaced over the course of the nineteenth century by a more missionary mode of philanthropy. This was in part the result of the imperial developments previously described.[36] As Donna Andrew has recently argued, the secular provisions of eighteenth-century philanthropy served vital national interests in a society widely believed to be facing a demographic crisis of underpopulation—relative, that is, to the growing demand for human capital to invest in Britain's rapidly expanding colonial settlements. In other words, the corporeal ministrations of Hanoverian philanthropy served the useful political and economic function of augmenting the physical health and reproductive well-being of those sectors of the British population from which potential settlers were recruited. Particular attention was paid in this regard to the reproductive capability of the young and female poor. Lying-in hospitals for pregnant women, foundling societies for abandoned children, and lock-hospitals and Magdalene societies for the treatment of venereal disease and the reclamation of prostitutes were all designed to improve infant mortality rates and to restore to usefulness the bodies as much as the souls of those lost to respectable society as a result of vice.[37]

The colonial spoils that Britain accrued from its victory over France in the Seven Years War dealt the first blow to this mercantile colonial vision. The acquisition of heavily populated territory in areas of Africa, Asia, and the Caribbean required that the British colonial establishment devote ever more of its attention to governing indigenous populations rather than to transplanting British settlers to take their place.[38] The American Revolution was an even more significant turning point. The loss of the American colonies was a terrific blow to Britain's settlement policies; at the time, Britain possessed few other territories with comparable potential.

The resulting decline in official interest in promoting European settlement in Britain's colonies weakened an important rationale for the provision of "humanitarian" or material forms of relief to the poor. The philanthropic public in Britain became ever less inclined to invest its wealth in charities that enhanced the reproductive capacities of a social grouping whose demographic increase the colonies no longer needed and could no longer absorb. The impact of these colonial developments on metropolitan philanthropy was exacerbated by contemporaneous developments in the metropolitan economy, which lessened the need for labor's application on the empire's British home front. The commercialization of agriculture in the closing decades of the eighteenth century was, at least initially, accompanied by high levels of unemployment and underemployment in Britain. The nascent industrial sector—limited in its extent as we now know it to have been, especially in the south of England—would not be able to offset the decline in demand for labor for years to come.[39] What industry that existed in this period needed not more but better, that is, more disciplined workers. The swelling ranks of those unemployed by agriculture's simultaneous improvement increased the pressure on the poor rates. This coupled with thefts against property occasioned by distress, contributed to the rise of Malthusian anxieties about overpopulation during the tumultuous decades that bracketed the nineteenth century's turn.[40]

These imperial and metropolitan developments converged to transform the forms of charitable outreach in Great Britain. The first order of response to the nation's social crisis was an intensified paternalism based on the outdoor (that is to say, outside the workhouse) provision of material relief to the unemployed. This so-called Speenhamland solution, named for the Berkshire parish at which these policies were pursued most aggressively, was the preferred response of especially southeastern farmers, who were concerned about preserving a ready supply of labor.[41] But growing numbers of propertied people, including but not limited to the evangelical middle classes, deemed such policies the cause of and not the solution to the problem of poverty. In this emergent critique of humanitarian philanthropy, secular assistance (in the form of alms, health care, housing, food, coal, blankets, etc.) was increasingly viewed as a very cruel form of kindness, which simply encouraged the kind of "irresponsible" behavior, such as "over-breeding," on which poverty was increasingly blamed.[42] "It fosters habits of idleness and vice, of luxury and waste, of thoughtlessness and improvidence, of servility and discontent," and it was itself held responsible for "most of the evils which have lately pressed so severely upon the poorer classes of society."[43]

Evangelicals promoted missionary philanthropy as an alternative to such misguided forms of outreach to the poor. Ministering to working-class souls rather than providing for working-class bodies was touted as a "charity of the most enlightened nature; charity which no just views of political economy, no general speculations on the condition of mankind, can for a moment render questionable."[44] Reforming manners and saving souls took increasing precedence over saving lives. The founding of the Proclamation Society in 1787, the Religious Tract Society in 1799, the Society for the Suppression of Vice in 1801, the British and Foreign Bible Society (BFBS) in 1804, and numerous Sunday schools and itinerant societies from the 1780s on, were all manifestations of a fundamental shift from a humanitarian to a missionary mode of philanthropy, a shift that prefigured the transformation of political philosophies of governance culminating in the reform of the Poor Law in 1834.[45]

The Problem of Authority for the Free-Born Englishman

The poor were not, of course, the only social group targeted by the new missionary mode of philanthropy. Colonized peoples were made available for missionary philanthropy by the same shift in British imperial focus from settlement to conquest that had made the British poor available, although the two groups of missionary beneficiaries were affected in decidedly different ways. The laboring poor in Britain were rendered in need of missionary outreach as a result, at least in part, of their imperial obsolescence. Colonized peoples, by contrast, figured ever more centrally in the colonial project. The British colonial establishment faced a novel constellation of forces and interests in its new colonies in the East. The indigenous people of Britain's first North American empire had been treated primarily as objects to be removed; their souls were of minimal concern to a colonizing population that coveted their land and not their labor. By rendering indigenous removal and European settlement alike effectively impossible, demographics pressed the problems of governing indigenous populations to the fore.

This was taking place at the very same time that Britain's governing classes were being forced to rethink their basic approach to colonial government in the wake of the American fiasco. Britain's governing classes drew

from their humiliation at the hands of the American colonists the lesson that
their mistake had not been their abuse but rather their neglect of the prereq-
uisites of power. Under the ostensible rationale of checking the excesses of
colonial elites left too much to their own devices—which was publicized most
dramatically in the impeachment trial of Warren Hastings—the British government initiated a series of reforms designed to strengthen London's authority in the day-to-day managing of colonial affairs. The indigenous elites as well
as European expatriates through whom Great Britain had heretofore ruled indirectly were rapidly displaced during the opening decades of the nineteenth
century by the personal representatives of the Crown. This enhancement of
the colonial executive was accompanied by a "growing and orchestrated contempt for the Asian, African and even European subordinates" whose purportedly innate corruption provided the ultimate rationale for the reforms that
were being undertaken, at least ostensibly, on indigenous people's behalf.[46]

  This transformation of colonial policy posed a serious problem for a nation taking shape in an age of revolution. For the increasing authoritarianism
of British colonial rule at the turn of the nineteenth century exposed contradictions at the heart of a national identity whose origins were very new. As
Linda Colley has recently argued, British national identity coalesced over the
course of the eighteenth century around a dynamic admixture of religious
and colonial appeals in which France figured prominently as the British nation's defining Other. The diverse peoples of England, Wales, and Scotland
were persuaded that their differences could be contained within a unitary national identity by a discourse that emphasized their similarities by contrast to
the French. And religion figured prominently in this new language of the nation. It was to religion that eighteenth-century Britons increasingly attributed the distinctive rights and privileges of free-born British citizens: "wherever there was any degree of liberty, the Protestant religion" was said to have
prevailed. And it was religion that they blamed for the autocratic forms of
governance to which their counterparts in France were subjected. As Congregational minister Rev. David Bogue put it: "wherever there was arbitrary
power, by its sanguinary aid Popery kept its place."[47] Colonial expansion figured in this nationalist equation as the divine reward for Britons' religious
and political virtues; the military weakness of Britain's vanquished rival was
laid at the feet of an unchecked absolutism from which the British had been
rescued by the Glorious Revolution and the Protestant succession.[48]

  It is more than a little ironic that the very colonial spoils that Britain accrued in its century-long succession of wars with France posed what was perhaps the most serious challenge to the fundamental meanings of Britishness
to date. How were "free-born" Britons to govern such a densely populated

and far-flung colonial empire (which included a quarter of the world's population by 1820) without resorting to the autocratic and militaristic methods
of rule of their despised French foils? This problem was further exacerbated
by the succession of acts of resistance of colonized peoples and colonists alike,
which destabilized European colonial authority in this period. The American
Revolution was followed in its turn by the execution of Captain Cook, by
scandals in India, by slave revolts throughout the empire, and, most threaten-
ingly, by the Haitian revolution. The demise of autocracy in France made
colonial resistance all the more damaging to the British nation's claim to a
distinctive proclivity for liberty.

On the most general level, missionary philanthropy helped to reconcile
the contradictory imperatives of Britain's constitutionalist traditions, however
invented these latter might have been, and the perceived necessity of authoritarian colonial practices through which the empire was increasingly being
governed. Missionary propaganda claimed divine approval for the British
colonial project, ensuring that British colonial expansion would be effectively
sacralized in the popular imagination as the means by which "the widespread valleys of Africa and the East may, ere long, yield a blessed harvest to
his praise."[49] In his Annual Sermon for the supporters of the LMS in 1819,
the Rev. John Angell James drew his audience's attention to the many occasions on which secular developments had ensured the gospel's advance.

> The world is given to Jesus, and he is incessantly employed in bringing it to
> himself. . . . Little did Julius Caesar imagine . . . for what purpose he disem-
> barked his legions on our coast; but we know that it was to open a door through
> which the Gospel might enter our beloved country. Little did the spirit of com-
> mercial enterprise imagine, when urged only the *auri sacra fames*, it fixed its es-
> tablishments at the mouth of the Hoogley or on the banks of the Ganges, that it
> was sent thither as the forerunner of Christian Missionaries. Little does the ge-
> nius of war imagine, when impelling its mad votaries to new contests, that
> Christianity is following at a distance, in the rear of victorious armies, to plant
> her stations.[50]

Secular officials paid their homage in turn. While often critical of missionaries in private and opposed to them in practice, colonial officials invariably referred to them in public in highly favorable terms. Margary Perham's
assertion that "the selfless work of the Christian missionaries . . . may prove
the most precious service of all" those that the empire allegedly performed
was typical in this regard.[51] It was a short step to the kind of grandiose claims
so frequently aired at the nineteenth century's close—claims to the affect
that the British Empire was "the greatest instrument of good that the world
has seen."[52]

Christian missions figured in official as well as missionary rationales as the ultimate gift exchanged in the colonial encounter, one that bestowed upon violent, superstitious, and perishing peoples the benefit of eternal salvation. Until that faraway day when the colonized had learned the lessons of Christian civilization, the British would govern, directly or indirectly, formally or informally, on their behalf. In this way did skill at wielding imperial authority in the interest of the governed take its unlikely place alongside love of liberty as a distinguishing feature of British national character.

Missions as a Politics of Middle-Class Opposition

My argument has thus far pitted the propertied classes in Britain against the laboring poor at home and the indigenous populations of the empire. But propertied Britons were themselves divided in ways that were registered and contested in missionary philanthropy's emergence. Not all Britons were convinced of the political efficacy of missionary methods of control. Indeed, the deployment of missionaries at home and abroad was enormously controversial in Great Britain as well as in the colonies. I want now to suggest that missions were a distinctively middle-class alternative to gentry modes of authority, a means of controlling the lower orders at home as well as abroad that was in direct opposition to traditional or gentry forms of rule.

Religion more generally and missions in particular were an important marker and mediator of the considerable social distance that separated the largely provincial and industrial middle class, on which the missionary movement depended for the bulk of its support, from a landed elite that continued to control the institutions of the British state, at least at the national level.[53] Although it was not impossible to cross, the divide between the provincial middle classes and Britain's political establishment remained wide at the end of the eighteenth century. Even the most successful industrial magnates were outsiders from the point of view of Great Britain's political elite. The middling ranks of British society were not without social status and economic clout from the point of view of the laboring poor, nor were they without concomitant political influence at the local level. But they were a "dominated fraction within the dominant class," lacking formal political power, especially at the national level, at which colonial policy was determined.[54]

Religion would play an increasingly important role in the closing decades of the eighteenth century in mediating this sociopolitical divide. Membership in the Established Church of England was a prerequisite of national political office and a social marker of gentry status at the local level. Obviously the boundaries of the church were drawn more widely. Laborers were not absent, though their participation was increasingly limited to holidays and rites of passage.[55] And the prevailing stereotype of entrepreneurial dissent notwithstanding, a good many manufacturers, clothiers, commercial travelers, merchants, and the like appear to have found in the Established Church social connections that helped to compensate for the relative lack of status accorded to their bourgeois occupations.[56] Rubbing shoulders with the local gentry provided ties to politicians and placemen that were vital for acquiring government contracts and other political favors conducive to business success.[57]

The middle class did not, therefore, require dissent in religion, or in politics for that matter. Religious dissent did provide, however, an alternative and politically oppositional model of middle-classness. Dissenting institutions, particularly in the provinces, were dominated to a considerable degree by industrial entrepreneurs (in the case of Congregationalism men such as Titus Salt, Samuel Morley, John Crossley, Albert Spicer, and Henry Wills) who largely bankrolled their operations. For such individuals, temperament or social circumstance precluded the close association with the landed elite incumbent upon religious conformity; religious dissent, both rational and evangelical, provided a more protective haven in a world that was, if not heartless in its treatment of the wealthy, then slow to reward economic advance with enhanced social status or political influence.[58] Serious religion provided a powerful basis from which to attack the lifeways of the establishment as degenerate, frivolous, and immoral; it even served as evidence of the elite's basic unfitness to rule. Dissent functioned as a cultural weapon with which provincial and industrial capitalists could berate their gentlemanly superiors, a language and institutional practice through which an ambitious fraction within the industrial bourgeoisie could challenge the legitimacy of the establishment's social and political as well as religious power. Dissent would, in fact, comprise the religious precipitant of the oppositional radicalism from which popular liberalism took shape alongside its Whiggish variant in Parliament. It was no accident that in England, as elsewhere, freedom of religious worship would be one of the constitutive political concerns of a nascent liberal movement.[59]

These tensions within the propertied classes did not make themselves felt until the closing decades of the eighteenth century. The passage of the Toleration Act in 1688 and the influence of Enlightenment rationalism and humanism in Old Dissent and of latitudinarianism in the church helped to diminish the potential volatility of religious difference. At the same time, the specter of Catholicism appears to have overridden the social, political, and religious resentments with which the Dissenting fraction of the middle class viewed its betters. Dissenters seemed to have accepted their own disabilities as a judicious prophylactic against the everpresent threat of Roman Catholic advance.[60] There was considerable cooperation between Dissenting "saints" and Anglican clergy, and even the laity was increasingly inclined over the course of the eighteenth century to occasionally conform or dissent, as the case may be.[61]

During the second half of the eighteenth century, however, political discontent within the ranks of the respectable and propertied public became increasingly apparent. The possibility of a Stuart restoration was effectively removed in the aftermath of the Jacobite rising of 1745. It was not until the 1770s and 1780s that Dissent joined the ranks of political opposition. Dissenters who had been loyal to the government during the reigns of the first two Georges were increasingly alienated by government policies during the reign of George III.[62] Their political alienation was connected, no doubt, to the social transformation of revived Dissent. The increasingly plebian profile of especially provincial Nonconformity had its corollary in the prominence of Nonconformists within artisan radicalism from the 1770s on.[63]

Missions were a lightning rod for the heightened social tensions of this turbulent period. They were, as we have seen, a product of the transformation in the British colonial project, a means of governing colonies whose indigenous inhabitants could no longer be eliminated, enslaved, or removed. The Established Church's colonial missions (the SPG and the SPCK) would adapt themselves to this role, as would the missionary organization founded by the church's own increasingly influential evangelical wing, the Church Missionary Society.

In the hands of Dissent, however, the foreign missionary agenda was initially articulated in terms that were more critical of the empire's official classes. Foreign missions were conceived of, in other words, as an alternative to the increasingly authoritarian forms of rule by which the British state hoped to avoid a repetition of the American Revolution.[64] Dissenting missionary enthusiasts upbraided the ruling elite for a martial tyranny the American colonists were deemed right to have resisted, and they issued dire warnings that continuing its tyrannous ways would bring down upon the British nation the wrath of a vengeful god.[65] Missionary advocates accusingly commented on the vast and growing number of "distant countries . . . which our armies have overrun, and which we have seized as our own—countries which our troops are now wetting with the tears and with the blood of the innocent inhabitants—countries from which we have for a long course of years been dragging the wretched natives to worse than Egyptian bondage," asking "where is the country which we have exerted our zeal to rescue from pagan darkness or Mahometan delusion, and to bring to the knowledge and consolations of the gospel?"[66] Missionary philanthropy was promoted as a form of atonement, a way for the nation to confess and absolve itself of the sins it was committing in the colonized world. In 1811, the Rev. John Wilcox berated his nation, "this the land of privileges, this nursery of liberty," for "holding millions of its fellow creatures in iron bonds."

> Are we, the far-famed champions of freedom exercising such a tyranny as will not bear the light of scripture? It cannot be: or if it be a truth, a truth the patriot Christian can but mourn; allegiance to my country and my King commands me to admonish the state to repent the grievous wrongs inflicted, and sooner to renounce the sovereignty even of worlds, than hold it on such a tenure.[67]

These resentments might be understood as a middle-class tax revolt against a swollen imperial bureaucracy's growing demands for revenue. But such concerns found expression in early missionary propaganda in terms that would have larger political significance—political in the sense of involving the very means of producing and reproducing social power. Missions provided not just an occasion to criticize the colonial status quo but a prescription for a new world order. By contrast to the establishment's increasing reliance on coercion, the evangelical rationale for imperial expansion was predicated on an alternative mode of authority, one in which social order and political stability were linked to the production of consent among the governed. Christianity was explicitly promoted as "the only effectual barrier that could oppose the demoralizing and destructive career of atheism"; "religion and the religious" were deemed, in this regard, "the best friends to the well-being of the state."[68]

The same logic was advanced with regard to missions at home, although it was the religious establishment's neglect rather than its abuse of the lower orders that required home missionary redress. As the founders of the Essex Congregational Union put it in 1798, while "the British Nation hath long been favoured with the Glorious Gospel of the blessed God . . . it is exceedingly to be lamented, that in various parts of the Country, this privilege is not fully enjoyed, and that many persons are living in gross Ignorance, Irreligion, and Wickedness."[69] The challenge to the establishment in formulations such as these was obvious to all concerned. Whenever a "Methodist Preacher came to an Anglican parish in the spirit, and with the language of a missionary going to the most ignorant heathens, he asked the clergyman to lend him his pulpit, in order that he might instruct his parishioners for the first time in the true Gospel of Christ," the Anglican priest, not to mention his parishioners, could not fail to register the insult.[70]

Such analogies between the home and foreign mission fields will be discussed more fully in the next chapter. It is sufficient for our present purpose to observe the critique of the establishment implicit in home missionary claims that the British "people have been almost inevitably left as destitute of religious instruction, and as far removed from the personal cognizance of their legitimate pastor, as if they had colonized the oases of an African desert, or the interminable steppes of Siberia."[71] The affront to Anglican sensibilities became even more transparent when evangelicals openly assumed the guise of a missionary. As the nineteenth-century historian and Congregational minister, Rev. R. W. Dale, recognized, this gave "offense on the ground that it treated as heathen a nation that in name, at any rate, was Christian."[72]

My point here is that the politics of missions in their founding phase were implicitly if not explicitly oppositional, conveying as they did a critique of the political establishment's claims to moral authority. This is not to say that the missionary language of opposition was antiauthoritarian, much less antinational. As Hugh Cunningham has pointed out, the language of political opposition in this period was deeply patriotic.[73] Indeed, defining the nation's interest and claiming to represent it was the principal terrain on which social and political struggle took place in eighteenth- and nineteenth-century England. That it was oppositional, however, was not to say that it was democratic, nor that it was opposed to imperialism in principle. Evangelicals were not asking the nation to sacrifice its imperial interests; to the contrary, they claimed that missions represented an alternative mode of colonial control that was more efficacious than was that of their military or paternalist counterparts.

While they might have been intended to contain the aspirations of subalterns at home as well as abroad, missions sought to do so by means very different from those on which the establishment had heretofore depended and which it would continue to promote. Missions were not, therefore, simply a functionalist instrument of social control, deployed by and in the interests of a unitary ruling class. The birth of modern missions was a politically contested solution to the problem of social order; it was the contingent outcome of class struggles as much as it was an exigency of colonial or metropolitan social control. Missions were promoted as an alternative to the social relations of power sanctioned by the British ruling elite at home as well as abroad, and the missionary mobilization of the masses conveyed what traditional elites considered to be highly subversive messages about the spiritual equality of believers. As Victor Kiernan has put it, "to invite peasants [or colonized people, I would add] to read Scripture themselves, unguided [the reference here is to the BFBS] was to overthrow, in the end, all respect for law and order."[74]

The Primacy of the Foreign Field

Secure in its hegemony, Britain's governing classes tolerated, albeit uneasily, the mounting tide of missionary activism during the 1770s and 1780s. This uneasy truce, however, foundered abruptly with the outbreak of revolution in and then war against France. Evangelicals, and particularly the Nonconformists among them, were widely suspected of Jacobin sympathies. And their missionary expansion became, as a result, increasingly intolerable to the establishment. Interestingly, however, home and foreign missions weathered these storms with significantly different degrees of success. The intensification of metropolitan social tensions in this period resulted for historically contingent reasons in the privileging of the foreign mission cause over its home counterpart.

The Dissenting supporters of missionary outreach at home as well as abroad were often, as their critics suspected, involved in the radical and reform campaigns of the late eighteenth century, and many were also, at least initially, enthusiastic supporters of the French Revolution. Robert Haldane, one of Scotland's leading advocates of foreign missionary expansion, described himself as being "aroused from the sleep of spiritual death by the excitement of the French Revolution."[75] The Rev. Bogue—a Congregational minister in Gosport, a founding editor of the *Evangelical Magazine*, and one of the central figures involved in the founding of the LMS—was subpoenaed as a material witness during the infamous treason trial of Hardy, Horne, Tooke, and Thelwall in 1794, and it was suggested that he was involved in the naval mutinies in Spithead several years later.[76]

Bogue himself reacted with "severe mortification" to the charges raised against him, protesting his innocence of what he considered to be any "active interference" in politics whatsoever (an abstinence that extended to his failure to exercise his right to vote in county elections). And certainly, Bogue's circle of associates, however suspect in the eyes of the government, was far more respectable than were the working-class cadres of the London Corresponding Society or the merchant marine. But Bogue's radical opposition to the established order was also very real, as was its intimate connection to his evangelical ardor. The tensions between evangelical Dissent and the British political establishment are particularly evident in his infamous address to the Scottish Society for Promoting Religious Knowledge in the Highlands in 1792, a sermon that made Bogue's radical reputation in the eyes of a critical establishment.

Perhaps the most striking characteristic of this sermon to the present-day reader is Bogue's open enthusiasm for the revolutionary developments unfolding in France. Bogue pronounced the recent overthrow of the French monarchy a blow against "tyranny" that heralded the advance of the Kingdom of God. There is a level at which Bogue's analysis of the revolution could be understood as patriotic support for his own nation's governing system, since the primary evidence he cites of political tyranny is the French state's support for Roman Catholicism: "at the time of the reformation from Popery, there arose in every country in Europe men professing the Protestant religion; but why did not the Protestant religion every where prevail? The sole cause was this; the tyranny of human governments stretched out its iron fangs, and tore to pieces its professors, or drove them from their country and their home." Protestantism's victory in England would thus seem incontrovertible evidence of the liberal character of the English constitution.

But Britain's governing classes were almost certainly outraged if not frightened by Bogue's enthusiastic prediction that the revolutionary forces unleashed in France were certain to spread to the realms of England's most important allies: "this generation shall not pass away before the expiring groans of arbitrary power are heard through every country in Europe, and the lovers of mankind are called on to rejoice over her, as the murderer of the witnesses of Jesus Christ." Anglican listeners had good reason to suspect that Bogue's diatribes against false religion might apply to their own practices as well. Bogue's discussion of civil liberty, for example, as "the scaffold on which the builders stand to erect the fabric of the church of Christ; and . . . a preparatory step to the extending of the Redeemer's kingdom" seemed expressly designed to provide religious legitimization for the radical aspirations the revolution had unleashed in Britain itself. Civil liberty was the watchword of the campaign for the repeal of the Test and Corporation Acts, on which Dissenters embarked in the immediate aftermath of the outbreak of revolution in France, implicitly if not explicitly suggesting that the powers exerted by the British state, too, had arbitrary elements in need of reform.[77]

In the face of such vociferous opposition and in light of the debacle unfolding on the continent, the British government instituted one of the fiercest clampdowns on political opposition in its history.[78] While restrictions were aimed primarily at Paineite and working-class radicals, Dissenters were targeted as well. A torrent of anti-evangelical invective poured out of establishment organs of propaganda during the 1790s and 1800s; this invective drew direct connections between the religious wars of the seventeenth century and the present state of emergency. Typical in this regard was the alarm sounded in *The Anti-Jacobin* in October of 1800:

> The descendants of the puritans are still found among us, in great numbers; they retain the same principles which in England and America have produced so

much disturbance; they take care by their offspring and the seminaries, to transmit those principles to their posterity; and they have, with few exceptions, admired, extolled, nay even encouraged and promoted, to the utmost of their power, the French Revolution, because it was founded upon their own principles.[79]

Missions, both foreign and domestic, epitomized the subversive potential attributed to evangelical Dissent, and a concerted campaign was undertaken to contain their operation. The establishment's assault was two-pronged. There was a move on the part of evangelicals to set up agencies within the church that would make use of missionary means to counter Dissenting influence. Hannah More is perhaps the best known of the Anglican advocates of appropriating the home missionary method to conservative political ends.[80]

The other and related move was to close down Dissenting missionary institutions and to silence their promoters, a critical severance of the personal and institutional ties that had begun to unite evangelicals across the denominational and social spectrum.[81] Dissenting missions were subjected to vituperative abuse in establishment pulpits; itinerant preachers were physically assaulted by church and king mobs, prominent Dissenters were harassed by hecklers in their places of worship and arrested by local authorities on the flimsiest of excuses.[82] Rev. David Bogue, for example, was placed under surveillance by the Privy Council in 1792 for admitting in the course of a sermon that "it would give me infinitely more delight to hear of a few solitary missionaries crossing the Ghauts, than a well-appointed English army; of a town or a district submitting to the gospel of Christ, than yielding to our troops; and of the Mysore country receiving the religion of Jesus, than yielding subjection to the commander of our forces there."[83] The suspension of habeas corpus and the imposition of severe penalties on those found guilty of encouraging "contempt for monarchy or constitution" put all evangelicals, but particularly Nonconformists, in an extremely vulnerable position.[84]

While the French Revolution may have convinced England's governing classes of the need to ground its authority in religion in the long run,[85] its short-term effect was to render highly suspect the institutional means—particularly itinerant preaching before large public assemblies—whereby religion might acquire genuinely popular assent. This ambivalence was felt within the ranks of Dissent as well. Increasingly alarmed by the course the revolution was taking in France, propertied Dissenters began to distance themselves from home missionary ventures, whose social structure (large public meetings addressed by plebian enthusiasts) if not their political discourse closely resembled mass mobilizations on the continent. The stakes were too high, perhaps, in volatile times such as these, for property of any denominational suasion to risk the possibility that missionary association might unleash the forces of disorder and anarchy that were then wreaking havoc in France.

Home missionary operations were left, as a result, to the underfunded agency of impoverished and politically vulnerable plebian and radical elements within evangelical Dissent, from whom their respectable counterparts were increasingly alienated.[86] According to an early Victorian observer, home missionary work "was looked upon as inferior; it was dependent on charity; it was laborious; it was often dangerous; while it was in most cases necessary to persevere in the face of much ingratitude and neglect."[87] Foreign missions, by contrast, continued to prosper. In 1847, the Church Missionary Society, the BFBS, and the SPG all had incomes in excess of £100,000, the LMS's income was over £75,000, and the Baptist Missionary Society's income was over £25,000. The income of the London City Mission, Britain's best-known home missionary agency, by contrast, barely exceeded £14,000.[88] Home missionary activists were understandably resentful, complaining frequently and bitterly about their difficulty competing for funds with "the more exotic attraction of overseas missions."[89]

Evangelical support for home missions across the denominational board would remain negligible, according to Kenneth Inglis, until the second half of the nineteenth century.[90] This leaves us to explain why foreign missions flourished. How did foreign missions manage to avoid the ignominious fate of their home missionary counterparts? Foreign missionaries and their supporters were, as we have seen, no less critical of the establishment than were their home missionary counterparts. But their harangues about colonialism do not appear to have aroused the same level of concern among the governing classes as did the activities of their itinerant colleagues at home. Even as the British government was taking measures (in the form of Lord Sidmouth's bill of 1811) to restrict the movement of the itinerant ministries on which Nonconformity's domestic expansion depended, the very same government was pressuring the East India Company to allow foreign missionaries to enter its territories.[91]

It has been suggested that the missionary ambitions of evangelical Dissent were deliberately deflected in colonial directions, where their subversive potential would be of considerably less consequence to Britain's governing elite.[92] I would like to propose an alternative explanation of the more receptive response to foreign versus home missionaries. My explanation underscores rather than minimizes the importance of the colonies in the minds of British statesmen. Simply put, the very same missionary practices that endangered the hegemony of the British political establishment at home facilitated its power in the colonies, where it invariably faced a very different balance of social and political forces.[93] There the primary threat to the British state's authority was increasingly posed by other sections of the European colonial community: settlers, traders, planters, and businessmen. These groups were becoming more and more frustrated by the centralization of colonial authority after the American Revolution. Murmurings of revolt were heard among planters in the West Indies, Protestants in Ireland, and Company officials in India, all seeking greater control over their colony's management (and especially over native policy) as their right as "free-born" Englishmen.[94]

While missionaries were frequently a nuisance to colonial officials, they had less power than did other Europeans to challenge policy or disrupt practice. Nor did they have, perhaps, the same incentive. They were far more likely, in fact, to need the British state's protection against that vast majority of Europeans who were hostile to missionary influence over the indigenous labor force. And the British state found in missionaries a useful ally in its struggle to contain other discontented Europeans. The Colonial Office would find particularly serviceable precisely that characteristic of the modern missionary movement that rendered it dangerous at home: namely, the institutional channels through which missionaries gained access to a broadly based, self-conscious, and politicized evangelical public. The ability of settlers and other private colonial interests to mobilize electoral support in Britain could be checked by the missionary lobby's usually superior ability to do the same. The "dreaded propaganda machinery" of Exeter Hall was a double-edged sword, to be sure; but it generally worked in the interest of the British government in many parts of the world well into the nineteenth century.[95]

This was particularly the case in Britain's plantation colonies in the Caribbean. Tensions reached their flashpoint during the campaign for slavery's abolition, and missionaries bore the brunt of an enraged planter resistance. In 1823, John Smith, an operative of the LMS, was convicted by a planter-dominated legislature in Guinea for inciting a slave rebellion. Smith was sentenced to hang, but he died in prison before his scheduled execution.[96] The missionary and antislavery movements joined together in a massive protest. The ensuing public outrage facilitated the Colonial Office's continuing centralization of authority, making possible its attempt to emancipate the empire's slaves in what Thomas Holt has characterized as a modernizing manner. While hardly a neutral party (that planters would remain in control of land and labor was never questioned), the British colonial administration was as determined to transform planters into rational employers of wage labor as it was to transform former slaves into a working class. And missionaries were vital to both agendas. They aided the state by helping it establish sufficient distance from the planter regime to discipline the latter where necessary, and, as is more widely acknowledged, they helped the state inculcate the "civilized" wants that would make free men wish to work for wages.[97]

Missionaries cooperated to varying degrees with British colonial officials in what was a not unreasonable belief that it was in their religious interests to do so. British officials were usually more sympathetic to missionary operations than were indigenous or settler authorities. And the imposition of colonial rule provided missionaries with legal guarantees of freedom of worship and military protection of their property and person that were seldom enjoyed under indigenous or settler regimes. Moreover, the secular concomitants of imperial expansion—the spread of western technology, scientific knowledge, and philosophy—were widely credited in missionary propaganda for laying the groundwork of Christian advance. The consolidation of colonial rule brought with it positive incentives to conversion that had not existed in precolonial times. Comparatively lucrative employment opportunities in colonial bureaucracies required educational credentials that missionaries, and few others, could provide.[98] For missionaries and their supporters, there was the additional advantage of displaying a patriotic face in and with regard to the colonies, a posture that helped assuage concerns about their radical associations at home.[99]

These practical considerations never prevented missionaries from criticizing colonial policies. Though they seldom questioned the legitimacy of imperialism as an ideal, they did exert what pressure they could in efforts to liberalize colonial practice. It was missionaries' support for colonial reforms that earned them the enmity of other Europeans in the colonies. The religious ties that bound missionaries to the colonized pitted missionaries and their supporters against other colonial lobbies in ways that mattered in the empire as well as in Britain and for forging effective links between these distant geographical sites. The ideals of conversion toward which missionary operations were directed attributed souls and the rights of man incumbent therein to people that their European compatriots were determined to despoil of their land, labor, and personal freedom. Missionaries were compelled by the logic of their civilizing mission and the demands of simple justice as they construed it to promote educational provisions, wage scales, land ownership patterns, and living standards conducive to a Christian lifestyle. All this put them on a collision course with Europeans whose primary concerns were to keep wages low, labor acquiescent, and land in European hands wherever possible. The ability of missionaries to serve the reign of princes, as they referred to secular interests, was also constantly being undermined by the complications inherent in ministering to the rebellious slaves, runaway wives, and outcast populations who flocked to their stations.[100]

Missionaries did not have to criticize or oppose what their fellow Europeans were doing in the colonies in order for their presence to interrupt the smooth workings of colonial exploitation.[101] In order to be effective agents of empire, much less cultivators of Christian souls, missionaries had to work and live in close physical proximity to colonized peoples, standing side by side in the same schools, hospitals, chapels, gardens, villages, and compounds. This degree of intimacy was a clear violation of the segregationist proclivities of those within the colonial community for whom racial difference reconciled Britain's liberal pretensions and imperial interests. Missionaries were punished for their transgression in their construction by other Europeans as a virtual race apart. Missionaries were characterized by their European enemies as "devotees of fanaticism, and the propagators of wild and enthusiastic notions," "their tenets as dangerous to society, and their principles as subversive of existing governments."[102] John Smith was one of many missionaries to come under attack, literally as well as figuratively, because of his sympathy for colonized people.[103]

The historical significance of these tensions within the European community is obscured when missions are dismissed as simply rhetorical camouflage for colonial exploitation. Colonized peoples were able to use missionaries to their own ends and to take advantage of European infighting. These tensions were also of great importance on foreign missions' British home front. For the missionary ties that bound many Britons to their empire were forged, in part, as a means of supporting outgunned missionaries in their struggles with other European interests on the colonial ground. British missionaries had to wage their battles for the "conscience of the Victorian state" from the lower rungs of a colonial social structure that was even more castelike in its hierarchy than was the class system at home. Most missionaries were recruited from the skilled working and lower-middle classes and would not have been welcomed within a colonial community that was composed of people from middle- and even-upper class backgrounds, for the most part.[104] As the "dominated fraction of the dominant class," the direct influence missionaries were capable of wielding in the colonies, at any rate, was minimal.[105]

Missionaries sought to offset their vulnerability in the foreign field by cultivating the considerable support they enjoyed at home. The elaborate institutional mechanisms by which the missionary movement raised its funds had ideological and political potential that was long without contemporary rival. Whereas the SPG and the SPCK had depended, for the most part, on the financial support of a relatively small clique of wealthy patrons with a direct interest in the colonies, their evangelical successors, by contrast, were voluntary associations, which meant that they raised the money to finance their more extensive operations abroad by collecting small contributions on a regular basis from large numbers of people. This intensified the necessity to attend to home organizational matters, to raise ever more money to support the growing number of volunteers recruited for service abroad. Organizing agents were sent on provincial fund-raising tours, and local associations or auxiliaries were formed to raise money on a more regular basis for the central organization's coffers.

These organizational initiatives succeeded in mobilizing a more popularly based constituency in support of foreign missionary expansion than was enjoyed by almost any other social or political movement of the day, with the possible exception of the antislavery campaign, in which missionary supporters were actively involved. "For the first time a substantial minority of laymen and clergy" were connected to the mission field through very personal investments of their money, time, and prayer.[106] And missionary operatives in isolated foreign outposts invariably embraced these ideologically potent institutional ties to the British public as an opportunity to secure the political protection that was almost as vital to their day-to-day operations as was financial support. It was by these means that the missionary project generated one of the most ideologically potent of the institutional channels through which the British public encountered the colonies and the colonized.

Conclusion

This chapter has located the birth of foreign missions at the intersection of the Evangelical Revival, middle class formation, and the transition from the first to the second British Empire. It was the combined and converging forces unleashed by the industrial and the Methodist revolutions in Britain and by colonial revolutions in North America, India, and the Caribbean, all of which took place in the shadow of the unfolding revolution in France, that transformed relations of authority in Great Britain and its colonies alike in ways that were marked, mediated, and connected by an emergent missionary philanthropy. Unintended consequences, moreover, played a central role in this process. The foreign emphasis of evangelical missionary philanthropy was the product, at least in part, of class formation on the missionary movement's British home front. Moreover, the class struggles that shaped missionary philanthropy were not only the struggles between the propertied and the poor. However complicit they may have been in the ruling establishment's colonial project abroad, the middle-class "fathers and founders" of evangelical missions included prominent political radicals. And they were as a group vilified by Britain's governing establishment, which took energetic measures to curtail their growing influence. That said, these tensions within the propertied elite were at bottom waged over competing modes of securing the political order on which property's power rested, at home as well as abroad.

The missionary impulse was thus a more complicated phenomenon than the binary opposition between ruler and ruled, complicity and resistance, religion and social control, metropole and colony that has dominated scholarship to date on both sides of the divide between recent postcolonial cultural studies and more conventional approaches to British history in its domestic as well as its imperial variants. Neither the missionary contribution to colonial social control nor missionaries' evangelical inspiration are sufficient separately or even together to explain the timing or the geographic focus of the emergent missionary impulse. These questions require our attending as well to the contingent political struggles through which the evangelical fraction of the British middle class was taking shape in relation to its gentlemanly capitalist superiors and to a nascent working class.

This chapter has attempted to demonstrate when and how missions emerged as a crucial institutional medium through which developments in the foreign mission field could reverberate on the British Empire's home front. The next chapter will suggest some of the ways in which the missionary movement influenced the subsequent cultural formation of the evangelical fraction of the English middle class. During the first half century of the missionary movement's existence, the Dissenting middle class made its move from the political margins of British society to its cultural center. And missions, I will argue, assisted in paving the way. The missionary project helped to associate the Dissenting middle classes with the nation and the nation, in turn, with evangelical middle classness, in the eyes of British society and of the world at large. Although it may have failed to transform colonized peoples in its image, the missionary project did succeed in articulating a distinctively middle-class vision of the nation.

CHAPTER 3

"Congregationalism's Special Mission":
Missions and the Making of an English
Middle Class, 1795–1845

The social relations of production grounded in economic life were not
the only objective determinants of class formation. All kinds of other
institutions, created out of the "middling sort" the middle class of nineteenth-century England.
> —John Seed, "From 'Middling Sort' to Middle Class in Late
> Eighteenth- and Early Nineteenth-Century England"

If there be a human association, which bears a perfect conformity to
the primary principles of the gospel, I must profess my deep conviction
that it is the Missionary Society.
> —John Pye Smith, *The Connections of the Redeemer's Heavenly*
> *State with the Advancement of His Kingdom on Earth*

In doing this thou shalt both save thyself, and them that hear thee.
> —1 Tim. 4. 16

During the first half century of the LMS's existence, the political valence
of evangelical Dissent underwent a marked transformation. Those who had
been vilified during the 1790s as politically subversive and socially disrep-
utable "descendants of the puritans" would increasingly be viewed as the
"thinking, active, influential classes," "the modern movers and moulders of the
world." Or so the Rev. Thomas Binney put it in a sermon delivered in 1848,
an auspicious year for bourgeois self-congratulation.[1] This was very much the
social constituency that the Rev. Binney, himself considered to be "the representative Nonconformist of his generation,"[2] encountered in the London
chapel where he ministered. King's Weigh House Chapel was located in the
heart of the City, just off the entrance to London Bridge, and it catered to the
families and clerks of City businessmen. George Williams, who founded the
YMCA with the intention of servicing the latter constituency, was a member

of Binney's congregation, as was Samuel Morley, the Liberal MP and million-aire proprietor of the *Daily News* who was purported to be one of the world's largest employers of labor in the textile industry. King's Weigh House, more-over, was far from unique in the "fit and proper" profile of its membership.[3] Binney's congregation had numerous counterparts throughout London and in the provinces, in all those chapels where attended "the most considerable per-sons" of "the best fashion."[4] For church and especially chapel attendance was an almost inviolable fashion among members of the early Victorian middle class.[5] Some of the most eminent representatives of the Victorian bourgeoisie were to be found in Congregational chapels come Sunday morning and many weekday evenings as well: the carpet manufacturer Sir Francis Cross-ley of Halifax; the Wilsons of Sheffield, whose fortune was made in that city's steel industry; the Baineses of Leeds, father and son who edited one of the leading organs of provincial liberalism, the *Leeds Mercury*; the Wills brothers of Bristol tobacco fame; the wool stapler Titus Salt of Bradford, who built the model industrial village of Saltaire to accommodate his workforce; and the Spicers, whose London branch was made up of well-known and prosperous stationers. This elevation in the social status of Dissent represented "a new el-ement in the life of the country and one that was bound to have great and in-creasing influence in public affairs."[6] Congregationalists were certainly prom-inent in the political movements with which the Victorian middle class has conventionally been associated. George Hadfield, one of the founders of the Anti-Corn Law League, was a leading light in Manchester Congregational circles, and Congregationalists formed the largest bloc among the ministers who assembled in Manchester in August 1841 to demonstrate in the League's support.[7] The Rev. James G. Miall, one of the LMS's most active provincial directors, was Edward Miall's half brother. Edward Miall was himself one of the most politically active Congregational ministers in the nation; he founded the Liberation Society and edited *The Nonconformist*, the influential mouth-piece of radical Dissent. Also active on the LMS's board of directors was the Rev. J. P. Gledstone of Sheffield, who, with his chapel's leading layman H. J. Wilson, provided crucial support in Josephine Butler's campaign for the re-peal of the Contagious Diseases Acts.[8] These were the quintessential repre-sentatives of those "classes which fill neither courts nor cottages, but which, gathered into cities, and consisting of several gradations there," to which Congregationalism, according to Binney, had a "special mission."[9]

The contribution of organized religion to the making or remaking of the English middle class during the first half of the nineteenth century is widely recognized.[10] A language of class did not take shape until the decades that bracketed the nineteenth century's turn, when it was voiced first and foremost by evangelicals of middling rank.[11] And as R. J. Morris has pointed out, evangelical institutions also played a critical role in providing the institutional structure on which middle-class formation depended. It was largely if never exclusively through the associational opportunities provided by organized religion that middle-class Victorians secured credit and employment, procured marriage partners, cemented political alliances, displayed personal piety, and otherwise established the social ties that bound them to similarly situated individuals.[12] Organized religion was in these and other ways preeminent among the cultural practices in and around which an influential fraction of the Victorian middle class cohered. It was a principal institutional site at which a middle class fractured at the point of production managed to combine forces long enough and well enough to promote its interests against the claims of social groupings above as well as below.[13]

And it was primarily under the auspices of organized religion, in the institutional forum of foreign missions, that middle-class evangelicals encountered the colonized and soon-to-be colonized peoples of the world.[14] Foreign missions were, in fact, the single most popular of the associational activities in which middle-class evangelicals were involved.[15] The establishment of a chapel branch or auxiliary association of the LMS was almost always among the very first undertakings of those myriad new chapels that sprang up in such large numbers during the opening decades of the nineteenth century. And while the number and variety of religious societies in competition for Congregational loyalties and largesse multiplied steadily over the century's course, foreign missions retained their privileged place in Congregational affections throughout. By the middle of the nineteenth century, the "missionary spirit" was widely regarded, by friends and foes alike, as the "characteristic feature" of the religious piety that was in turn the characteristic practice of the English middle class.[16]

The unrivaled popularity of foreign missions is often observed in social histories of middle-class formation.[17] But historians have only recently begun to plumb its ideological significance, particularly with reference to connections that missions established between their middle-class supporters and the mission fields of empire.[18] The assumption behind the latter's historiographical neglect would seem to have been that foreign missions were popular precisely because they did not matter in any real—that is, immediate or material—way to those involved. Conventional accounts of the place of missions in the life of the middle class presume that middle-class individuals were only able to escape the fratricidal impulses of the market in venues that were essentially void of any intrinsic meaning, in venues in which they had no real or direct "interest."[19]

Certainly the empire in which missionary operations were largely if not exclusively conducted is widely assumed to have been just such a venue. Middle-class Victorians more generally, and especially the provincial and industrial fractions therein from which Nonconformity drew the bulk of its support, have typically been portrayed as insular "little Englanders," for whom the empire was an abhorrent violation of their liberal principles of peace, retrenchment, and free trade.[20] The dominant consensus among British historians, domestic and imperial alike, has been that interest in the empire was effectively confined to the "gentlemanly capitalist Establishment." As P. J. Cain and A. G. Hopkins have recently put it, "even among the super-rich, most had no wider ambitions than to concentrate their political and social talents on their localities."[21]

The local and the imperial were not, however, mutually exclusive or even discrete frames of reference. To the contrary, the same institutional networks through which the provincial middle class exercised its "political and social talents" at the local level—namely organized religion—were simultaneously directing middle-class attention to the empire. And it was from this conjunction that the missionary project derived much of its ideological potency. It was, in other words, *because of*, not in spite of, organized religion's contribution to the immediate and material experiences of middle-class formation, that missionary identifications and their imperial frames of reference acquired much of their ideological significance. Even if the middle class exercised relatively little influence over colonial policy, even if the middle class had relatively little economic interest in the empire, its attachment to empire was nonetheless intense, and for the very good reasons that middle-class identity had been made dependent on it. And, as we shall see, the consequences for the culture of capital and the social relations of power within Britain itself were considerable.

This chapter then will argue that the missionary imperial project was central to the construction of Victorian middle-class identity, or at least to one influential version of it. Missions affected middle-class formation in several distinct ways. They significantly enhanced Congregationalism's capacity to provide the associational opportunities on which the concerted action and cohesive identity of middle-class Congregationalists depended. They also provided ideological material with which middle-class Congregationalists defined or rather redefined their relationship, as they saw it, with the governing establishment above them and with the laboring poor below. As E. P. Thompson reminds us in *The Making of the English Working Class*, class comes into being through the experience of conflict.[22] While economic interests, broadly understood, set limits to the cohesion that culture could effect among members of the middle class, this does not negate its significance, for class is inevitably a relationship whose form and content is fluid and continually contested.[23] This chapter will suggest some of the ways in which missionary institutions and their propaganda helped to shape the relationships from which evangelical middle-class identity drew its meaning and through which Victorian evangelicals constructed their case for respectability.

Missions as a Medium of Middle-Class Association

The ideological potency of missionary imperial propaganda was a product, at least in part, of the singular importance of missionary institutions as venues of middle-class association. Associational opportunities are widely acknowledged to have been crucial preconditions for the transformation of the middling ranks of early modern England into the nineteenth century's middle class. And the rise of voluntary associations, like the rise of foreign missions, came about as the result of the contradictory gap between the middle class's economic success and its continuing political impotence, locally as well as nationally.[24] To effectively pursue their interests in a polity controlled by the landed interest, even after the reform of the Parliamentary franchise in 1832, Britain's increasingly prosperous commercial and industrial classes had to unite, or, as Asa Briggs has put it, while "their philosophy, like their wealth, depended on 'individualism,' . . . their social action had to be concerted."[25]

Foreign missions contributed significantly to Congregationalism's capacity to facilitate the association of its increasingly prosperous and ambitious middling rank. Until the establishment of the LMS, eighteenth-century Congregationalism had been almost completely decentralized. Independent chapels enjoyed, as their denominational label suggests, almost complete theological, administrative, and financial autonomy. The members of each gathered congregation called and ordained their own ministers, determined theological disputes, nurtured the suffering, and disciplined the wayward within their midst.[26]

This fiercely guarded independence, however, left Congregationalism vulnerable to evangelical inroads. Considerable opposition to the Methodist message was initially voiced by prominent Congregationalists, who were, like so many of their Anglican counterparts, suspicious of enthusiasm, but an evangelical outlook eventually triumphed.[27] Indeed, while Methodism originated in the established Church of England, its effects were felt most strongly in the realms of old Dissent, and nowhere more strongly than among Independents.[28] In the absence of a central denominational authority, individual Congregational ministers and their congregations were freed to embrace the new religious precepts and practices being promoted at Wesleyan revivals. Conversely, entire Methodist communities, chafing under the rigid centralization of Wesleyan authority, often transferred their denominational allegiances en masse to the more flexible and democratic forms of the Congregational church order.[29]

The tenor of Congregational church life underwent a dramatic transformation in the revival's wake. The quiet confidence of the Independent elect was increasingly if not entirely displaced by a more fervent pursuit of salvation. Services were more and more often noisy and emotional, or as their enemies put it, ruined by enthusiasts "screaming with some hideous noises and unbecoming gestures."[30] Audiences spontaneously erupted in "groans and sobs" at their minister's increasingly vocal admonitions, fainting in distress upon remorseful meditation on their sins.[31] There were even spectacular accounts of souls transported at the very sound of the gospel message. Two men were struck dead in the course of a sermon delivered by the charismatic George Whitefield himself during the 1760s at Booth Congregational Chapel near Halifax, whereupon the survivors were said to have remained fixed in their pews, each fearful that "the next call may be to himself," each trembling while he listened "as to the voice of his own doom."[32] God worked upon the heart in mysterious ways, before which Christian men and women could only quake in fearful awe.[33]

The Evangelical Revival was not in itself sufficient, however, to encourage Congregationalists to sacrifice their independence in the interest of association. In fact, revived Congregationalism put many obstacles in the way. The secular rivalries that divided the Congregational bourgeoisie seem to have been exacerbated by the intensification of their religious faith. The ever-present anxiety about divine retribution brought with it the temptation to attribute one's enemies' earthly misfortunes to the wages of sin. Disruptions were commonplace. In the aftermath of a bitter dispute among the members of the Tabernacle Congregational Chapel in Lewes, Sussex in the 1830s, Charles Wille recorded in his diary with grim satisfaction the business setbacks, family quarrels, illnesses, and even deaths with which God had punished his rivals, who had seceded from the Tabernacle Chapel to form a separate congregation of their own.[34] Lewes was not unique in this regard; the revival exacerbated the fissiparous temptations to which Dissent had long been prone.[35]

The revival also complicated the social composition of Congregationalism in ways that were at least potentially discouraging of middle-class association. For most of the eighteenth century, Congregationalism had been the exclusive preserve of the propertied classes.[36] But in the aftermath of its revival, the plebian presence within Congregationalism increased significantly. For the better part of the nineteenth century, not all, or even most, Congregationalists would be from the propertied or employing classes. The majority were from lower-middle and artisanal-class backgrounds, while the massively popular Sunday schools of all evangelical denominations were populated almost exclusively by the children of the laboring poor.[37] For every King's Weigh House Chapel there were two or three and often more chapels in a district, borough, town, or village in which gathered congregations far less prosperous and powerful than those to whom Binney and his cohort ministered. Agricultural laborers and domestic servants, miners and milliners, artisans, and even factory workers far outnumbered leisured gentlemen and employers of labor within Nonconformity as a whole as well as within most chapels.[38] While a greater percentage of the middle-class population may well have been regular churchgoers, the 15 to 40 percent of the working-class population that did attend religious services meant that it was the latter who made up a clear majority in most chapels, including those of Congregationalism.[39] And this working-class majority, in turn, rendered the assertion of Congregationalism's "special mission" to the middle classes a peculiar claim indeed.

It was the revival's missionary offshoot that helped Congregationalism fulfill this mission. To be sure, as an interdenominational undertaking, the LMS set its course against evangelicalism's divisive potential from the outset. But denominational divides proved insurmountable, and the LMS very quickly became in practice if not principle a denominational adjunct of Congregationalism.[40] Nor did the LMS at the outset pose an organizational challenge to the much-vaunted autonomy of Congregationalism's fiercely independent chapels. During the first decade of its existence, the society collected funds in a manner that did little to intrude upon the isolated existence of independent congregations. The LMS financed its early operations much in the way that its High Church predecessors (the Society for the Propagation of the Gospel, and the Society for the Promotion of Christian Knowledge) did, which is to say it raised funds in the form of large one-time contributions from sympathetic notables. This mode of fund-raising brought a narrow circle of individual Congregationalists into occasional contact with individual representatives of the Missionary Society, but it did not provide extensive opportunities for social intercourse among the donors, nor did it encourage the increase in the latter's numbers on which middle-class formation would depend.

The home organizational structure, or, rather, the lack thereof, was predicated on the assumption that heathenism would quickly succumb to the missionary revelation of gospel truth, and that foreign missions would quickly become self-sufficient, supported by grateful converts who would quickly form their own financially independent congregations. This was not so much an underestimation of the challenge of communicating Christianity across cultural lines as the assumption on the part of the "fathers and founders" of the LMS that a task of such magnitude could only be accomplished through the intervention of the divine. Saved men were required to place themselves in God's service, but human agency was itself powerless to achieve the missionary plan. The missionary obligations of Britain's evangelical public would consist, then, largely of start-up costs—transporting missionaries to the foreign mission field, whereupon they "would practically be able to support themselves." At this point, the success of their mission would be entirely up to God.[41]

The LMS dispatched its first emissaries to the South Seas with what would prove inordinate dependence on the Lord to provide the means to their success. Thirty missionaries and their families departed England on September 24, 1796, only one year to the day from the society's massively attended inaugural meetings, in full expectation that their act of faith would be rewarded by large-scale conversions.[42] The expectation of immediate and miraculous divine intervention rendered these missionaries' departure an emotional event of unprecedented intensity. Services ordaining and honoring this first missionary party were attended by "several thousands"; "immense" crowds also gathered at Woolwich to watch the missionary ship (the LMS purchased its own, which they named The Duff) set sail. Delayed by the weather and the difficulties of obtaining a military escort while Britain was at war with France, the missionaries spent almost a month in dock at Spithead, where they were visited daily by "multitudes . . . from all parts."[43]

The founders' faith that missionary success would ultimately depend upon divine intervention was reflected in the society's minimal attention to the selection and preparation of these first missionary parties.[44] This faith was quickly put to the test. Of the 30 missionaries who arrived in Tahiti in March 1797, 20 deserted the mission within its first four years. Eleven missionaries (including most of the married men in the party) abandoned their posts after only a year. Two missionaries were expelled from the church for marrying indigenous women (although their accusers were careful to insist that the crime lay in their wives' unrepentant heathenism rather than in their race).[45] Three missionaries were murdered in the course of a civil war after ignoring repeated advice not to take sides. All told, only seven of the initial party proved to be "effective workers." A second group of missionaries, sent out in December 1798, was even less successful. Their ship was captured by a French privateer in February, and its party was sent to France. Shortly after their release they were recaptured by the Portuguese. By the time they were finally allowed to return to England in October, most of this party, "reasoning, as imperfectly educated men might in such circumstances," that God did not intend their mission to succeed, resigned their connection to the society.[46]

It was the failure of the society's first missionary parties—which was the result, in large part, of indigenous resistance to missionary overtures—that precipitated the transformation of the institutional structure and organizational culture of metropolitan Congregationalism on which the making of a Congregational middle class would so largely depend. The LMS's leaders and supporters back in Britain attributed their first missions' ignominious collapse to inadequate human agency rather than to divine disapproval, and they embarked on an ambitious program of organizational reform. There was more than a semblance of social condescension toward the men and women, most of whom were skilled laborers, who comprised these early parties. Only four of the first party, for example, were ordained ministers. The remaining 26 included 6 carpenters, 1 shopkeeper, 1 harness maker, 2 tailors, 2 shoemakers, 1 gentleman's servant, 1 gardener, 1 surgeon, 1 blacksmith, 1 cooper, 1 butcher, 1 cotton manufacturer, 2 weavers, 1 hatter, 2 bricklayers, 1 linen draper, and 1 cabinetmaker.[47] Their London employers blamed their dismal performance in the foreign field on their "impure and inferior motives" and on the fact that their educational background was not sufficient to secure them against heathenism's many temptations.[48]

A more rigorous course of missionary recruitment and preparation was prescribed, the latter to be taken at the Rev. David Bogue's own theological seminary at Gosport.[49] The Rev. Bogue, among others, had argued from the beginning that fervor alone was not adequate to the task of combating heathenism. Missionary agents required careful selection as well as considerable training and preparation. This was especially the case for those sent out to so-called civilized heathens, but even those dispatched to the purportedly primitive mission fields of the Pacific, Africa, and the Americas needed to be carefully screened and trained if the society wanted to avoid further embarrassment, namely the theological and social capitulation to heathenism's temptations to which its first missionaries succumbed.[50]

The costs of training, maintaining, and supervising missionaries at the standard required for survival if not success in the foreign field quickly disabused British evangelicals of their initial assumption that foreign missions would be financially self-supporting, at least in the foreseeable future. The institutional structure that had characterized eighteenth-century Congregationalism was grossly ill-equipped for the task of raising the vast sums of money required to realize this course of action. The society found it increasingly necessary to broaden the social base from which it solicited support and to cultivate among its supporters an awareness that its financial needs would be greater than had been initially recognized, and that they would be ongoing. To these ends, in 1806 the society's board appointed a home committee that was charged with promoting "the enlargement of the Funds" by "means of a more extensive circulation of our Reports, Transactions, &c." and by appeals to ministers and prominent individuals.[51] Under its auspices, a vast institutional network, through which the LMS's operations and needs would be brought to the attention of ordinary Congregationalists on a day-to-day basis, was established during the opening decades of the nineteenth century.

The institutional culture of Congregationalism was transformed in the process in ways that would encourage middle-class association across chapel lines on a regular basis. The high costs of operating in the foreign mission field would also render missionary and other Congregational institutions ever more dependent upon the propertied classes. In the self-supporting chapels of evangelical Dissent, those who paid the bills inevitably enjoyed influence out of proportion to their numbers. As Brian Stanley has pointed out with regard to the Baptists, the growing popularity of missions increased such chapels' normal expenses significantly. And in the process, it increased the already considerable political clout of the propertied minority therein.[52]

It was in this institutional sense, then, that foreign missions helped to make Congregationalism and its missionary offshoot a distinctively middle-class domain. The middle-class minority in Congregational chapels, and typically the most prominent individuals therein, were the ones who served as church trustees, deacons, Sunday school superintendents, and officers of the chapel branches and regional auxiliaries of the LMS. And it was this institutional power base that enabled any chapel's propertied elite to ensure that the mission cause would be presented in ways that served distinctively middle-class ends.

Much of the impetus behind the institutional innovations of this period seems to have come from Congregationalism's middle-class supporters. The founding fathers of the LMS were forced by popular demand, for example, to move their early meetings from conference boardrooms to the sanctuaries of the capital's largest chapels to Exeter Hall itself, where the society met from 1831 to 1891.[53] Audiences at the society's annual meetings in London grew rapidly. Dozens and then hundreds of the LMS's leading activists attended the society's first meetings, but by the 1840s audiences numbering up to 4,000 and 5,000 reported. Crowds began to collect hours in advance to find good seats from which to observe proceedings that might themselves last another six hours.[54] The novelty of these mass meetings was manifested in their exuberance, which was reflected in one supporter's relief that

the style of speaking at our public meetings has, we think, on the whole, im-
proved during the last twenty years. There are now fewer vulgar jokes than
there used to be, fewer instances of fulsome flattery of "the ladies", and fewer
instances of that excessive mirth which must surely be "not convenient", when
the object before the meeting is the salvation of mankind.[55]

The May missionary meetings became a signal event in the Congregational
social calendar, equivalent perhaps to the London season itself in better social
circles. Indeed, the LMS was suspected in the more austere circles of the
Baptist Missionary Society of staging its anniversary celebrations for the express purpose of providing its supporters with the opportunity to display their
considerable and growing wealth. While Baptists condemned the "noise and
ostentation" of LMS meetings, Congregational ministers viewed the opportunity to deliver the society's Annual Sermon in London as the "proudest
challenge" their denomination had to offer.[56]

Although extremely popular, these London meetings were still by themselves unable to meet the financial demands of the foreign field, and the Society began to encourage even greater organizational initiatives, which enhanced considerably the opportunities for association that Congregationalism
provided. The Home Committee devolved many of its responsibilities at the
local level to the numerous branches or local auxiliaries of the LMS that
were established to mobilize the support of Congregationalists at the chapel,
town, and county level. The first mention of a local auxiliary (that of the
Rev. Roby in Manchester) occurs in the society's annual report for 1807. By
1820, a nationwide network of local auxiliaries had come into being, spreading quickly from the LMS and the Bible Society to the missionary and other
philanthropic organizations in Congregationalism's sister denominations. This
auxiliary system proved to be "the most fruitful method of sustaining and
augmenting the funds."[57]

The auxiliary movement replicated on the regional and local level the associational functions of the national missionary meetings. Local auxiliaries
brought together missionary activists from individual chapels on a citywide,
regional, and countywide basis. The primary mode by which they brought
middle-class supporters together was in their staging of public missionary
meetings. These meetings were held annually (or sometimes biannually) in
cities, towns, and villages all over Britain, and they were the occasion on
which the British public received firsthand accounts from the colonies where
British missionary organizations largely concentrated their efforts.[58] And
these meetings were everywhere the unrivaled highlight of the evangelical
calendar.[59]

This was in large part due to the presence on the stage of foreign missionaries, who were required to travel the provincial fund-raising circuit when home on furlough from abroad. Missionaries returned to England from their sojourns abroad as conquering heroes of an uncharted heathen wilderness and were greeted by receptions not unlike those that would be accorded to military heroes and monarchs later in the century.[60] The Rev. John Williams, for example, was overwhelmed by the evangelical public's welcome upon his return from Tahiti in 1836, and the publication of his *Missionary Enterprises* a year later intensified popular enthusiasm for his work. The investment in missions on the part of those who had been galvanized by William's personal and printed testimony was further deepened by the news of Williams' murder on the island of Tanna in the New Hebrides in 1839. A similar cult of personality quickly developed around Robert Moffat, one of the LMS's pioneers in South Africa, during his first furlough from service that same year. According to his son and biographer, Moffat's "reception in London was a surprise for which he was scarcely prepared. He found himself at once plunged into a whirlpool of public meetings even before he could get his luggage through the custom-house."[61] But it was Moffat's son-in-law, David Livingstone, whose missionary exploits in Africa informed "the greatest myth of the century," according to the foremost historian of imperialism's popularization, John M. Mackenzie.[62] Livingstone arrived in Bechuanaland in 1841 at the age of 28 to begin his service as a medical missionary for the LMS. He returned to England in 1856 to an extraordinary welcome in London and in cities throughout provincial England. Livingstone was feted by commercial, civic, and scientific organizations as well as in Congregational and other religious circles. He was received by the queen and appointed a consul by the British government, and more than 70,000 copies of his book, *Missionary Travels and Researches in South Africa*, were sold. Even lectures about Livingstone were likely to attract large audiences, or so the Rev. William Garland Barrett, one of the society's organizing agents, gleefully assured the society's home secretary, Rev. Ebenezer Prout, in January 1857, having just had the good fortune to address 500 factory hands in Ashton-under-Lyne on the subject of Livingstone's recent explorations.[63]

Great excitement was also incited by the presence on the missionary podium of the occasional native convert to Christianity. Mary Carpenter recalled that her chapel in Bristol "was more crowded than I ever remember to have seen it" on the occasion of an address by an Indian Brahmin convert, whose person exceeded in her view all other manifestations "of the wonderful power of Christianity."[64] In 1849, the Rev. D. John accompanied Rafaravay, Andrianinianana, and three other Malagasy converts on a speaking tour that brought Congregational missionary enthusiasm to a fevered pitch. These converts described to enthralled audiences in London as well as throughout the provincial auxiliary circuit the mass executions and enslavement of the society's converts in the aftermath of the LMS's eviction from Madagascar. Fish Street Chapel in Hull "was crowded in every part" to greet this party of martyrs. The Rev. James Sibree recalled that "the appearance of these Christian fugitives on the platform, as they stood arrayed in their native costume— especially the white, flowing lamba, gracefully covering the whole person— produced a startling impression on the audience. . . . [N]one who were present will ever forget."[65]

The homage paid to converts was framed in ways that reinforced rather than subverted the missionary public's assumption of its superiority to colonized and soon-to-be colonized peoples. Native deputations, as they were referred to by the Society and its representatives, invariably flattered their listeners by denigrating the heathen condition from which they had been rescued and in which most of their peers remained mired. Jan Tazatzoe, a "Christian Caffre chief," who accompanied Rev. John Philip to Hull in 1836, is reported to have said that "when the Word of God came among us we were like the wild beasts; we knew nothing. . . . I thank the English nation for what we have received at their hands. You are our own friends; we are your children."[66] These carefully staged displays were deemed by many contemporaries positive proof of evangelical Christianity's miraculous power to transform.[67]

The missionary achievement was to integrate the miraculous into the evangelical everyday. Missionary speakers were recruited to attend the most important occasions in the life of local Nonconformity, such as ordinations and the anniversary celebration of a chapel or its Sunday school.[68] The "warm and tender ties" that bound home supporters to the mission fields of empire were all the more powerful when missionary speakers could draw on local connection. A Birmingham supporter of the LMS commented on the unusually "respectful attention" with which members of her chapel listened to a missionary address in the early 1830s.[69] The speaker to whom she was referring was Henry Nott, a former bricklayer from Bromsgrove who served the LMS in Tahiti from 1797 until 1844. Before leaving England, Nott had been an active member of Carr's Lane Chapel, where this meeting took place, and this was surely a factor behind the warmth of his reception.

There were any number of British congregations enjoying such personal connections to the colonial mission field. The holding of missionary ordinations in provincial chapels enhanced considerably the local interest in the missionary ordinand's work abroad.[70] And the connections between missionaries and home chapels were encouraged from the field. Mary Moffat, whose husband Robert was one of the most popular of the LMS's missionaries, remained in contact with their former chapels in Manchester and Ashton-under-Lyne, which helped to engender a sense of personal responsibility within these congregations for the mission work in southern Africa in which she and her husband were engaged. Her letters home "were treated as circular epistles. Copies were made and sent round, and the station received many proofs of the heart felt liberality which spoke in practical language, and made many things possible which otherwise would have been left undone."[71]

Home ministers were fond of claiming a special passion for the mission field in order perhaps to move their congregation to higher levels of Christian passion. And nothing, apparently, moved a congregation more than the not infrequent announcement of the missionary intentions of a worshipper or even a minister. An example of such an announcement is the one made at Theddingworth Congregational Chapel in Leicestershire in December 1840, when the Rev. J. T. Jepson "announced, amid the tears of an affectionate people, his intention of vacating the Pulpit which he had occupied for six years; having been appointed to Tahiti in the South Seas to protect the cause of the Redeemer there against the threatened encroachments of Popery."[72]

The 1830s and 1840s were the high point of the missionary movement's popularity. Missionary reports back from the mission field of conversion and martyrdom alike were widely credited with "quicken[ing] the sympathies and zeal of the church at home." Booth Congregational Chapel near Halifax, for example, experienced "a remarkable revival of religion . . . chiefly among the young persons" in the early 1820s as a result of missionary services; the minister at the Congregational chapel in nearby Sowerby similarly reported that "by seeking to interest the minds of his people in the salvation of others, he led them to feel a deeper and more tender concern for their own."[73] The occasions on which a Robert Moffat, John Williams, or David Livingstone addressed a congregation were recalled for years thereafter as "red letter days" in the life of a town or chapel auxiliary.[74] Expressing their grateful thanks to Robert Moffat for visiting their city in 1842, the society's Edinburgh supporters testified to the reverence with which all missionaries were viewed in this period:

> Your visit to us we never can forget. Our little children are already, in their infantine chronology, beginning to date from the time "when Mr. Moffat spoke to them." . . . We have reaped a real and pure pleasure from the pictures you have given us of missionary life—your romantic adventures, your hair breadth escapes, your bold exertions, your surprising successes. You have opened before us a new page of human society and character, and have confirmed our attachment to the missionary cause by showing that there is no tribe too degraded for the gospel to elevate, no heart too polluted for Christianity to purify.[75]

Thus did missions render simultaneously the familiar sublime and the sublime familiar, translating at public missionary meetings as well as in its printed propaganda the miraculous work of missionaries abroad into local and even personal idioms. This was accomplished at the most basic level in the person of the missionary himself (and during the first half of the nineteenth century, all of the society's missionary employees were men), most of whom were from working-class backgrounds. Robert Moffat worked as a gardener and John Williams as an ironmonger's apprentice before they joined the LMS's foreign field force; David Livingstone began work as a piecer in a Blantyre textile mill at the age of ten.[76] It is certainly likely that Theddingworth's minister was drawn to the foreign field by the straitened circumstances of his congregation. Theddingworth was built in 1833 at the sole expense of a single local notable, John Sims; by 1836 it numbered only ten members.[77] The chapel's records indicate that his removal was accompanied by the emigration of several of its members to America, which was another symptom of its struggling constituency.

Historians of missions have found in the biographical profiles of missionary candidates evidence that foreign missions were a variation on the larger nineteenth-century theme of the anti-industrial and anti-modern sensibility of Europe's lower-middle and upper working classes who sought to resist its inexorable and, for them, murderous logic. Foreign missions were purportedly embraced along these lines as an opportunity to escape the pressures of an emergent industrial capitalism for the classes of people who were to be its chief victims, hence the frequent framing of the mission fields of empire as rural idylls wherein could be recovered the worlds that were disappearing in the empire's metropolitan heartland.[78]

While instructive, such readings do not exhaust the social meanings conveyed by foreign missions on their British home front. Foreign missionaries may themselves have been from lower-middle- or working-class backgrounds, but they were dispatched and their operations financed by the middle and upper-middle classes who controlled the institutions of evangelical Dissent and who were industrial modernity's chief agents and beneficiaries. Their interest in foreign missions stemmed no doubt from very different sources. The social logic of the missionary project with respect to its entrepreneurial benefactors lay in a large part, I would argue, in the relationships it helped to establish between the disparate social groupings that comprised evangelical Dissent.

Nowhere was the social diversity of nineteenth-century Congregationalism more apparent, in fact, than on the foreign missionary platform, where plebian missionaries stood surrounded by adoring local notables. The rela-

tionship displayed encouraged, in the large and popularly based audiences attracted to these occasions, a more immediate and personal identification with
the missionary cause than would have been the case had foreign missionaries
been from the patrician backgrounds of their benefactors. This was one of the
ways in which missions helped to democratize the imperial process, giving
very large sections of the population an investment in securing a world that
would be saved by their viewing.[79]

Such displays served a disciplinary function as well, a function more in
keeping with the view that missions helped construct the social relations of
power on which industrial modernity rested than with the view that missions
simply facilitated the missionary's escape. Or, rather, the foreign missionary's
escape was staged in ways that justified the subordination of the majority of
working people who witnessed it. The working-class missionary was often
represented in missionary hagiography as the exception to an immoral rule,
his achievement of virtue requiring a physical separation from his working-
class community of origin. The turning point in missionary biography typically entailed the sinning hero's conversion at the hands of a middle-class pa-
tron, who then brought the properly contrite plebian to the LMS's attention.[80] And even where the uplifted missionary was himself concerned, the
social logic of missionary performances conveyed mixed messages. They may
well have been the single most important instance of lower-class valorization
in an emergent public sphere. But their middle-class patrons were not above
congratulating themselves on the indifference to class as well as race that
made possible their social intercourse with the likes of foreign missionaries—
an indifference belied in its very profession.[81] And implicit in the homage
paid to working-class missionaries was a socially condescending theology that
delighted in the fact that the Lord could work miracles *even* through human
instruments such as these.

Though honored on the public platform, then, missionaries were clearly
treated like second-class citizens when they were off it. This was regretted in
some quarters; the Rev. John Angell James urged his audience at the Annual
Meeting in 1819 to regard missionaries "not as the menial servants of our Institution, but its respected and beloved agents."[82] That missionaries were in
fact regarded as servants is suggested by the fact that they were not allowed
to sit on the society's board of directors, and by the close scrutiny to which
they were subjected, even in the field.[83] Missionaries were very carefully selected and trained to accept without challenge the superior wisdom of their
middle-class employers. Deference was a condition of their entry into the Society's employ and a central emphasis of their formal missionary training. The
LMS declared in 1800 that "the principal point" of missionary education

"must chiefly refer to the heart, and instead of cherishing the desire of shining in the world by distinguished talents, must aim at subduing every elevating thought, and at mortifying the vain propensities of our nature." While ordinary seminaries to which middle-class candidates for the ministry were sent emphasized

> the principles of logic, the rules of composition, the rudiments of language or of science . . . our students are to learn how they may be patient and submissive under disappointments, persevering under long discouragements, ready to meet sufferings or even death, if such should be the divine appointment. . . . Thus he may be expected to unite great activity with great meekness, faith with patience, and at length, we trust, great success with humility and praise.[84]

Praise for plebian missionaries' achievements in the field was also undercut by simultaneous expressions of regret that the Society was not more successful in its efforts to recruit more respectable volunteers. Missionary activists bemoaned the fact that far from encouraging their children to become missionaries, most middle-class Congregationalists taught them by example "to despise the missionary's life, to shudder at its hardships . . . [and] to trample underfoot its honours."[85] And it was in these terms that calls for improving the conditions of missionary employment were cast. If the Society were going to recruit a "better class" of missionary, it would have to make concessions to middle-class sensibilities. This the Society would increasingly do in the second half of the nineteenth century, in calls for reform that provide us with evidence of the mentality by which missionaries had been deployed in previous decades. "The old system, though now carried out I daresay with the greatest delicacy and consideration possible, may do very well for men who in education and feeling are not above the rank of school-masters," but the "surveillance and dependence" to which the latter had been subjected "will not be acceptable to such men as you now require for India and China."[86]

In these and other ways the celebration of plebian missionaries' achievements subtly reinforced the authority and the prestige of the missionary movement's middle-class promoters, while allowing (if not requiring) them to remain safely at home. Middle-class evangelicals were, in return, extraordinarily energetic on behalf of the foreign mission cause. Rare are evangelical autobiographies and memoirs that don't make reference to extensive missionary involvement. Rare are the chapels in which foreign missions did not enjoy pride of place. Historians of the middle classes widely if fleetingly acknowledge the fact that attendance at missionary meetings was de rigueur for the Congregational elite. The LMS's auxiliaries' anniversaries were invariably graced by the most prominent citizens of a locale.[87] Such involvement, I have tried to argue, afforded local dignitaries the opportunity to display their generosity to the excited masses of their chapel and their town, and in so doing to assert their superiority over the lower orders in their midst in the very course of honoring the latter's most celebrated individuals.[88]

Foreign missions were in fact the principal occasion upon which Congregationalism's local notables came into contact with one another across the chapel lines that divided them. The significance of the missionary achievement in this regard is suggested by the fact that for many years foreign missions would remain the only cause for which the middle classes who controlled Congregationalism would be willing to sacrifice their much-prized local autonomy.[89] The LMS was in fact the only centralized religious organization to which Congregationalists were collectively attached until the founding of the Congregational Union of England and Wales, and because the latter was dominated by the clergy, the LMS remained for a long time thereafter the principal site of lay association on a nationwide organizational basis. The primacy of the LMS is tellingly reflected in the fact that it was in the society's offices that the Congregational Union of England and Wales was called into existence.[90]

The LMS was thus a critical site at which the social ties that united the Congregational middle class and made its concerted political action possible were forged. Missions had in this regard to work against the competitive individualism for which market pressures as much as philosophical inclination were responsible. Tensions within the middle-class public were always in evidence, but their articulation in relation to the mission cause ensured that they facilitated rather than undermined middle-class cohesion. Gift-giving invariably took on competitive inflections, as donors determined to translate their missionary virtue into the capital of reputation enhanced. They insisted that their names be printed in national missionary publications, and they were often reprinted at the donors' insistence in local chapel, regional, and denominational publications as well. This competition was carried over into the society's other fund-raising initiatives. Private breakfast meetings, for example, of the Congregational elite with missionaries and other representatives of the parent society were among the most successful fund-raising initiatives of the LMS Auxiliary in Leeds. The atmosphere was akin to that of an auction or sale, with participants trying to outbid each other in displaying their generosity and support. The contest extended into the public realm, as well. Large contributors were rewarded with positions on the platforms at public meetings, and the amounts of their contributions were published in chapel manuals and auxiliary newsletters as well as in the LMS's publications. This costly outlay was vehemently defended on those occasions when the society proposed their elimination or at least their scaling down (that is to say raising the level of the donation necessary to receive individual public acknowledgment) in order to economize on its home expenditure.[91]

These returns were closely scrutinized, and there was considerable jockeying for moral advantage. Thomas Simpson, a supporter from Preston, corresponded regularly with the society's home secretary on the subject of his fellow entrepreneurs' failure to discharge their missionary duties as he saw them. Simpson urged the society to ask local Congregational ministers to provide a list of all spinners and other manufacturers in their congregation, whose profits, he argued, constituted in themselves a "large and special debt" to the colonies, which could only be repaid by their supporting foreign missions. Simpson himself provided at least one such name, a Mr. Kershaw of London, whom Simpson claimed had profited from trade in cotton textiles to India somewhere on the order of £15,000 in this year alone. "Surely then God claims some return for India, out of such liberal profits, and if ever the Missionary Society had a claim it is now . . . whatever Mr. K. may have given before, if it is allowable to judge for others, I believe he could now well afford largely to add to it."[92]

The LMS also sought to benefit from the emergent civic consciousness of this period, and in so doing it may have exacerbated local rivalries. LMS auxiliaries were organized primarily on a townwide or citywide basis, and their contributions were often weighed against those of other towns. The titles of official histories of these auxiliaries, for example, categorize the contributions of individuals, chapels, or auxiliaries according to locale, usually a city and its district: "A short history of the part played by Hull and the East Riding of Yorkshire in the society's Foundation and Work," "The LMS in Reading," "Story of the Sheffield Auxiliary," "Colchester and the Missionary Movement," and so forth.

Such symbolic enactments of the ruthless competition that characterized the economic lives of those involved was no doubt an effective means of neutralizing or containing the conflicts of interest that divided them. On the most obvious level, their competition was in service to a national and imperial cause behind which middle-class evangelicals were obviously and very publicly united. In addition, the potential for conflict between local elites through the stimulation of individual, chapel, and civic pride in LMS auxiliaries was circumvented by the society's home organizational structure. Auxiliaries and their locales were knitted together, for example, by their sharing of missionary deputations (retired or vacationing missionaries were required to advocate for missions on the auxiliary circuit), as well as by their exchanging the services of their own local celebrities. The chairmen of such meetings, for example, were drawn wherever possible from other provincial cities or even from London.[93]

Indeed, the LMS and its auxiliaries were widely hailed for providing "a bond of union encircling the Congregational Churches of the district and providing a common meeting ground," that joined the districts of its auxiliaries into a viable national network.[94] Through its very institutional structure, the foreign missionary movement helped broaden the geographical horizons of middle-class Congregationalists from the local arena, where their economic interests and political power was no doubt concentrated, to a national frame of reference. Attention was directed to such a frame of reference by printed propaganda, traveling agents, and representation on the society's board of directors. It was also thus directed, of course, by the obligatory trips to London for Congregationalism's middle-class elite; at the wildly popular national meetings, middle-class individuals experienced a similarity of vision and circumstance with those of others of their ilk from across the country. Experiences such as these provided crucial preparation for middle-class collective action at the national political level. The LMS was neither the only associational opportunity available to the middle class nor the only institutional framework to link their local worlds into a national network. However, the LMS was for many members of the middle class the first such framework, and for a long time it was the most sacred. Moreover, the pressure groups through which middle-class Congregationalists engaged in concerted political action in the period between the First Reform Act and Second Reform Act were modeled on its institutional example, their personnel, and the links between them borrowed from its culture.[95]

The Missionary Language of Opposition

This chapter has argued thus far that foreign missions provided the primary occasions on which Congregationalists associated across local and regional geographical divides. This association was staged in ways that contributed to middle-class hegemony in the communities that were called into being. The contribution of these associational opportunities to middle-class formation lent missionary propaganda, in turn, much of its considerable potency. Although ostensibly about the foreign field, missionary texts, such as the annual sermons I will now survey, conveyed messages that were addressed explicitly as well as implicitly to the domestic and social concerns of their Congregational audience. In them, representations of the colonies were constructed and deployed in ways that positioned what it meant to be middle class at home in relation to those social groups above and below as well as in relation to the colonized. In this section I will explore the ways in which missionary discourse was used to question the values of the Anglican establishment, or, rather, the values attributed to the establishment by evangelical Dissent. Far from diverting middle-class attention from the domestic politics of opposition, as some historians have argued that foreign missions did, the foreign mission cause was promoted in terms that challenged the legitimacy of gentlemanly capitalist rule at home as well as abroad.[96] Seriousness and sacrifice were, as Leonore Davidoff and Catherine Hall have argued, the tender with which evangelical Nonconformists defined their class culture as more righteous than that of their social superiors in the Anglican establishment.[97] And the missionary cause was an effective weapon within this larger arsenal. Missions provided a vivid canvas, biblical in its scope and reference, on which the virtues of the middle class could be promoted in the very process of condemning the sins of their social betters.

Chief among the sins castigated in missionary propaganda was the conception of civilization by which Britain's governing classes justified their right to rule. The ruling elite in Britain in this period had been installed in the settlement of the Glorious Revolution. It was no simple ancien regime; theirs was a modernizing agenda, responsible for the innovations in commerce, finance, insurance, and agriculture that fueled Britain's unrivaled economic growth in the early nineteenth century. Against Dissenters' Methodist-inspired enthusiasm, the Anglican elite advanced rationality. Against evangelicals' leveling demagoguery, the Anglican establishment argued that wise and judicious authority be exercised by the able. The ability to rule, moreover, could not be acquired in the practical curriculum of the Dissenting academy; it was a matter of character ingrained rather than knowledge applied. The establishment's understanding of its capacity to govern would be predicated for most of the nineteenth century on a preparatory education at public schools and Oxbridge, from which Dissenters were excluded and in which classical languages and history figured prominently.[98]

Foreign missions provided materials with which Dissenting evangelicals called into question the cultural foundations on which the British establishment justified its authority. The annual sermons delivered at the public meetings of the LMS during its first half century of existence repeatedly invoked the example of classical Greece and Rome in ways that challenged the cultural pretensions of Britain's governing elite. That these manifestly civilized empires were as damned to eternal perdition as was the most primitive pagan called into question whether civilization without Christianity was truly possible. As the Rev. John Angell James put it in the annual sermon he delivered in 1819, Greece in all its grandeur was to the Apostle Paul "nothing but a magnificent mausoleum, decorated it is true, with the richest productions of the sculptor and the architect, but still where the souls of men lay dead in trespasses and sins." He went on to say that "men without Christ are in the very depths of misery, though they may stand in other respects, upon the very summits of civilisation, literature and science, and for such an opinion we can plead the authority of the great Apostle of the Gentiles who bewailed a city of *philosophers*, with more intense and piercing grief, than any of us ever did, a horde of idolatrous *savages*."[99] The "chief object of Missionary exertions," argued the Rev. William Borrows a year later, was "not only to introduce predatory hordes of savages into the habits and refinements of civil and social life," for "if they be viewed as the principal object of our exertions, even ancient Rome, or Greece, might peradventure have sent out better Missionaries than ourselves." It was not civilization or for that matter commerce that would save the heathen world. The "object which far transcends them all . . . the preaching of the gospel of the blessed Lord . . . without which even Athens herself, in the meridian of her literary and philosophical glory, was in total darkness."[100]

The recurring condemnation of "civilization" in missionary texts in the opening decades of the nineteenth century was, I think, a barely veiled indictment of the cultural terms on which the political establishment justified its political and social hegemony. In this regard, the homage paid to the simple (spiritual as opposed to worldly) virtues of evangelicalism's plebian missionary emissaries underscored the Dissenting middle class's dismissal of the merits of civilization by which they were themselves disdained, without, as we have seen, calling into question the moral superiority of the middle classes vis-à-vis their working-class compatriots.

This social agenda rested upon constructions of purportedly heathen people that are relatively egalitarian, at least by comparison to the more explicitly racist discourses that took shape during the second half of the nineteenth century.[101] Advocates of missions in this their first half century stressed the underlying nature that all men (and the emphasis here, by contrast to the period discussed in chapter 4, is very clearly on men) had in common. To the orientalist critics of missions who argued that Christianity was not suited to the diverse cultures of the world, the Rev. John Johnston argued that the gospel

is wonderfully adapted to mankind, howsoever their condition may be modified and varied by external or adventitious circumstances. . . . It addresses itself to man in that character which under every combination of circumstances he uniformly sustains; it addresses him as an ignorant, and guilty, and helpless creature. . . . This is his character, both in his civilized and in his savage state—a character which no attainments in science and no progress in the arts can remove from him.[102]

And that no lack of, in turn, could further indict. As the Rev. James Steven noted in 1811, "So far from making any distinction between Jew or Gentile, savage or sage, bond or free; Jesus commands that the everlasting gospel shall be published for the faith of all nations."[103] British audiences were reminded that there but by the grace of God's ancient missionary representations would Britons still dwell, in the heathenism that debased their lost "brethren" the world over. Thus spoke the Rev. Clayton in a sermon delivered at the society's annual meetings in London in 1821:

> it will be salutary to remember what we ourselves once were, in order that our motives may be invigorated, our resolutions confirmed, and our compassion awakened in favour of those who are still "without God and without hope in the world," and whom we are determined by the assistance and blessing of the Most High, to place on an equal footing with ourselves, in all the light and liberty and joy, of which Christianity is the parent and the source.[104]

Heathen people are typically represented in this period more as sinners than as sufferers, or rather as suffering from sin rather than from their social condition.[105] Christianity's virtues, moreover, are evidenced in the hope that it offers the weak.

> How tenderly should we commiserate the state of the blinded nations, and how should we employ our utmost endeavours to spread the light and influence of true Christianity amongst them! Possessing, as they do, the same feelings of nature as ourselves, the same moral wants, the same faculties of improvement, the same dread of misery, the same desire of happiness, and the same capacity of enjoyment, ought we not zealously to endeavour that they may also become partakers of like precious faith with us, and sharers in the same common salvation?[106]

Here the imperial ends to which missionary means were directed were at their most egalitarian: the spread of Christianity would eventuate "in a period, when ignorance, superstition, and violence shall yield to the reforming influence of a pure religion—when man shall cease to be the enemy and oppressor of man—when all the varying tribes of men shall be united in one faith, and trust in the same Redeemer, when they shall be of one heart and of one mind, and the same songs of praise shall be heard in all their dwelling places."[107] The attraction of the cross lay in the fact that "It removes every obstacle out of the way of the sinner's approach to God; it puts an authorized and perfect satisfaction to justice in his hand . . . and invites the whole family of man to the feast."[108]

The relative egalitarianism of missionary discourse in this period endorsed the virtue of humility, particularly when juxtaposed with other of the colonial discourses to which its audience would have been exposed, especially the hugely popular travel literature, in which the targets of missionary operations abroad were portrayed as wildly exotic, primitive, and inferior.[109] Those who professed "to rejoice in the extension of the Redeemer's kingdom" and, to an even greater extent, those who did not, were urged to "enquire with diligence, whether his dominion has been established in our hearts, and if we have yet been brought into captivity to the obedience of Christ."[110] The pointed insinuation of remarks such as these to the non-evangelical elite, whose theology did not require of them obedience or humility, was obvious and obnoxious; as the Duchess of Buckingham remonstrated, "it is monstrous to be told you have a heart as sinful as the common wretches that crawl on the earth."[111] It was no wonder then that the official classes were less than enthusiastic about missionary operations during most of the society's first 50 years.

And it was these "fashionable scoffers" within colonial officialdom who were pointedly rebuked from missionary platforms for their godless privileging of civilization over Christianization. The Rev. James was contemptuously dismissive of "those who would restrict our benevolence to the temporal interests of mankind. Civilise the savage, say they, cultivate his intellect, teach him to till the ground, and deliver him from the galling fetters of slavery, but leave alone his religion." James bitingly retorted that "such an admonition is in character from the man, who having no religion of his own, would gladly find himself countenanced in the dreadful deficiency, by the universal suffrages of a world of atheists, or idolaters."[112] The Rev. John Pye Smith was even more acerbic in his condemnation of those "monsters, miscalled philosophers"—I would guess the Utilitarians to be his target—who "vamp up their daring impieties" by making "the name of nature . . . the idolatrous and senseless substitute for the name of Jehovah."[113]

Foreign missions did not provide their middle-class public in Britain with enough power to influence colonial policy. They did, however, enable middle-class evangelicals to use the British public's growing fascination with colonized and soon-to-be colonized regions of the world to their social advantage in Britain, if not in the colonies. Missionary reflections on heathenism were deployed in ways that undermined the Anglican establishment's moral credibility. Missionary propaganda therefore contributed to the recasting of respectability, gentility, and civility in distinctively middle-class terms.

This social logic makes better sense of middle-class support for foreign missions than does the more familiar, and more easily discounted, recourse to the profit motive.[114] Promises of profit were, to be sure, bandied about from the very outset. That Christianity produces civilization was an incontestable fact, the Rev. William Harris argued at the Annual Meetings of the LMS in 1817, that "would remain unaltered, even on the impossible supposition, that the Gospel were demonstrably a cunningly devised fable. For these reasons, therefore, unbelievers ought, on their own principles to encourage the propagation of evangelical truth."[115] Commercial interests were certainly the target of missionary activists' claims that Christian conversion and the productivity of native labor would increase hand in hand; as the Rev. John Angell James put it in the LMS's Annual Sermon of 1819, "industry is enjoined by the weight of a heavenly authority, and enforced by motives of eternal importance."[116]

Narrowly material considerations of colonial profit were not, however, the main or at this point even a prominent concern.[117] Indeed, one of the most noticeable features of missionary discourse in its first quarter century is its insistent devaluation of the civilizing mission. In the sermon just quoted, the Rev. James went on to remind his audience that "the object of the Redeemer's visit to our world was not to teach men the arts and the sciences, not to instruct them in letters, not to introduce the reign of philosophy, not to break the yoke of civil tyranny, nor to promulgate the best theory of human government. . . . No, my brethren there is but one object in the universe, which, according to all the ideas we can entertain, is sufficiently dignified to justify the humiliation of the Son of God, that is, the salvation of the human soul."[118]

Middle-class Congregationalists embraced a missionary cause whose colonial ambitions were framed in terms that were primarily if not exclusively spiritual. Motivations relating to spirituality, faith, or piety are not something about which secular historians write easily. As Joan Scott has recently reminded us, the emotional and expressive nature of religious observance, regardless of the social complexion of those involved, has long disabled social historians from engaging its manifestations or taking its agents seriously.[119] But it is only by acknowledging the spiritual ambitions of early missionary supporters directly that we can glimpse their social logic. The missionary contribution to middle-class formation included a language in which to voice opposition to the hegemony of an allegedly corrupt landed elite. This language was, in turn, dependent upon a piety whose social efficacy would be diminished by any worldly advantage accrued.[120]

Missions were one of the primary mediums through which middle-class Congregationalists framed theirs as a culture of sacrificial benevolence, which they did in response to the establishment's efforts to depict middle-class people as soulless materialists.[121] Congregationalists were, in fact, required to invest an enormous amount of time and money in the demanding practice of their faith. Complaints about missionary services running upwards of six hours in the early years provide a foretaste of the intensity of this associational life.[122] Regular worship services began in the early morning; afterward the most pious members would teach Sunday school and perhaps attend the day's second evening service. The memory of these endless and gloomy Sundays is a commonplace of Victorian biography and fiction.[123] In addition to regular services, Congregationalists spent many weekday evenings attending prayer and bible study meetings, as well the meetings of voluntary associations, of which foreign missions were but the most popular and demanding of a steadily growing number. And the amount of money given to foreign missions by middle-class evangelicals was often vast. Sir Francis Crossley, for example, a Halifax MP whose family fortune came from West Yorkshire textiles, donated £20,000 to the LMS near the end of his life.[124] The Baxters of Dundee, particularly Edward and his niece Mary Ann, were also very generous, the latter donating more than £15,000 to the society. The most spectacular of such donations was the £350,000 left to the society in 1905 in the will of Robert Arthington.[125]

And all of this was given on behalf of a cause from which the donors could expect little in return, even in the spiritual currency of souls won to Christ, on their investment. Only a small minority of the Indian population ever embraced the missionary gospel. Missionaries were somewhat more successful in the West Indies, the South Pacific, and Africa but not, for the most part, until after the consolidation of British colonial rule, which did not take place in many of these regions until the opening decades of the twentieth century. Hence the paradox: foreign missions enjoyed their greatest metropolitan support during their least successful period in the field. For most of the nineteenth century in most places in the world, the foreign missionary experience was one of cultural isolation, political marginalization, and general rejection.[126]

Failure abroad, however, did not stem the enthusiasm of the missionary movement's supporters at home. To the contrary, failure was embraced as a badge of honor, evidence of the missionary movement's transcendence of worldly values and concerns. The lowly missionary who held fast to his beliefs in isolation from the culture that paid him homage was exalted above those who needed human forms of support and worldly encouragements. The foreign missionary was singled out for praise for having worked and lived in regions of the world "where the flattering commendations of men could not reach him with injurious effect. He had known the *reality* of the long and patient conflict with idolatry and wickedness; and perhaps the praises of men at home seemed to him only so much talk."[127] Thus could both heathen opposition to and heathen embrace of missionary overtures embody the persecution for righteousness's sake, for whose sufferance abroad and at home Dissenting evangelicals hoped to reap an earthly as well as a divine reward.

"The Conversion of Englishmen and the World Inseparable"

The awful sincerity with which wealthy philanthropists earned their pious reputations was demonstrated in the extreme by Robert Arthington (1823–1900). The Arthingtons, a prominent Yorkshire Quaker family, related to the Jowitts, the Fryers, and the Peases, had made their fortune in brewing, but upon their conversion to temperance closed down their brewery in 1850. The family survived this sacrifice; Robert inherited upwards of £200,000 from his father. Regarding his wealth as a "high trust," Arthington spent virtually none of his inheritance on himself. He was known locally in Leeds as the "miser of Headingley," where he lived a reclusive life in a single room. Arthington apparently spent most of his days reading missionary literature and corresponding with various societies and their agents in the field. By the time of his death at the age of 77, Arthington's fortune had grown through careful investment to over a million pounds, most of which was divided between the Baptist Missionary Society and the LMS, to form the largest single bequest to a missionary organization in the history of modern missions. The domestic and social logic underlying Arthington's philanthropy is suggested by his virulent antipathy for the poor: as his biographer put it, Arthington "was not greatly moved by poverty, saying that he knew from experience that it was possible to live on very little."[128]

Missions helped middle-class evangelicals like Arthington position themselves in relation to the laboring poor below them as well as in relation to the Anglican establishment. And there was a connection, of course, between these social poles of the Dissenting middle class's self-constituting frame of reference. It was the Established Church's neglect of its pastoral duties and particularly of its obligation to minister to the souls of the poor that forced evangelicals and especially the Dissenters among them to embark on a missionary crusade at home. Looking back from the vantage point of the mid-1880s, in the midst of the moral panic over "outcast London" he had himself helped to incite, the prominent Congregational minister Andrew Mearns concluded that "had it not been for Sunday Schools, which from the first were largely supported and conducted by Nonconformists, nothing could have prevented the masses of the people from lapsing into utter barbarism."[129]

As discussed in chapter 2, the founding of the major foreign missionary societies at the eighteenth century's close coincided with the establishment of a range of home missionary organizations. The London Itinerant Society was established in 1796, the Congregational Society for Spreading the Gospel in England was established in 1797, and the Home Missionary Society was established in 1819. And many of the same individuals were active promoters of both home and foreign missions. The founders of the LMS also helped found the Religious Tract Society (RTS), the BFBS, and the numerous Sunday schools and Itinerant Societies, through which evangelical Dissent targeted plebian constituencies. Joseph Hardcastle, the LMS's first treasurer, also convened meetings of the RTS and BFBS at his offices and helped to found the Village Itinerancy Society. Rev. David Bogue, perhaps the most influential of the LMS's founders, was the founding editor of the *Evangelical Magazine* and was also active in the work of the RTS.[130]

But with the important exception of Sunday schools, these initiatives were feeble and often short-lived by comparison to their foreign missionary counterparts.[131] The Congregational Society for Spreading the Gospel in England was dissolved in 1809; the Village Itinerancy Society in 1847. According to Mearns these were "dark times" in which Nonconformists were made to suffer for their reputation as "friends of the poor and the oppressed"; their ministry purportedly "fomented sedition" and "unfitted the poor for labour."[132] Whether as a result of a pragmatic desire to avoid confronting the establishment on this, its home, terrain or of the middle class's own fears of the politically disruptive potential of home missionary encounters, the evangelical public was considerably and noticeably less generous with the home missionary institutions that appealed for its support than it was with their foreign counterparts.

The contrast between the enormous popularity of foreign missions and the comparative neglect of those at home did not escape the attention of home missionary advocates, who complained repeatedly about widespread disparities in press coverage and in attendance at public meetings, and, most important, in contributions made to the home as opposed to those made to the foreign cause. These differences were explicitly attributed to the respectable public's association of home missionary outreach with political radicalism.[133] Frustrated home missionaries and their supporters sternly reminded their fellow evangelicals that "if the obligation of Christian benevolence extends to men of every tongue and people of every nation, its claim must possess peculiar force at home."[134] Some occasionally went so far as to call it downright "preposterous to weep over the perdition of distant millions, and set at nought the claims of countless multitudes who are dropping into hell all around, at your doors, and before your eyes."[135]

But even those least sympathetic to the foreign missionary cause were forced to defer to the latter's popularity in order to raise money and otherwise mobilize support for their own undertaking. Such competition was not necessarily acrimonious. Remember that most home missionary advocates were also active supporters of foreign missions; that they generally avoided the sort of resentful hyperbole cited above should come as no surprise. What they did try to do, and on a very large scale, was to turn the popularity of the foreign field to home advantage. However, this fiscal pragmatism would have the important discursive consequence of connecting foreign missionary constructions of heathen peoples in foreign lands with home missionary constructions of the poor.

Home missions were, for example, explicitly promoted as vital and necessary means to foreign missionary ends. Home-missionary outreach was promoted as a means of enlarging the social base from which foreign missions could look for funds. More and better Christians in England would translate into more contributions for foreign missionary coffers, argued Rev. John Angell James in his aptly titled sermon "The Conversion of Englishmen and the Conversion of the World Inseparable": "Every minister who is raised up to preach the gospel at home, is another advocate for missions abroad. . . . Every new congregation that is formed is a new home and foreign mission at the same time. . . . See what a connexion [exists] between home operations and the spread of the gospel abroad?"[136] "I am convinced," urged another Congregational minister in 1850, "that if during the last five and twenty years we had been spending more in wise and well-directed effort in England, the London Missionary Society's income would be double what it is. I speak in the interests of India and China and Africa, when I appeal to you on behalf of our great English interests in this matter."[137]

The renewal of large-scale emigration represented another way in which home missionary exertions in Britain would benefit the foreign missionary and imperial cause. The Rev. John Blackburn warned of the "baneful influence" that "ignorant or profligate British settlers would exert on the character of the natives and labours of the brethren, were they to take up their future home near one of our missionary stations," and he urged his audience to remember "that the children that crowd our schools, and the humble rustics who hear our village lectures, may be shortly called, as seamen, soldiers, or settlers, to go far away amongst the Gentiles, and let this thought excite us to labour and pray for their conversion, that they may be the means of converting others."[138] Similar arguments were advanced by home missionary activists; the following sentiments were expressed in an annual report of the Baptist Home Missionary Society:

> That large numbers, in the course of a few years, will emigrate, there can be little question; and if they are to go forth as a blessing, not as a blight, to aid distant missionary effort, not to neutralize and destroy it; to propagate not the worst evils which characterize the parent country, but the blessings which with

all its faults, give it so high a place in the scale of nations;—they must be Christianized before they leave their native shores.[139]

Interestingly, these arguments were taken seriously by proponents of emigration, who sought foreign missionary support for their efforts abroad. W. Campbell Gilliam, the Honorable Secretary of the South African Colonization Society, solicited the LMS's backing for its application for land grants in 1859, arguing that a British settler presence would provide missionaries with protection against both Boer and "Kaffir" invasions.[140]

The interests of British patriotism as well as Christian charity were invoked in arguments that home missions were the precondition of imperial as well as foreign missionary success—and the two were clearly viewed as fundamentally intertwined. "We must become a 'chosen generation, a royal priesthood, an holy nation, a peculiar people,' ere we can occupy the fields of usefulness that are before us, and lead the heathen nations, that are subject to our sceptre, to rejoice in that dominion which brought with it the unspeakable blessing of Christian liberty."[141] Unfortunately "the melancholy discrepancy between the sacred books and the personal characters of the English residents [in the colonies] has often excited the surprise and the disgust of the more thoughtful heathen."[142]

Alongside the instrumental argument that home missions served foreign missionary ends was the more amorphous and pervasive assumption of their underlying similarity. It seems to have been almost impossible for evangelicals to describe, and arguably even to think about, the laboring poor, who were the explicit target of home missionary operations, without comparing them in some way to the empire's heathen races.[143] Home missionaries complained incessantly that England suffered from a "heathenism as dense as any in Polynesia or Central Africa"; comparing reports of local conditions in rural areas to "the survey of some unknown district of Africa by a missionary"; or describing the inhabitants of rural and village communities "as heathen and barbarian as the natives of darkest Africa."[144] No more effective analogy was apparently to hand to underscore the vices of the unchurched in Britain than the one suggesting that they were necessitous of "missionary interposition as energetic and devoted as in any heathen land."[145] At an 1830 service honoring a newly appointed city missionary of the Christian Instruction Society, Rev. Joseph Fletcher bemoaned the "awful degradation" of those in London "as ignorant of 'the true God' as if they had lived under the meridian of heathen superstition, and paganism were still the religion of the villages!"[146] Scottish Congregationalist Rev. Ralph Wardlaw similarly pleaded on behalf of those "many thousands of our own countrymen, who pass under the common name of Christian, and yet are living in the ignorance of heathens, and dying in this ignorance."[147]

Foreign missions were frequently invoked in home missionary appeals. In "A Plea for Home Evangelicisation," the Rev. Joshua Wilson opposed proposals to increase the educational requirements for home missionary agents by arguing that

> so long as a large number of the inhabitants of such counties are living in a state of practical heathenism—neglecting all religious ordinances (except a mere formal observance of the baptismal rite for their children), and habitually absenting themselves from all buildings set apart for divine worship and public religious instruction,—they equally need the preparatory labours of the evangelist, as the inhabitants of heathen and Mahometan lands.

These preparatory labors, he goes on to argue, required the spiritual rather than the intellectual gifts of piety, zeal, love, and pity, as well as a "robust corporeal frame"; what the home field requires "in a word," he concludes, are "real labourers."[148]

The capacity of our evangelicals to make such comparisons suggests that "race" and "class" had not yet taken their present shape as antithetical or even discrete axes of identity. By contrast to contemporary scholarly assumptions that race and class are alternative explanatory frameworks or modes of exploitation, British evangelicals seem to have assumed, for most of the first half of the nineteenth century, their underlying similarity; to have been struck, as Thomas Holt has recently put it, more by their similarities than by their differences, convinced by the very symmetry in representations of poor and colonized peoples that both forms of subordination were just, both prejudices true.[149] Or, to put it somewhat differently, sin was certainly a great equalizer in missionary discourse during the early nineteenth century.

The relative egalitarianism displayed in missionary constructions of colonized peoples did more than enable middle-class evangelicals to subvert the worldly claims to respectability of the Anglican Establishment. This same relative egalitarianism also made possible the comparisons between the metropolitan poor and the purported beneficiaries of foreign missionary ministrations. Here, however, missionary discourse circumvented those social boundaries we distinguish today by reference to race and class in such a way as to reinforce rather than to subvert domestic social hierarchies and to contain potential challenges of the colonized alike. Theirs was, in other words, a profoundly and consistently negative equality; from their comparison neither group of heathens derived moral or political benefit. It was not until and not unless he embraced Christianity that "the wild Hottentot" who was only on "the verge of humanity, learns to reason, to feel, to speak, as a Man."[150] And the same was believed to be true of the laboring poor with whom the Hot-tentot was explicitly compared. As the Rev. James Steven grimly concluded in 1811, "in surveying the moral condition of mankind, of every age and country, whatever varieties may be found amongst them in colour, language, customs, and manners; the same gloomy features of inherent depravity, the same sad proofs of estrangement from God are visible in all."[151]

This impulse to compare would have increasingly negative consequences for the British working classes in the aftermath of slavery's abolition. Evangel-icals more generally and Dissenters in particular were among the most active proponents of the abolition of the transatlantic slave trade and then of colonial slavery itself, in part if not only because of slave owners' hindrance of mission-ary operations in Britain's plantation colonies. The missionary public's antipa-thy to slavery had roots elsewhere as well. These were central to "the self-justification of emergent middle-class groups, and thus to the *ideological*, though not directly economic, needs of an expanding capitalism."[152] As David Brion Davis has argued, slavery was the ultimate violation of Christian political econ-omy. Evangelicals viewed "free" labor and its corollary, "legitimate" trade, as the economic mechanisms through which Christianity distributed its political and social benefits, as well as, and perhaps more importantly, its punishments. The movement for slavery's abolition was in these terms critical to the British middle class's efforts to normalize and valorize as free emergent labor relations on its home front that were the subject of profound contestation.[153]

Antipathy to slavery remained prominent among middle-class evangeli-cals' concerns even after the slave trade was abolished in 1807, followed by the abolition of slavery itself in 1834. At this point, however, the geographic fo-cus and political signification of antislavery sentiment began to shift from a moralizing condemnation of Europe's demand for slaves for its New World plantations to a condemnation of Africa's willingness to supply them. Eman-cipation succeeded in transforming slavery from something that depraved Europeans did to innocent Africans to something that guilty Africans did to one another. The problem of slavery in the aftermath of emancipation was, then, increasingly framed as a problem whose solution would require Euro-pean intervention in the form of a civilizing mission. The rationale for for-eign missions shifted accordingly, from atonement for Europe's complicity in slavery to the means by which Christian Europe might save Africans from themselves.[154]

Heathenism, meanwhile, became an ideological repository for the British public's well-honed repugnance for slavery. And thanks to the connective tis-sue constructed by the missionary movement, this would have, in turn, important consequences for the language of class taking shape in this period. The fact that the heathen people abroad to whom missionaries compared the poor at home were themselves being constructed in increasingly hostile ways in the aftermath of slavery's abolition rendered missionary comparisons of working people to colonized races all the more negative.

The propensity to compare subaltern groupings across the colonial divide did not prevent evangelicals from invoking contrasts to their advantage. As Stuart Hall has reminded us, race and class combine to form what is invariably a "complex structure: a structure in which things are related as much through their differences as through their similarities."[155] Home missionary propagandists frequently tried to outdo their foreign missionary competitors in condemning the alleged beneficiaries of their operations. To underscore the urgency of Britain's need for missions, they characterized the heathen classes at home as even more degraded than their overseas counterparts. As one report put it, "the outcast thousands of the people, whom we have culpably suffered to grow up in the heart of our country, [are] more profligate and more perverted than Hindoos."[156]

> If they could be selected and separated into a city by themselves, they would present a population as blind, corrupt, and brutish, as could be furnished from any city of the heathen world—they are seared in conscience, almost divested of moral sense, and sunk into all but hopeless degradation. They are in all respects "earthly, sensual, devilish," without God and without hope in the world.[157]

In 1847, the *Annual Report* of the London City Mission similarly urged its claims on the public purse by portraying its targets as more sinful than heathens elsewhere:

> Of all places in the world, London has the first claims upon us. Here within a walk of this place (St. John's) we know that hundreds of thousands are living without the public worship of God; and we have reason to fear that they are living without religion altogether; we know that many are sunk in vice and sorrow; more guilty than the Heathen, because they have greater means of knowledge, and they have the prospect of a more awful end. Untaught and unreclaimed, they disgrace the kingdom. . . . NEVER WAS THERE, I THINK, SO LARGE A MASS OF UTTERLY UNREGARDED HEATHENISM IN IT AS AT THIS MOMENT.[158]

This rhetorical strategy, however, was not without risk to the home missionary quest for a fairer share of the evangelical purse. Foreign missionary promoters played this scenario to their advantage. Missionary deputations claimed to have established abroad the reverse of the situation that prevailed in Britain. "Even in your enlightened country," they admonished their listeners, "the few are the spiritual, religious, orderly and correct; and the multitude are the impious . . . but here, the many are the worshippers of God, and the keepers of His commandments; and the few are the wicked and disobedient. . . . O that we could say this of London, and the [other] towns of Britain!"[159] Foreign missionary activists occasionally went so far as to argue that even if British heathens were more degraded than their foreign counterparts, their degradation was the reward of their own perverse moral choice and thus neither susceptible to nor deserving of missionary redress. Such was the logic of William Carey, founder of the Baptist Missionary Society, who pointed to the fact that "our own countrymen have the means of grace, and may attend on the word preached if they chuse it" to argue for the priority of the foreign cause.[160]

Implicit in the moral economy of formulations like this latter was a widespread belief that the poor at home had been coddled enough. It was at this point in missionary discussions that representations of the British poor and of colonized Others diverged. What is interesting here, however, is the disciplinary function that this quasi-racial distinction performed in the home missionary language of class. Even, or perhaps especially, those characteristics that the poor had in common with the missionary middle classes—their racial or national heritage—constituted benefits whose apparent waste served merely to further indict their possessor. It was this racial kinship, oddly enough, that helped in the rationalization of the aggressive social distancing that characterized the period in which the British working class was being formed. As E. P. Thompson has argued, "the years between 1790 and 1830 see an appalling declension in the social conscience of Dissent." There was a "virtual unanimity of complicity on the part of official Nonconformity" in terms of child labor, with middle-class chapelgoers resisting all efforts at reform.[161]

The poor could exonerate themselves from these demonizing charges by paying homage to the missionary project in which their own subordination was inscribed. Self-help was poverty's only cure in the minds of our missionary political economists, and charities that stimulated self-help were regarded as the most effective means of alleviating the suffering of exceptional "deserving" individuals. Such charities were also looked upon as a revealing index of a beneficiary's potential worth (the logic being that those who would help themselves were deserving).[162] At the same time, the act of philanthropy on the part of the laboring poor was considered to be an important stimulant of some of the most crucial components of self-help, namely thrift and responsibility.[163] The problem, of course, lay in finding sufferers in sufficiently dire straits to evoke the philanthropic pity of the poor. Foreign missions claimed to constitute just such a cause. They purportedly elevated the poor at home by exposing them to the uplifting example of middle-class missionary activism as well as by stimulating their fiscal prudence—all the while re-deeming heathens abroad by financing the global spread of gospel truth. The auxiliary movement was expressly designed to enable "the poor of the flock, by the periodical contribution of small sums" to "materially enlarge the funds and . . . to offer up their intercessions for the prosperity of this institution."[164] The society instructed its auxiliaries to collect the contributions of those "persons, not blessed with affluence, and whose convenience it would not suit to become Annual Subscribers." A printed circular to LMS supporters in 1812 similarly referred to auxiliaries as enabling the collection of the "contri-butions of the poor."[165]

And if they rejected this opportunity to participate in the mission cause, then they removed themselves from the pale of Christian charitable consid-eration. "If there be an impenitent and unbelieving sinner present, this day," warned the Rev. George Clayton at the annual meeting of the LMS in 1821, "who is still without Christ, in a land that is full of Christ, let him know, that it will be more tolerable for Sodom and Gomorrah, for Tyre and Sidon, in the day of judgment, than for him."[166] The culmination of this disciplinary artic-ulation of race and class in the missionary discourse of the Dissenting middle class lay in support for the punitive reform of the Poor Law of 1834.[167] De-signed to distinguish between the undeserving able-bodied and those ren-dered dependent through no moral failing of their own, the reformed Poor Law had the effect instead of stigmatizing poverty across the board, associat-ing it in the Dissenting middle class's eyes with the increasingly negatively charged condition of heathen pauperism.[168]

Conclusion

This chapter has argued that the foreign missionary movement was an influential site at which race and class converged in the making of an evan-gelical middle class. Missions did not so much deflect a metropolitan social process—namely class formation—from its purportedly natural course as give culturally specific shape to the relationships in and through which a middle class was made, or rather remade into that respectable and influential grouping to which the Rev. Binney paid tribute at this chapter's beginning. Organized religion's capacity to "make class" depended on the existence of an institutional culture able to generate out of or translate into the essentially local social practices of everyday religious life a practice and a vision of a na-tional community, an institutional capacity created in the case of Congrega-tionalism by the birth of foreign missions. Foreign missions also provided ide-ological material with which middle-class Congregationalists defined themselves in relation to Others above and below, at home and beyond. The language of class generated in home missionary operations was, as a result, inflected and informed by recurring comparisons, contrasts, and other references to the peoples and policies of the imperial mission field.[169]

Historians are only just beginning to recognize how modern is our scholarly assumption of the fundamental distinctiveness of race and class as ways of seeing, naming, containing, and resisting, and how anachronistic, therefore, our scholarly division of labor that keeps the study of industry and empire safely apart.[170] Missions were by no means the only or even the first institutional or discursive site at which the languages of class and race intersected. Comparing the poor to colonized peoples had become, by the turn of the nineteenth century, a familiar trope in European social discourse. That peasants were an alien race was a central plank in aristocratic cosmology; in fact, this social divide was, according to Benedict Anderson, where racial thinking originated.[171] The Irish, moreover, had also long been construed as both a lower class and an alien race.[172] But missions did contribute in important and concrete ways to making what were emergent conceptions of class and race conditions of each other's existence. The missionary contribution to this process enjoys distinctive claims to our attention, moreover, in terms of both the numbers of people exposed to missionary texts and the institutional practices that lent these texts their immediate and material resonance.

The next chapter will describe the transformation in the relationship between home and foreign missions during the second half of the nineteenth century. As a result of this transformed relationship, the tendency toward the convergence of class and race in the evangelical language of mission was reversed. It was in this period, the second half of the nineteenth century, that class and race acquired their contemporary antithetical connotations. This occurred, at least in part, I will argue, as a result of missionary philanthropy's feminization. It is, then, to the subject of the role of women in the missionary movement at home and abroad that I will now turn.

CHAPTER 4

From Telescopic Philanthropy to Social Missionary Imperialism: The Antinomies of Class and Gender in Missionary Conceptions of Race, 1845–1895

The history of every religious and benevolent society in the civilized world shows the female sex pre-eminent in numbers, zeal and useful-ness, thus attesting the interest women take in Christian labours for the welfare of society.
    —Clare Lucas Balfour, *Women and the Temperance Reformation*

There is a certain moral sense in which the free churches may be said to have created the working-classes of this country.
    —Joseph Parker, *The Larger Ministry*

    The LMS entered the second half of the nineteenth century at the height of its popularity. The much-heralded missionary tours of the 1840s reached their apogee in the triumphal return to England in 1856 of the LMS's most famous missionary son, David Livingstone. Livingstone's geographical ex-ploits—he was credited with being the first European to cross the African continent—spread his celebrity beyond the already broad social confines of the evangelical public to the upper reaches of British political culture. Livingstone was granted an audience with the queen and appointed a British consul. His book, *Missionary Travels and Researches in Africa*, sold 70,000 copies.[1] He was feted by commercial, civic, and scientific organizations as well as by religious groups; Roderick Murchison, president of the Royal Ge-ographical Society, observed in 1858 that "the name of Livingstone was suf-ficient to attract an assembly larger than any room in London could hold."[2]

    The enormous popularity of foreign missions was widely if not always approvingly acknowledged. Missionary enthusiasts, obsessed to tragicomic lengths with the progress and pitfalls of isolated missions in "exotic" foreign lands, were a staple feature, for example, of literary caricatures of evangelical piety during the middle decades of the nineteenth century.[3] It is the missionary aspirations of Jane Eyre's admirer, St. John Rivers, that perfectly capture his incapacity for true intimacy.[4] Support for missions was also conspicuous among the pieties in which Pitt Crawley and his mother-in-law, the Countess Southdown, took such unbecoming pride in William Thackeray's *Vanity Fair* (1847). Charles Dickens, whose enmity toward missionaries and their foreign beneficiaries alike was notorious, characterized Mrs. Jellyby's missionary concerns in *Bleak House* (1852) as an obsession that would have been merely humorous had it not been pursued at the expense of all those who knew her. Two decades later, George Eliot would still be castigating evangelicals, like Mr. Bulstrode of *Middlemarch* (1872), as those "whose charity increases directly as the square of the distance."

These still-familiar caricatures obscure the piety and the power on which missionary philanthropy was predicated. But they do flag for us the gendered nature of the intersection of home and foreign missions on which this study focuses. For it is evangelicals' relative preference for foreign over home missionary philanthropy that draws the bulk of this critical fire. "Loud-sounding, long-eared Exeter Hall" (which was the London location of the annual meetings of most of the major missionary organizations) was repeatedly attacked by the secular intelligentsia for agonizing over the plight of heathen races in the colonies while evincing scarcely a thought for the conditions of factory operatives or the urban poor who resided on evangelical philanthropists' very doorstep. What about the suffering of "sixty thousand valets in London itself who are yearly dismissed to the streets" or "to the hunger-stricken, pallid, *yellow*-coloured 'Free Labourers' in Lancashire, Yorkshire, Buckinghamshire, and all other shires!" queried an irate Thomas Carlyle.[5] Dickens similarly admonished evangelicals: "The work at home must be completed thoroughly, or there is no hope abroad. To your tents, O Israel! but see they are your own tents! Set them in order; leave nothing to be done there."[6]

The dire consequences of evangelicalism's reversal of these priorities are revealingly represented in what are anti-feminist dystopias, whose missionary inhabitants personify a subversion of the gender status quo. Among the characters who embody missionary enthusiasm, women, or, at the very least, pointedly effeminate men, figure prominently. Dickens scathingly refers to the male leadership of the evangelical lobby as a bunch of "weird old women";[7] Thackeray similarly has Pitt Crawley dismissed by his schoolmates as well as his by soldier brother, Rawdon, as "Miss Crawley." If male missionary supporters are disparaged as somehow not real men, their female counterparts are similarly portrayed as not quite women. Pitt Crawley's sister-in-law, the tract writer Lady Southdown, is all but unsexed by her missionary involvement, "having but faint ideas of marriage, her love for blacks occupied almost all of her feelings."[8] Dickens similarly attributes the unhappiness pervading Mrs. Jellyby's household in *Bleak House* to her unnatural preoccupation with the foreign mission field—there is effectively no mother, mistress, or wife at the helm, these identities having all been invested in the foreign mission cause. Note the slippage that pervades this discourse between the foreign missionary movement's domestic or home front, which is to say the geographical space of the nation, and the missionary enthusiast's middle-class home. It is her dirty and neglected children, drunken and mismanaged servants, and emasculated husband who are made to represent the domestic casualties of a missionary philanthropy that takes women like Mrs. Jellyby outside the respectable confines of Victorian domesticity. Thus were the causes and the consequences of Dickens' "telescopic philanthropy" gendered at their core.[9]

This chapter will explore the social realities toward which these literary representations gesture, namely the influence of gender on British evangelicals' engagement with the mission cause. As we shall see, foreign missions were being feminized in fact as well as in fiction during the second half of the nineteenth century. From the 1840s and 1850s on, women began to play an ever larger role in the propaganda and the practice of the LMS as objects and agents of missionary outreach in the foreign mission field. Moreover, British women's support was courted on the missionary home front in increasingly gendered terms. And just as missionary involvement helped give shape to English middle classness, so too were evangelical conceptions of femininity constructed, at least in part, out of material provided by the missionary cause.

Contrary to what literary conventions might lead us to expect, however, evangelicalism more generally became less rather than more telescopic in its focus during this period. Dickens et al. appear to have been correct in their suspicions that evangelical women preferred their objects of philanthropy "at a distance." However, this gendered predilection for foreign missionary philanthropy was simply not sufficient to override class and colonial developments that pressured evangelicals to invest their philanthropy elsewhere. As a result of these developments, the LMS would find itself at a serious disadvantage in its efforts to compete with increasingly popular home missionary agencies for its share of the Congregational purse.

In response to this competitive environment, the LMS's promoters began to recast the terms on which they staked their claims to Congregational support in ways that brought racial difference to the forefront. By contrast to their critics' depiction of them as blind to racial difference, missionaries and their supporters' purported "love for blacks" was predicated on a relatively fixed hierarchy—fixed, that is, with respect to the middle-class colonizer. As we have seen in the preceding chapter, however, it had not been fixed with respect to the laboring poor. Colonized peoples and the metropolitan working class were frequently compared if not conflated in missionary discourse for at least the first three quarters of the nineteenth century. The impulse by century's end, however, was toward their racial dissociation.[10] During the second half of the nineteenth century, missionary discourse becomes, in other words, ever less concerned with asserting the similarities between the home and the foreign targets of missionary ministrations (which are increasingly invoked less as common sense than for their shock value) than with underscoring their distinctive features. Comparisons continued to be invoked, to be sure, in urban ethnographies such as General Booth's "In Darkest England."[11] But these are, increasingly, disciplinary exceptions to an intensifying rule of racial difference, on whose terms a new regime of metropolitan as well as colonial social controls was constructed.

These then are the three basic narratives this chapter will pursue: the feminization of foreign missions, the rising competition of home missions, and the advent of racial distinctions between home and foreign mission fields. While connected, these narratives do not coincide; this chapter will not in other words tell a single, self-contained story. Rather it will expose multiple and often contradictory forces that were impinging on the missionary movement in this period and will assess the historical pressures that favored one of many possible outcomes of their convergence. Each of the master narratives of gender, race, and class at work here are repeatedly disrupted, but it is, of course, precisely their dynamic interaction that is of interest.[12] For the larger thrust of this chapter, indeed of the book as a whole, is that neither gender nor race nor class exists outside of or prior to this history; they are, to the contrary, constituted in and through it. And it is in this period, when the relationship between home and foreign missions is in the process of being reconfigured, that their inchoate interdependence is most visible.

Missionary Imperial Feminism

That gender takes precedence over women's history in the story I am going to tell (or, rather, that the women's history I will relate was made possible by changing conceptions of gender that affected men as much as women) is suggested by the fact that the literary caricature of missionary philanthropy as feminized predates considerably the social relations it pur-

ports to describe.[13] To be sure, "Female Societies" were established in connection with local auxiliaries of the LMS and its mainstream counterparts
from the outset, which is to say from the 1810s and 1820s.[14] However, the
missionary involvement of these mothers of the Victorians should be distinguished from those of Mrs. Jellyby by the degree of institutional autonomy
and professional recognition—or, rather, the lack thereof—that the former
were accorded. During the first half of the nineteenth century, women's auxiliaries were subsidiary adjuncts of their male counterparts. It was the male
officers of local missionary branches who planned the extraordinarily popular anniversary meetings; wrote the auxiliary's reports; forwarded their district's receipts to the London office; spoke on behalf of missions at public
meetings and in their chapels, churches, and affiliated Sunday schools; and
otherwise publicly associated themselves with the increasingly popular mission cause. Women's involvement was largely confined to the more behind-
the-scenes tasks of serving tea, sewing fancy goods for sale at missionary
bazaars, and collecting subscriptions door-to-door. The latter activity was an
intensely personal affair in which women's maternal powers of persuasion
over society's weaker beings—children, other women, and especially the
lower classes—as well as their having sufficient time, unlike their employed
male counterparts, to "spend hours calling on non-subscribers in the hope of
enlisting their sympathy" were believed to stand them in good stead.[15]

During the second half of the nineteenth century, however, the nature of
women's involvement in the foreign mission campaign was transformed in
the more autonomous directions that Dickens seemed to fear. Rather than
simply serving as fund-raising adjuncts within institutions controlled by men,
evangelical women began to establish independent linkages to the foreign
mission field. Their circumvention of the male-dominated institutional channels through which they had heretofore been connected was manifested most
dramatically in the paid professional employment of middle-class women in
the foreign mission field. The first steps in these directions took place outside
the institutional purview of the mainstream missionary organizations. The
Society for Promoting Female Education in the East, which was founded in
1831, and the Indian Female Normal School and Instruction Society, which
was founded in 1854, were both designed to promote the deployment of single women in the foreign mission field.[16]

During the 1860s and 1870s, the major evangelical missionary societies
set up their own committees and auxiliary organizations for recruiting and
deploying women candidates. Ladies' committees were formed for these purposes in connection with the Wesleyan Methodist Missionary Society in
1858, the Baptist Missionary Society and the Society for the Propagation of

the Gospel in 1866, and the LMS in 1875.[17] Progress thereafter was rapid. By the close of the nineteenth century, the percentage of women in the foreign mission field force had grown from virtual nonexistence (save for the considerable but unacknowledged labor of missionary wives) to almost full parity.[18]

Most evangelical women remained, of course, in Britain. But their missionary involvement was qualitatively transformed as well during the second half of the nineteenth century, when local ladies' missionary auxiliaries began to display what was to their critics within the evangelical community as well as without a disturbing desire for autonomy.[19] No longer content to perform the preparatory labor for the male auxiliary's annual meeting, ladies' societies began organizing their own separate meetings, to be addressed whenever possible by women—female missionaries for the most part, but also the leading women activists in the locale. British women embraced this increasingly gendered mission cause with enormous enthusiasm, and their contributions by century's end totaled some 70 percent of the income of the major missionary organizations.[20] Indeed, the foreign mission cause was very probably the largest mass movement of women in nineteenth-century Britain.[21]

While its importance in the history of British women cannot be overstated, I would like to suggest that the origins of the missionary movement's feminization lay as much in colonial relations of power as in gender relations at home. Or, rather, the opportunity for British women to exercise their agency on behalf of foreign missions was opened, at least in part, by developments in the colonies. Colonized peoples' rejection of the gospel message forced many missionaries to rethink their mode of outreach. Although the situation varied enormously across the LMS's vast and diverse foreign field, the refusal of many societies to receive missionaries into their midst unless they were promised or provided worldly benefits of some sort (often firearms and diplomatic protection, but also trade, employment, education, and health care) led many missionaries to view the purportedly heathen targets of their ministry less as recalcitrant individuals than as members of an unreceptive culture that would itself have to be changed *before* Christianization would be possible. Effective proselytism was increasingly believed to require a basic minimum of social support, and bible preaching was increasingly supplemented with secular forms of outreach. Teaching domestic as well as industrial arts, providing health and education as well as spiritual services, were now touted as means of displaying Christianity's "civilizational" superiority.[22]

By the middle of the nineteenth century, then, the missionary movement began to embrace the once-despised premises of the civilizing mission. Gender was central to the conception of civilization on which this new missionary praxis rested, for women were believed to hold the key to opening heathen hearts to the civilizing influence of Christian love. In keeping with the gendered norms by which evangelical women were sheltered in the private sphere, heathen women were increasingly viewed as the key to their families' salvation. Evangelicals deemed women nurturers by nature whose purpose in life was to bear and rear children.[23] Their lack of selfish or sexual desire made women the natural repositories of religious piety as well. Women's innate religiosity and their maternalism, moreover, went hand in hand, for one of the most important ways that women fulfilled their obligations as wives and especially as mothers was by making the home a haven safe from worldly temptations and the family the critical unit of worship.[24] Women's piety was thereby deemed the crucial precondition of any culture's salvation, their influence "as wives and mothers, on the next generation would alone be a sufficient argument for endeavouring to rescue and to raise them."[25]

This gendering of the object of missionary outreach triggered a radical revision in the missionary movement's relationship to the imperial project. As discussed in chapter 3, early missionaries juxtaposed the Christian missionary agenda with the civilizing missionary ambitions of secular elites, past as well as present. Greece and Rome, they were fond of saying, had excelled in the arts of civilization but were no less damned for it: "Even the most polished nations of the heathen, both in ancient and modern times, amidst all their improvements in civilization, literature, and the arts, have, in glaring contrast to this displayed the grossest ignorance of everything belonging to the divine science of religion."[26] The missionary lobby's insistence that it was Christ and Christ alone through whom salvation could be secured was not too obliquely directed against a classically educated political establishment widely represented as indifferent to religion. The "civilization" of which this elite was so proud was denigrated as a distraction from a saving focus on the divine.

This critical perspective on civilization was gradually displaced by its opposite during the middle decades of the nineteenth century. The worldly accoutrements of British imperial as well as commercial expansion were increasingly validated in missionary propaganda as divinely ordained albeit secular means to missionary ends. On its surface, the missionary movement's newfound respect for civilization advocated only the informal support of private economic interests. Livingstone, in particular, stressed the importance of establishing British commerce in the African interior as a legitimate alternative to an African slave trade that he claimed was even more nefarious than its transatlantic predecessor.[27] The Nonconformist bourgeoisie hesitated, however, to invest its own capital in such a risky venture.[28] But its cheers were raised in massively attended meetings when the British state was called upon to take the initiative. "The object was of national importance," argued J. A.

Turner, MP, in his introductory remarks at a Manchester Auxiliary meeting held to honor Livingstone's achievements, and "it was hardly reasonable that all should be left to private exertion, or private mercantile capital, to develop a country in which much would have to be done before commercial operations could be fairly entered upon."[29] Or, as the Bishop of Oxford argued at a meeting convened on behalf of the Universities Mission to Central Africa (a High Church organization founded to carry out Livingstone's vision), while "it was the work of the Church and not of the nation to Christianize the earth; the work of the nation was to open the way in which the Church must pass." And it was, of course, God himself who "had made it in the direct pecuniary interest of men that this work should be carried out."[30]

Imperialism figured prominently among the worldly interests that God in his wisdom (rather than mankind in its sinful weakness) ensured that Christian missions would serve. Indeed, the missionary lobby found itself on the vanguard of expansionist sentiments in this period. At the very moment when key representatives of the nation's governing elite were complaining that Britain's existing colonies were unprofitable burdens, "mill-stones" around the nation's neck, as Disraeli put it, missionary celebrities like David Livingstone were drawing evangelical attention to the national benefits of increased commercial interaction with the non-European world, and urging the British nation to colonize the foreign mission fields that remained beyond its formal reach.[31]

Missionaries' mounting enthusiasm for colonial expansion was further encouraged by their increased (though obviously never exclusive) emphasis on women and children. This gendered split of the colonized targets of missionary intervention helped to reconcile the contradictions between missionary and more coercive imperial visions. The imperious exercise of British authority in relation to colonized men could be rationalized as the necessary means to the more liberal end of emancipating colonized women. This was one of the disciplinary subtexts of missionary propaganda's emphasis on the "heart-rending details" of female infanticide, child marriage, forced prostitution, polygamy, widow burning, and the like, that were designed to move "the spirit of every reader" to an awareness of "the deplorable debasement to which females are reduced in the nations of the heathen."[32]

This protofeminist indictment of the culture of the colonized thus enabled imperial and missionary expansion alike to be represented in England if not received in the colonies as a liberal project of freeing oppressed women and children from the debilitating throes of heathen patriarchy. Colonial officials were quick to give imperial credit to missions where credit was due. "By spreading Christianity Great Britain had been able to gain to herself whole nations of people," claimed Sir George Grey, British colonial secretary, in an address to a missionary gathering in 1859.[33] And how did Christian missions facilitate this process? By making Britons known as "the tribe who love the black man." This, according to the Earl of Shaftesbury, was the missionary movement's real achievement.[34]

And it was this marriage, which became happier and happier over time, between missions and imperialism that provided British women with the opportunity to negotiate the terms of their own subordination by playing an ever more active and autonomous role in the foreign missionary crusade. This was in many ways a historically contingent coincidence. This is to say that it was inadvertent; it was not intended by the male missionary promoters of the civilizing mission, much less by their new allies in the colonial establishment. It nonetheless linked at the level of experience (a more powerful, less easily contested form of attachment than logical inevitability, anyway) the pleasures of participating in the missionary project with the maintenance of racial and national hegemony in the British Empire for the British women involved.

It was the agency of British women themselves, of course, that was critical in the end. It was their showering of financial and other forms of support upon an increasingly gendered missionary praxis that ensured the latter's preeminence. And the reward for their support lay in the missionary rationale for European women's professional employment in the foreign mission field. Christian women were the only agency through which the heathen family could be remade, especially in those cultures that prohibited male missionaries from engaging in personal contact with indigenous woman. And even where male missionaries could address native women, their doing so always risked the possibility of scandalous liaisons (of which there had been many). Male missionary outreach to women or children would also result in most places in a loss of face with the indigenous male population, whose conversion remained the missionary movement's ultimate end. It was the women of England alone who would be able to "find their way into the zenanas and rescue the unhappy section of humanity they found there."[35]

Missionaries' wives, to be sure, had long been doing just such work, but their labor was now deemed intrinsically inadequate to the missionary task at hand.[36] Domesticity was invoked to argue that their familial responsibilities did not leave missionaries' wives with sufficient time or energy to conduct missions to women on the requisite scale. The paid professional labor of single women was thus the only adequate means by which the massive job the missionaries faced could be tackled. Its mobilization would require, in turn, the autonomous agency of female supporters at home. Local women's missionary auxiliaries began to direct their energies ever more exclusively toward

the special object of missions to women, sending sewn and other goods, letters, prayers, and money directly to individual women missionaries in the
field, cultivating in the process, or so it was claimed, a more intimate connection or "living relationship" with the foreign field than their male counterparts enjoyed.[37]

By means such as these, middle-class women were encouraged to identify with the mission fields of empire in a powerfully personal way. Much of
what it meant to be a respectable middle-class woman was connected to or
rendered dependent upon the foreign mission cause. And, as was the case with
respect to the missionary influence on an emergent middle-classness, femininity itself was being reconstituted in the process. Missionary propaganda
represented British women as "elevated to their rightful station and dignity,
the equals and beloved associates of men . . . by the heavenly principles of
'the glorious gospel of the blessed God.'" British women's status was invoked
as evidence that the gospel held the key to reversing "the present degradation
of their sex in Pagan and Mohammedan countries." Thus, "If all Christians
are bound to exert themselves in this cause, surely the obligation which rests
on Christian women is fourfold! They, far more than men, owe to Christianity their present free and happy state—while it is on their sex that, in other
lands, the hard bondage of heathenism presses with the heavier weight."[38]

What did this missionary-inspired conception of the feminine actually
entail? Was it the subversive escape from women's separate sphere of domesticity that Dickens feared it to be? Or was women's missionary philanthropy
domesticity's realization, as mission and feminist historians have since tended
to assume?[39] At first glance, the latter would seem to have been the case. Missionary propaganda celebrated the prevailing state of gender relations in Great
Britain: "to think of the difference" between heathen women and their British
Christian counterparts, argued a missionary speaker in 1883, "was to excite
feelings of grateful wonder."[40] Missionary outreach to women abroad was expressly designed to extend to heathen women precisely those advantages that
Victorian women reputedly enjoyed on their domestic pedestals: "can you be
content to sit at ease in Zion," queried a typical missionary publication in
1898, "whilst millions of your sisters suffer untold shame and anguish?"[41]

Missionary discourse thus projected the problem of British women's oppression outward, onto the empire; the obvious implication of the missionary
critique of heathen patriarchy was that Britain's Christian homes were a ful-
filling and safe haven.[42] "Wives, who are happy in the affectionate esteem of
your husbands—mothers, who enjoy your children's reverence and gratitude—children, who have been blessed by a mother's example, and a mother's
care—sisters, who have found in your brothers your warmest friends,—

Christian women, who feel that you can lend to society its charm, and receive from it a loyal courtesy in return—protected, honoured, and loved"— these were the subject positions to which the missionary movement appealed.[43] England's "happy Christian homes" were identified as "the foundation of all her real greatness" in missionary propaganda.[44]

There is a sense, however, in which these tributes to domesticity subvert by exaggeration. The celebratory descriptions of Victorian gender relations in missionary propaganda may well have encouraged the imagination of feminist alternatives to women's confinement to the domestic and private sphere. Addressing British women as those whose "minds are intelligent and cultivated," whose "lives are useful and happy" (as well of course as those who "can look for a blessed immortality beyond the grave") set up a cognitive dissonance between missionary representation and the lived experience of middle-class women. Cultivated intelligence and useful lives were far removed from the leisured and ornamental existence toward which respectable women were increasingly encouraged in this period.[45] Such gaps between gender conventions and missionary prescriptions were as likely to encourage as to contain British women's resistance to the actually existing gender relations missionary propaganda was pretending to uphold.[46]

Such a reading is supported by the actions of those women who embraced the mission cause, actions that often though not always belied rhetorical celebrations of the gender status quo by implicitly and sometimes explicitly challenging the foundations of the domestic ideal. Marriage itself, the central relationship toward which Victorian women's lives were directed from all sides, was called into question, for example, not only by those independent women who flocked to missionary opportunities for paid employment in the second half of the nineteenth century, but by many of their married counterparts as well.[47] In the years before going out on their own became an option, female missionary enthusiasts deliberately and openly sought entry into the field by marrying missionary candidates. These marriages were often arranged by sympathetic ministers and took place after the man and woman had known each other only a few weeks. The mission cause would remain the central preoccupation of many of these women after their marriages and even after the arrival of their children, most of whom seem to have been sent back to Britain at an early age.[48]

All the more dramatic was the challenge to the premises of separate spheres posed by the paid employment of women in the foreign mission field. The gravity of this innovation in British gender relations was widely acknowledged, but the proponents of women's missions generally concluded that missionary ends more than justified such radical measures.[49] Rationales for employing (British) women in the mission field were implicitly and sometimes explicitly critical of the lives prescribed for middle-class women on the missionary home front. As Jemima Thompson, author of an early biographical tribute to women workers in the foreign field, passionately insisted in 1841,

> All human beings, whether they are men or women, require an object for which to live; i.e., not merely the grand object of preparation for the future life, but a subordinate and immediate one for the present. Women, a little removed from the humbler classes of society, commonly labour, in this respect, under a disadvantage not experienced by men. The latter have some profession on which to enter, as soon as what is usually denominated education is completed; but women, at that period, for the most part, have none. Many girls leave school at sixteen or seventeen, and spend . . . the most valuable part of their lives in a kind of restless indolence. Had they before them some great and benevolent object, such as taking a share in the regeneration of the world, they would be much happier, and much more amiable. Their mental powers, instead of being frittered away, would be increased,—their moral character would acquire a higher tone,—they would be more, rather than less, fitted for the enjoyment of domestic life in after years,—and many of the regrets of a death-bed would be avoided.[50]

Jemima Luke, a prominent Congregationalist who was active in support of LMS women's missions, explained her own missionary enthusiasm in similar terms, as a decision not to settle for "the luxurious ease of a beautiful country home, reading interesting books, writing chatty letters to friends, receiving and paying calls, doing Berlin woolwork, and making wax on paper flowers as then in vogue, and knitting babies' socks and anti-macassars for bazaars," a life she considered to be a waste of "an excellent constitution, untiring energy, and years spent in mental cultivation."[51]

The mission cause, in short, sanctioned the obvious desires of at least some Victorian women to invest their energies outside family and domestic life, in public endeavors that they themselves explicitly likened to the professional opportunities enjoyed by men. The missionary project also provided British women with the institutional space in which to engage in activities traditionally the purview of men: to act collectively, handle money, organize meetings, and, most importantly it seems, to speak in public on behalf of the cause.[52] Missions were one of the few such spaces available to women in evangelical churches, whose nineteenth-century history was characterized by the silencing of women and by their exclusion from positions of influence.[53] This is the context in which we are to understand the repeatedly acknowledged importance that ladies' missionary auxiliaries attached to having women speakers address their meetings. The enthusiasm of female audiences, gathered to hear a speaker of their own sex, suggests the sense of personal empowerment that these women derived from even vicarious involvement in this breach of separate spheres.[54]

To be sure, gestures were almost always made to the latter's continuing purchase; female missionary enthusiasts testified over and over again to how difficult it was to bring themselves to speak. When opening a women's missionary bazaar in Newcastle in 1883, for example, Mrs. Arthur Coote admonished her audience that "it was time the ladies were coming forward to speak on such occasions as the present. (Applause.) She knew how difficult it was for ladies to do so, she knew how difficult she felt it at first, and she had great sympathy for those who tried (hear, hear, and laughter) but it was their duty to help in such good works. (Applause.)"[55] Indeed, at least one female missionary deputation who had never spoken in public before suffered a nervous breakdown under the strain.[56]

But part of the transformative power of the missionary project was its sanctioning of such transgressive behavior. It was the pious woman's duty to overcome her "natural diffidence" in order that she might better serve the mission cause, and scores of women embraced the opportunity to do so with open arms.[57] Louisa Spicer Martindale (1839–1914) is an instructive example. Eldest daughter of James Spicer, a successful London stationer, and sister of Albert Spicer, chairman of the London Chamber of Commerce and long-time treasurer of the LMS, Martindale dedicated herself at an early age "to the cause of women as well as to the cause of religion."[58] In addition to serving as a director of the LMS, in which capacity she frequently hosted furloughed missionaries in her home, Martindale was a moving force in the Brighton Women's Liberal Federation from 1891 as well as being active in the National Union of Women's Suffrage Societies.

Martindale did not experience her missionary and her feminist aspirations as discrete much less as contradictory spheres of interest. To the contrary, they were mutually constitutive concerns. The empire enabled British women to promote their own suffrage in terms of the traditional rationale of service to others. The vote for British women was, in other words, represented as the precondition of colonized women's salvation. When lecturing British women's groups on the condition of women in India, she admonished her audiences "that if they did not desire votes for their own sakes, they ought, at any rate, to work for them on behalf of their Indian sisters for whose life and freedom they had a deep responsibility."[59]

However, as Antoinette Burton has so eloquently reminded us, the global sisterhood espoused by feminists like Martindale inevitably bore the marks of being forged in an imperial context.[60] And this was a context in which race, moreover, figured with ever increasing intensity. Racial attitudes were hard-

ening in the middle decades of the nineteenth century as a result of a number of different influences, among which the purported failure of emancipation figured prominently. Frustrated abolitionists found racial exemptions
from human nature's rules useful for explaining the refusal of freed slaves to
work in ways their emancipators intended.[61] A similar logic operated in colonial officialdom's recourse to race to explain all forms of resistance to colonial authority. The middle decades of the nineteenth century saw a wave of
anticolonial revolts break out in British North America, in Jamaica, in India,
in Ceylon, and elsewhere.[62] On all these fronts, race protected the rationales
by which waged labor and colonial subjugation were represented as free labor
and the civilizing mission. Rather than acknowledging whose interests were
being served, race was called upon to legitimize the testimony of those who
refused civilization's purported gifts. To these social and political determinations must be added intellectual developments relating especially to the social
application of Darwinian evolutionary theory.[63]

The missionary movement was, unfortunately, not exempt from this new
racialism. This hardening of racial attitudes was registered in the literary indictment of missionary philanthropy described at this chapter's beginning. Gendering missions as feminine was at one level a rhetorical strategy to discredit
liberal forms of outreach to racially demarcated Others the world over.[64]
Foreign missions were represented as a sentimental and irrational misreading
of colonized peoples' character and capability, "useless, futile, and we will venture to add . . . wicked," Dickens argues, because of the "great gulf" that separated "the civilized European and the barbarous African."[65] Brute force was
the only mode of authority viable in the colonies in Dickens' view. Dickens'
own racialist proclivities hardened considerably after the Indian Mutiny in
1857, about which he opined: if "I were commander in Chief in India, I
should do my utmost to exterminate the Race upon whom the stain of the
late cruelties rested . . . to blot it out of mankind and raze it off the face of
the Earth."[66]

The missionary movement was, unfortunately, not exempt from this new
racialism. Extremely negative views of colonized peoples were frequently
expressed, even in popular periodicals such as the LMS's *Quarterly News of
Women's Work*, whose purpose was to incite the kind of sympathy that would
encourage the bestowal of generous gifts. A Miss Rowe wrote from her new
station in Canton, South China, that while "the natives were invariably civil
and pleasant . . . I feel as Ezra and Nehemiah and Zerubbabel did in the
midst of a people that had backslidden and forgotten their first love, and
grown careless in every way." Although assuring her readers she will "stick to
them until my heart breaks, or my body gives out," she concluded her communication with a bizarre aside:

I do not say of them, as a missionary once declared of a certain African tribe, that a second deluge sweeping them off the face of the earth would be the best thing that could happen to them; but a fiery persecution would, I am convinced, be a fierce and salutary trial of the faith that is in them. . . . That would test them, purge out the dross, and bring the pure gold to light.[67]

Most missionaries stopped well short of genocidal extremes. Nonetheless, the gendered opportunities secured by their participation in missionary institutions did give evangelical women a stake in the unequal social power inscribed upon the missionary gift. Missionary articulations of British women's identity as women rendered their very piety dependent upon their Hindu sisters' needing help. It was predicated, in other words, on an assumed absence in colonized women and their societies of qualities, strengths, and virtues that the missionary project implicitly attributed to their English benefactresses. Nor did their missionary-reforming concern about heathen women preclude critical assessments of their moral state. However much social conditions were held responsible, British missionary enthusiasts often viewed their colonized sisters as needing "a great deal of helping up before they can get even half as high as English girls are."[68] Whatever benefits colonized women may have accrued from missionary interventions, British women almost invariably emphasized their own dominance in the missionary gift exchange.[69] They were, at the very least, elder sisters or, more often, maternal substitutes who cared from a great distance of space, culture, and moral character.

That relations of power were being imaginatively formulated or reformulated by this missionary-feminist discourse is further suggested by the frequency with which British women's maternal concerns for heathendom find expression in orphan motifs. Heathen women were believed to have been rendered incapable of being real mothers by the abject conditions of their existence; "rare" were the mothers who "really had their children's best welfare at heart."[70] "There was no home life in India, there being no mothers in the real sense of the term," or so the Ladies Missionary Auxiliary in Leeds was informed by LMS missionary Miss Barclay in 1897.[71] Heathen children's only hope, therefore, was to be removed from their parents' care. Heathen children are instructed "to flee from their mothers"[72] and allow themselves to be reared by sympathetic missionary substitutes able to provide proper moral guidance. "If we could give to orphan girls, or to the daughters of our very poor members," argued one female missionary, "even a short experience of what a happy Christian home should be . . . we should do for them a work which we cannot do at present."[73] As is evident from the example given above, even converted parents were not safe from missionary designs on children.

> It is very hard for those who have become Christians to throw off at once the influences which have bound them so long with a power more than human. . . . We need to get the children of Christians away from their influences during the years in which impressions for good or evil are so easily made. If some of these tender years are spent in Christian boarding-schools, then the chains of fear which have bound the parents, and whose traces are still visible, can never in the same way, or to the same extent, influence the minds of their children."[74]

Gendered missions sought to establish a different kind of power than that to which their critics aspired. But they sought power nonetheless. Indeed, their desire to appropriate the children of their colonized "sisters" was a gendered validation and considerable extension of the imperial state's displacement of indigenous political authority. Caring and control went hand in hand for imperial trustees, missionary sisters, and social mothers alike.[75]

Race, Class, and Contagion

It should be obvious from the discussion above that British women's attitudes toward their foreign beneficiaries were more complicated than the sentimental identification Dickens attributes to Mrs. Jellyby and her ilk. Or, rather, the latter's purported "love for blacks" did not preclude and was often predicated upon colonized people's subordination to European authority. A hierarchy that was fixed, at least in theory, by race (though we must remember that despite racialist pretensions to the contrary, racial boundaries are always permeable) was the precondition of the opportunities that drew evangelical women to the foreign mission cause. Rather than the repudiation of white supremacy, missionary feminism represented a liberal variation on an emergent racialist theme that was no less racial for its distinctively cultural emphases.[76]

In this section I want to suggest some of the often-contradictory connections between the intersection of gender and race just discussed and the transformation of class relations on the missionary movement's home front. Here, again, the missionary movement's home and foreign fronts illuminate as well as influence each other's development. The examination of class dynamics below suggests that race rather than reverence was responsible for the missionary movement's telescopic predelictions, especially where women were concerned. For it was race that rendered, and more than a little ironically, missionary contact with the colonized less threatening to middle-class women's respectability than was contact with the British poor.

That race may have played a role in metropolitan class relations is seldom considered in the social histories of this period. But the deepening of racial divides in the colonies facilitated the expansion of the political nation and the unification of British society across the class divide. Mary Poovey has recently characterized this process as a recasting of the political nation away from early modern conceptions of "body politic" to the modern "social body."[77] Viewed from the perspective of the body politic, the British poor were not qualitatively different from colonized peoples, in that they were both excluded from the political nation. This formulation has its parallel, I would suggest, in the comparisons of heathens at home to heathens in foreign lands that riddle early nineteenth-century missionary texts.

During the middle decades of the nineteenth century, Poovey argues, the political nation was reconceived as a social body, which, unlike the body politic, included the working classes. The incorporation of the poor did not approach equality, to be sure. The social body, like the human body, has different parts that play different roles in ensuring society's survival. While middle- and upper-class men and women were likely to see themselves as head and heart, respectively, in their minds the poor were likely to be relegated to hands and legs, organs whose movements are directed from elsewhere. Vital to the organism's survival, yes, but equal to other organs in no way.

What were the ramifications of the incorporation of the laboring poor into the political nation for the intersection of race and gender discussed above? On the one hand, the emergence of a unitary or organic conception of society was the basis for the growing domination of women in the implementation as well as the administration of philanthropy. Anthropomorphized by a medicalized language of health and disease, society was increasingly conceived of as a body in need of care. Although the authors of this discourse were men—Poovey cites the usual suspects: Utilitarian politicians, doctors, statisticians, and other scientists of the social—the terms on which they promoted their professional expertise created, without their having intended them to do so, opportunities for women as well. If society was a body, and, like all bodies, needed care, then who better to do it than society's natural nurturers? Thus could women justify their interventions in the public spheres of philanthropy and reform in terms of their innate maternal talents. They would be the social mothers of society itself.

There was, however, a significant obstacle in the way of this public application of women's domestic mission. Their caring for Others did not simply threaten to displace, as Dickens feared, evangelical women's responsibility to care for their own home. Even more dangerous, perhaps, was the closely related possibility that the very qualifications that enabled middle-class women to lift up Others would be endangered by their excursions outside the home's protective confines. As Leonore Davidoff and Catherine Hall have argued, women's confinement to a separate domestic sphere was justified on the grounds that it insulated them from the worldly contacts and temptations to which their male counterparts were exposed. It was their confinement in the home, in the separate domestic sphere, that secured for women their superior moral character. And it was their superior moral character, in turn, that ensured women's privileged capacity to secure others' salvation.

Contact with the poor was rendered more dangerous in this respect as a result of the working classes' incorporation within the nation's social body. The fact that the poor were now deemed members of the nation's social body did not necessarily improve middle-class assessments of poor people's limitations. It did, however, transform the terms on which the necessity for intervention in working-class lives was justified. Such initiatives were increasingly defended in a language of bodily disease—the poor were like a diseased organ whose treatment was necessary for the self's survival. However, while heightening the interests of the propertied elite in effecting a cure, such formulations carried with them the inevitable threat of contagion.[78]

Herein lay a crucial contradiction that was never fully resolved: the lack of moralizing contact with the middle class, and especially with middle-class women, was the key to what ailed subaltern groups at home as well as abroad. However, the moral classes and especially the moral gender therein had to be very carefully protected from contaminating social contacts that might deprive them of their social power to heal. The more nurturing women did outside the home, in other words, the greater the danger, because nurturing established intimacies, physical as well as spiritual, and intimacy with the poor was considered particularly dangerous in this regard.

Children were largely exempt from these concerns, childhood being conceived of as existing prior to class to some degree.[79] And middle-class women as well as men engaged in Sunday school work with relatively few qualms (though as we shall see in the next chapter, considerable anxiety was expressed about middle-class children coming into contact with their working-class counterparts). Adults were a different matter; and a middle-class desire to avoid compromising contact accounts, at least in part, I think, for the rise of the socially segregated missions to which evangelicals lent their support during the 1840s and 1850s.[80] The rationale for segregation was, admittedly, typically voiced in terms of what the poor themselves might find appealing, as in the following description of a mission station established by Queen Street Congregational Chapel in Leeds in 1863, which voiced the hope that "a plain, small, and *free* place of worship, might succeed in drawing persons who could not be persuaded at once to enter a large place of the ordinary sort, and that when assembled very much by themselves, this class of people might be instructed and blest by a kind of service specially fitted for them."[81] The results of such home missionary initiatives were that the missionary middle classes and especially the women therein were protected from potentially compromising liaisons.

That contact was particularly problematic for middle-class women helps us to account for the care with which Ellen Ranyard's well-known and widely emulated Female Bible Mission avoided it. This female mission (its targets, its agents, and apparently the majority of its contributors were all women) was distinguished from its male counterpart, the London City Mission, not only by the fact that its field operatives were women but also by the fact that they were from working-class backgrounds.[82] This may well have enabled, as Poovey suggests, a less hierarchical relationship between Ranyard's bible women and their plebian targets than was the case with the LCM. However, I also suspect that Ranyard's advocacy of "native agency" (a term she borrowed from the foreign mission field) reflected the reluctance of the Female Bible Mission's middle-class bankrollers to undertake extensive contact themselves.

Foreign missions would have represented an even safer involvement by this calculus. This is due to the simple fact of the geographical space that protected female missionary supporters in Britain from their sisters in foreign lands. But race as well as space seems to have functioned as a prophylactic against contagion for those middle-class women who volunteered for missionary service abroad. The call for women to serve in the foreign mission field was explicitly addressed to those "female disciples, who have wealth, cultivation and leisure to lay at His feet"; and the LMS was particularly insistent upon the necessity of their recruits being "women of education and refinement," rejecting the applications of those deemed deficient in this regard.[83] Female missionaries in the foreign field were more rather than less likely than their male counterparts (whom you will recall from chapter 3 were recruited primarily from the upper-working and lower-middle classes) to be from middle and even upper-middle class backgrounds.

That racial difference enabled intimacies precluded by class is further suggested by the missionary movement's rejection of "native agency" in the foreign mission field. In contrast to the preference shown for working-class agents at home, indigenous candidates for missionary service faced considerable discrimination. Few such applications made it through the disapproving gauntlet of the society's foreign missionary field force. Those that did, such as that of a woman from Bombay "with some native blood in her," were encouraged by nonmissionary sympathizers, in this case, the Rev. Alexander of Manchester. In rejecting her application, the Ladies Committee of the LMS acknowledged that their policy, circa 1876, was to deploy abroad "only English ladies of thorough English education at present."[84] Working-class white women were only slightly more acceptable than were indigenous converts.

To sum up the discussion thus far, the foreign mission field was a middle-class woman's preserve. It was so, at least in part, I believe, because missionary intimacy with the inhabitants of the foreign mission field was not considered to be as dangerous to middle-class women's respectability as were similar forms of contact with Britain's heathen classes. Ironically, it was their racial difference that made foreign heathens safe in Victorian eyes. Race resolved contradictions in missionary practice that made home missions dangerous. And it was race that enabled the intimate social contacts that were the ultimate expression of Christian love. As one medical missionary immodestly concluded about her own presence in the mission field, "for a foreign lady, who is so scrupulously clean in her own person and surroundings, to be willing to cleanse and bind up the loathsome sores of the dirtiest of Chinese women, without any other expression but that of tender sympathy, is surely one of the most practical lessons in Christianity which we can set before the Chinese."[85]

Reversal of Fortune

Despite the advantages that race bestowed, the foreign mission field was eventually overtaken by a resurgent home mission. Their tremendous and growing popularity among women notwithstanding, foreign missions began to face stiffer and stiffer competition from home missionary efforts to assuage the resentments of an increasingly organized and militant working class. The census of 1851 was the immediate catalyst of renewed interest in missionary outreach to Britain's "heathen" poor. The census revealed to the great alarm of contemporaries that over half of the British population (including the majority of its working classes) were not regular attenders of any of Britain's churches. In the words of the census taker: "The melancholy fact is thus impressed upon our notice that the classes which are most in need of the restraints and consolations of religion are the classes which are most without them."[86] Middle-class alarm deepened considerably during the decades to come as the unchurched working classes grew increasingly militant. The closing decades of the nineteenth century witnessed a dramatic departure from the relative quiescence of popular politics in the wake of Chartism's collapse.[87] The growth in trade unionism, the birth of socialist political organization, and, most importantly, the extension of the franchise to large sections of the skilled working class in 1867 and to agricultural laborers in 1884 an-

nounced a new epoch in British social relations. The onset of depression during the early 1870s called into question political economists' assumption that
the poor alone were responsible for their distress.[88]

The ministerial leadership of the religious community called for a radical revision in the churches' style of operation. The disciplinary predicates of
older forms of missionary outreach seemed increasingly inadequate to the
task of bringing the working classes under the moralizing influence of the
church. Typical were the Rev. William Stratham's remarks to the Yorkshire
Congregational Union meetings of 1873, which deprecated "the idea that
Congregationalism was adapted only for the middle classes."[89] Stratham's call
for Congregationalism to "readjust its spirit and its methods so as to reach the
working folk" echoed from countless pulpits during the half century before
World War I, and a great many heeded it.

Congregational efforts to reach the unchurched masses as well as to hold
onto the next generation of its own numbers had heretofore centered around
what is referred to as the Institutional Church. The Rev. U. R. Thomas of
Bristol (who was also an active supporter of the LMS) played a pioneering
role in encouraging the proliferation of innumerable ancillary organizations
in connection with the churches, organizations that catered to the interest of
constituencies self-consciously differentiated along lines of age, class, and gender.[90] Many of these organizations were designed to appeal to working-class
constituencies within the church and Sunday school.[91] Congregationalists also
embarked on organizational innovations aimed at reaching (primarily working-class) constituencies outside the church. Established chapels had long financed the building and maintenance of mission chapels in inner cities or
rural areas, but this practice accelerated considerably in the period after
1850.[92] The multiplication of philanthropic agencies was such that the Charity Organization Society was formed in 1869 to coordinate their efforts in
order to prevent their abuse by those deemed the "undeserving" poor.

In response to the heightened social tensions of the 1880s, church leaders began to advocate social integration. Congregational methods of outreach
to the working classes were marked, henceforth, by a mounting concern over
increasing the extent of direct personal contact between the missionary community and its plebian beneficiaries. In place of assembling working people
"by themselves," home missionary interventions were revised so as to multi-
ply the points of supposedly uplifting contact across class lines. The settlement
movement, for example, sought to civilize the slums of Britain's inner cities
by establishing residential outposts of middle-class influence. Congregationalists quickly emulated the urban settlements connected to the Established
Church, founding their own Browning Hall in Walworth and Mansfield

House in Canning Town.[93] During the same period, many chapels began sponsoring Pleasant Sunday Afternoon lectures for working men. By 1885, these lectures claimed over 100,000 attendants. In 1905, they were linked together in a national organization called the National Brotherhood Movement, which had its own periodical.[94]

The Brotherhood movement represented Congregationalism's most ambitious effort to welcome working-class constituencies into the chapel fold. Brotherhood meetings were, by the standards of other missionary institutions, fairly independent; discussions ranged widely and sometimes controversially across the spectrum of the political debate of the day. At the same time, however, Congregational propaganda aimed at these meetings pointedly interpreted the social reform interests attributed to the working-class membership in a language of self-help and social harmony. Brotherhood members were described as men who "have seen the miracle of the changed man, the home that was Paradise Lost transformed to Paradise Regained, the wife and children receiving with shining eyes and smiling faces the husband and father, whose homecoming before he joined the Brotherhood was a nightly terror." The transformation effected in working men was attributed to the personal influences of cross-class contact, contact that was "bridging the gulf between the 'classes' and the 'masses'" in a progressive alliance, "determined that the laws of the 'kingdom' shall be the laws of every department of social life."[95]

> Men of substantial social position and wage-earners meet in the Brotherhood on equal terms, get to know and respect and like each other, and this is preparing the way to supplant the hard-cash nexus by a living link of sympathy between the classes, that are drifting apart as a consequence of modern economic conditions, and more and more ranging themselves in order of battle against each other.

Social reform and social order went hand in hand, each the condition of the other: "it is saved men who will save the State, but the Brotherhood insists that the saved men shall do their duty by the State."[96]

These integrated missionary initiatives offered a preeminently liberal solution to the problem of social disorder. They resolved the threat posed by outsiders by bringing some within its boundaries, by teaching them to accept, even identify, with its rules as the price of their inclusion. The conversion process not only offered souls to God; it revealed a new site of social intervention or control in its positing of an individual "character," which leading Congregationalists hoped could be molded for the good of society and whose political consent to the social order could be won. "Character," in other words, constituted the terrain on which religious conversion effected social ends:

The building of character—Christ-like character—is the teacher's aim. . . . His influence cannot be expressed in the mere language in which the lesson is couched, but often *it is* the lesson the child's plastic nature most readily receives. . . . The teacher's influence is not, however, confined to the Church and School. It follows the scholar to his home, and, exercising its power there, does much to make less hurtful the surroundings of a bad, and to enhance the value of a good, home life. Thus in some degree the mischief caused by a vicious environment is counteracted, and the good of favourable conditions increased.[97]

Missions were, in this regard, a mode of power as well as piety, designed to produce citizens as well as converts. The Rev. Henry Ollerenshaw of Hull, like so many of his generation, considered this to be the central problem bearing upon the social and political, as well as the religious, health of the nation. Reflecting in 1868 on "The Best Method of Bringing Gospel Truth to Bear Upon the Working Classes of Our Land," Ollerenshaw insisted that there could be "no doubt of the extreme importance of this question, whether we view it in relation to the interests of Christ's kingdom or the welfare of our country. The working classes are the strength and sinew of the nation,— they are the basis on which the whole social fabric is built; if they be not worthy, no political change can bring salvation to the nation. . . . True politics, and all other efforts for social good, must have their basis in the religious progress of the nation, and of the working classes especially, as being the greatest in number."[98]

The massive increase in the British public's support for home missions inevitably diminished the funds available for their foreign counterparts. For the first time in their history, foreign missionary activists could not count on being the first priority of Congregational chapels or individuals. Agent W. J. Wilkins, the LMS's agent in the North, voiced a common frustration that all too often "some local charity, e. g. a children's hospital; or a charitable institution, e. g. Dr. Barnardo's home, takes its place on almost equal terms with the Missionary Society in the distribution of the funds raised."[99] The decline in home support for foreign missions in this period was relative, to be sure, and should not be overstated. Huge sums were still being expended; they were outstripped only by the numbers of people who continued to volunteer for service abroad.[100] But with the somewhat bizarre exception of the Forward Movement on the occasion of the society's centennial, retrenchment in the face of stagnation in funds was more and more frequently the order of the day.[101]

Home support for foreign missions was not only diverted by the domestic social fact of an increasingly organized and militant working class. Imperial developments were also undermining the foreign missionary movement's popularity at home. More specifically, foreign missionaries and their

supporters found themselves unable to counter home missions' urgent domestic political rationale with an imperial equivalent, because of the steady
marginalization in this period of missionaries throughout the British Empire. The push, for which the missionary movement had actively lobbied, to
add new colonies to the empire brought ever larger numbers of Europeans
with increasingly diverse interests into the British Empire where missionaries labored.

Race was as much a terrain on which the conflicts between various sections of the European colonial community were aired as it was the means to
European unification.[102] For the missionary variant of racism was at odds
with the kinds of racism being espoused by other sectors of the European
community, whose number and influence were steadily increasing (the result
in part of missionaries' own labors to encourage the empire's expansion).
Other Europeans were not, for the most part, interested in civilizing indigenous peoples, at least in the closing decades of the nineteenth century; to the
contrary, their aspirations for land and labor translated into demands for policies that would disrupt the sedentary lifestyles and family constellations on
which missionary outreach depended.[103]

Missionaries and their supporters objected loudly and in morally un-
equivocal terms to such policies. Theirs was not "the gospel of the mailed
fist," missionary enthusiasts angrily reminded their ostensibly Christian critics in the imperial mission field, but "the gospel of the pierced side and the
wounded hands."[104] Unfortunately for missionaries and their colonized beneficiaries alike, the mailed fist increasingly gained the upper hand in this period, at home as well as in the colonies. National interest and racial supremacy effectively displaced the welfare of the colonized, even in the rhetoric with which the British state justified its presence abroad. Soldiers and
explorers, settlers and businessmen, groups untroubled by the morals of colonial administration, more and more frequently personified the empire in
British imperial culture, displacing the Livingstones of their day as the embodiment of imperial heroics and the inspiration for metropolitan manly
ideals.[105] Missionaries' reformist concerns about the colonized were dismissed
as effeminate obstructions of the imperial project missionaries had done so
much to bring about—an argument facilitated by the demographic fact of
the missionary movement's feminization.[106] And in a marked example of the
polymorphous flexibility with which gender, race, and class could combine in
different ways to antithetical political ends, missionaries' purported "friendship with the native" was criticized as a betrayal of the British nation's imperial interests.[107] Race figured prominently, moreover, in such efforts to dele-
gitimize the missionary imperial vision. Missionaries were effectively deraci-

nated by their relatively intimate physical contact with colonized people, at least according to those Europeans whose operative understanding of race increasingly required rigid social segregation.[108]

Foreign missionaries continued, of course, to argue that theirs was "a great and imperial work."[109] And they urged their home supporters to ignore the "globetrotter's" "distant supercilious attitude toward missions" and to remember that it was "the missionary who was intimately acquainted with the inmost life of the people among whom he worked."[110] Their protests were muffled, however, by the jingoistic noise for which this period is noted.[111]

Social Missionary Imperialism

That foreign missionaries were on the defensive in the empire and in the imperial culture being reshaped in Britain did not help their efforts to counter the appeals of their home missionary rivals. Foreign missionary activists initially responded to the upsurge in interest in home missions with perhaps predictable resentment.[112] As had previous generations, they sought to challenge home missions' premise of first priority by arguing that "surrounded by religious influences, it is not through ignorance" that the poor "remain where they are," namely outside Britain's churches, but through deliberate personal choice. "No special mission is needed to them, as it is to those who have not their knowledge or their opportunities."[113]

When these arguments proved insufficient to quell their rivals' challenge, however, the foreign missionary movement readjusted its ideological strategy. Rather than trying to minimize the veracity of their rivals' claim on Congregational support, foreign missionary propagandists increasingly insisted, as had their home mission advocates in years past, upon the interdependence of their aims. An LMS pamphlet from the early twentieth century refused the juxtaposition altogether, insisting that foreign missions and the social question "rank together as twin investigations into Christian duty and Christian truth."[114] Or, in the words of an LMS spokesman writing in 1915, "the fight against the social heathenism at home and against the degradations of non-Christian lands abroad are simply one war."[115]

In these formulations was embedded a fundamental revision of the telescopic vision of missionary philanthropy that had held sway heretofore. In the manner of their home missionary counterparts in previous generations, foreign missionary activists now began to defend the foreign mission cause as a means to the home missionary end of winning the working classes to Christ. The foreign missionary movement increasingly shifted the focus of its fundraising activities in this period to target the working class, seeking ever more "scientific" ways of reaching working-class hearts and minds. The society engaged in a wide-ranging campaign to modernize its fund-raising apparatus. The Secretary for Funds, William Fairbrother, was forced into an early retirement in 1870 to clear the way for an overhaul of his department. The Bristol Auxiliary's historian recounts: "Fresh methods of organization arose. The interest of the Sunday-schools and young people were developed. The stilted phraseology of early Victorian days departed from the reports. In a word, modern methods touched and brightened every issue."[116] Auxiliary collectors were regularly reminded to collect from the entire constituency. In 1886, for example, an LMS agent reported that St. George Street chapel in Liverpool was making efforts to broaden the social base of its collections: "most of the churches have collectors for large amounts, but this plan of collecting will be extended so as to embrace the poorer members of the congregations."[117] The formation of a Penny-a-Week guild in 1903 was followed in 1915 by a special campaign to increase small subscriptions; in 1916 a separate agent was appointed to organize "penny a week and other small subscriptions among the working classes."[118] The society also sponsored tours of "missionary caravans" in rural areas, horse-drawn minimuseums with relics and literature pertaining to the mission field, which excited "great interest" in villages that often "had never been visited by a missionary or anyone else on behalf of the Society."[119]

The LMS replicated the Institutional Church in its internal organization as well, encouraging its local auxiliaries to form suborganizations, such as Women's Associations, Watchers Bands,[120] Young Men's and Young Women's Missionary Bands, Christian Endeavour Societies, and Missionary Study Groups, which were aimed at various social constituencies within the chapel. The society also made concerted efforts to make its publications more "popular."[121] In addition to its regular publications for Sunday schools, the society began publishing a series of quarterly leaflets on foreign missionary themes for distribution at Brotherhood meetings. In 1915 plans were made for a book "to be used by the industrial constituency and by speakers at Men's Meetings," which would consist of a "series of chapters on the social uplift in heathen countries, each chapter being related to some one of the Society's missionaries such as Livingstone, Morrison, etc., who had commenced life as an artisan." Will Crooks, mayor of Poplar and Labour MP, was approached to write the introduction, and George Lansbury was asked to author the book.[122]

Sunday schools, however, were the primary site at which foreign missions were drawn into home mission service. Sunday schools were perhaps the single most important institutional weapon in the religious community's continuing struggle to bring Britain's working classes into organized religion's fold. Working-class attendance at Sunday schools was extraordinarily high. Thomas Laqueur has estimated that "nearly every working class child" attended a Sunday school at some point in his or her life.[123]

The problem was not getting working-class children to attend Sunday schools; they did so in massive numbers. It was, rather, how to keep Sunday school graduates attached to the church. Rev. Ollerenshaw, for example, found it of immense concern that "so few comparatively who are educated in our Sabbath schools, become in after life attendants on the house of God," and urged that more attention be directed toward retaining the elder scholars in Sunday schools, where "we have an element of power which has not yet been properly estimated."[124] Rev. J. D. Jones of Bournemouth estimated that 75 percent of those masses outside the nation's churches had in fact "passed through" the Sunday schools.[125] Rev. Francis Wrigley claimed that in his working-class district in south Leeds, "nearly all those who are now outside our churches were once scholars in our Sunday Schools," and wondered "is it a task beyond the powers of Christian statesmanship to arrest this terrible drift?"[126]

Foreign missions found in these concerns a domestic raison d'etre that would give them a new lease on life in an age during which the forces of imperialism and democracy were converging to call earlier incarnations of missionary imperialism into disrepute. Promoting foreign missions in Britain's Sunday schools would serve, they argued, as a powerful antidote to working-class "drift," warning that any diminution of attention to the foreign mission cause in Britain's churches would result in "a very serious injury to the churches themselves."[127] Advancing a racialized theory of child development, foreign missionary activists argued that "the missionary idea appeals with peculiar power to the young" because of children's purported affinity with the childlike races of the foreign mission field.[128] According to a 1911 Congregational tract, "the teaching material provided by foreign missions is the finest in the whole realm of life for presentation to the child and adolescent. It is full of colour and movement, strangeness and wonder, inexhaustible variety and stirring heroic story, with all the glory of romance and the added strength of the fact that it is true."[129] Working-class children were thought to be particularly susceptible to the adventurous and imperial dramas of the foreign mission field. Missions were promoted in these quarters as "a living conquering power," an alternative to penny dreadfuls whose masculine excesses were apparently thought to threaten popular self-control. Here evangelicals contested the martial forms of masculinity that were hegemonic in this period by asserting in their stead a missionary version of manliness, predicated upon self-sacrifice and self-discipline.[130]

Are your lads fond of manly games? Tell them of C. T. Studd, the famous crick-
eter; of Stanley P. Smith, stroke of the Cambridge eight—both now Missionaries in China . . . and a host of others, and don't you think they may be led to
inquire what it all means? Is it not likely they will want to know something
more about that which, if worth dying for must certainly be worth living
for? . . . It is from the Mission-field that God would tell this doubting age,
young and old alike, that the Gospel has lost none of its power, nor the Bible
any of its inspiration.[131]

The lure of the exotic and of the heroic was the foreign missionary sugar
pill for the domestic missionary instruction in lessons of thrift, self-help, and,
above all else, gratitude for the manifold benefits of being English.[132] A few
excerpts from Sunday school lessons should suffice to give the flavor of this
literature. *Hindu Boys* was a Sunday school leaflet produced by the LMS
sometime during Rev. George Cousins' reign as editorial secretary (1885–
1898). India is depicted here via a vignette about an abandoned child starv-
ing to death when those around him refuse to help because they do not know
his caste:

Had a lower caste man given him food or drink, that would have destroyed the
caste of the child; had a higher caste man taken him to his home and allowed
him to live with his family, the caste of each member would have been destroyed. To English boys who see men start from a humble position and rise step
by step until they are equal almost to the highest, it seems strange that millions
of men should continue content to occupy the same position as that which their
fathers had. But it is easy of explanation. Every Hindu lad is taught that it is
God, and not man, who made these great distinctions of Society. . . . Who of
you will help us save them?[133]

Girls were similarly comforted by the contrast between the treatment of
women in heathen versus in Christian lands. In a Sunday school lesson titled
"Men and Manners" published during World War I, scholars were reminded
that men look after women in England, as is manifested primarily in men's
doing the bulk of work (except of course in emergencies like the war). This
was not the case, however, in heathen lands, such as the Congo, where "women
have to do all the hardest work. A Congo man does not regard his wife as being his equal or his companion. . . . A Congo woman or girl often has a very
hard life, and is beaten and scolded. I fancy I would rather be a girl in Britain
than be born on the Congo."[134]

The LMS targeted working-class adults as well as Sunday scholars; in fact
the Sunday schools were viewed as an influential point of entry into the
working-class home. The society also circulated its propaganda, however, in
other home missionary institutions, laying great stress upon the social aspects

of missionary interventions abroad. Missions were promoted as the foreign extension of the Brotherhoods' commitment to social reform, and they were a primary means whereby missionary progressives sought to make sure that working-class Christians' interest in the social question was articulated in terms of social uplift and not socialism. This was one of the primary "challenges of the modern situation," according to a Congregational pamphlet of 1911. A social gospel had evolved out of the churches' efforts to incorporate the working classes and the poor, but the church had to be on guard lest "Christ becomes the schoolmaster to lead them to Socialism, or to some other political activity." Missions channeled working people's concerns for social conditions along healthy lines: "it is not to stir the emotions and leave the matter there, but to cultivate the will and let the impression of love be followed by the expression of service."[135]

Class hatred was a central target of foreign missionary propaganda aimed at the poor and working classes. It was countered not only by the juxtaposition of the benefits of being English to the sufferings of heathendom, but also by allusions to the conciliatory ideology of brotherhood, which united Congregationalists from diverse social backgrounds behind the foreign mission cause. It was, in fact, its institutional capacity to bring together the working-class inhabitants of home missionary institutions and the middle-class members of Congregational chapels that constituted the foreign missionary movement's chief claim to a privileged capacity to heal the nation's social divisions.

The leakage of older scholars out of the religious community was frequently attributed to the segregation of Sunday schools, like other home missionary institutions, from the civilizing influence of the larger religious community. According to Rev. Ollerenshaw, the tendency to regard the Sunday school as "something apart from the church" alienated scholars and contributed to the high dropout rates once scholars began their apprenticeships or jobs. Ollerenshaw warned that brotherly love alone, manifested in the integration of the working-class beneficiaries of home missions into the broader chapel community, could offset the increasingly resentful sentiments of the industrial classes:

> In the Christian church we have the idea of Brotherhood, in opposition to Class-influence. We are one family in Christ. . . . We need more of this spirit, and especially more of its manifestation in business life, in the workshops and warehouses of professing Christian men; and this will be the true, as well as the most powerful, corrective of the antagonism which now characterises the relations of capital and labour.[136]

Similar considerations prompted Birmingham Congregationalist J. A. Cooper's recommendations in 1869 that the churches act affirmatively to incorporate their older scholars by giving them better seats in the chapel and waiving their pew rents.[137]

Congregationalism's claim that "In their church there were no lordships; it was a sort of Christian Republic" found its ultimate expression in the supraclass communities that foreign missionary auxiliaries were increasingly encouraged by their parent organizations to be.[138] While individual chapels and especially mission stations might reflect the social composition of the neighborhood around them, their differences were purportedly submerged by their joint participation in the local foreign missionary auxiliary. Within each chapel, the foreign mission cause would bring working-class Sunday scholars and the invariably more socially respectable chapel members together in concerted action. It was, in other words, primarily if not exclusively in relation to the colonized beneficiaries of their foreign missionary philanthropy that working-class and middle-class Congregationalists confronted one another at all in many cases and on anything like equal terrain.

This was, at least, the thrust of foreign missionary propaganda, of which *Mrs. Pickett's Missionary Box* constitutes a representative example.[139] Like much of the literature distributed throughout the nation's Sunday schools, this pamphlet was consumed across the denominational divide; its child-heroine was none other than Mary Slessor, one of the Church Missionary Society's most famous women missionaries. But adults were surely among its targets. The pamphlet is narrated by Mary's aunt, Mrs. Pickett, whose conversion is the central theme. Mrs. Pickett runs a boarding house and speaks in a broad ungrammatical dialect, which suggests that she is from a working-class or lower-middle-class background. Certainly at the outset of the story she is pointedly resentful of women who come from clearly middle-class backgrounds. Although Mrs. Pickett and her middle-class foils are all adults, the real heroine of the story is her young niece Mary, who converts her aunt from class struggle to Christianity with the aid of missionary pamphlets. Children are here openly engaged as evangelicalism's fifth column in the working-class community, pitted against working-class adults whose resentments they are sent to soften.

The story opens with Mrs. Pickett recalling for the benefit of the wife of the new minister her irritation when her young niece Mary first asked her to go to a missionary meeting:

> I'd got to have hard feelings against every on't looked's as if they got along eas-
> ier'n me, an' I'd most give up going to church at all. . . . I says [to Mary],
> "Pretty doin's 't would be for me to go traipsin' off to meetin's an' leave the
> i'nin' an' the cookin', an' sit alongside o' Lawyer Stapleton's wife, Learnin'
> about—what? Folks had better stay at home an' see to their work," says I.

Mary goes to the meeting alone, but returns with a missionary box for her aunt, inscribed "What shall I render unto the Lord for all His benefits to me?" Mrs. Pickett harumphs that she hasn't any benefits to spare the heathens, but later asks what "them geese" (as she later recalls in horror, remembering her disrespect) talked about at the meeting. Mary proceeds to describe the plight of widows in India, to which her aunt responds:

> "Well, if I be a widder, I'm thankful I'm where I kin earn my own livin', an' no thanks to nobody, an' no one to interfere!" Then Mary she laughed and said that was my fust benefit. Well, that sorter tickled me, for I thought a woman must be pretty hard up for benefits when she had to go clear off to Injy to find them. . . . An' next meetin', Mary she told me about Japan, an' I thought about that till I put in another because I warn't a jap.

One day Mary gives her aunt a missionary magazine, "seein' you're so interested in missions." Mrs. Pickett's reactions suggest something of the status associations common to this literature—that interest in missions, indeed the moral capacity for benevolence, would be a step "up" for the likes of a Mrs. Pickett.

> Me interested in missions! But when I come to think it over, I didn't see but what I was, in a way, an' I said it over to myself, kinder curious to see how it sounded. It was jest what they said about Mis' Stapleton, she't was the president of the missionary society. An' that night our new boarder he picked up the magazine, an' said, "Why, what's this?" An' I said, quite pleased, before I thought, "That's the magazine that my niece, Mary Pickett, she's subscribed to for me, seein' I'm so interested in missions."

The final step in Mrs. Pickett's conversion to the missionary cause interpolates the plight of heathendom, Mrs. Pickett's social resentments, and her love for her family:

> An one day—I'll never forget that day . . . she was a'tellin' me about Turkey, an' she told how some missionaries heard a little girl sayin' how the smallest thing in all the world warn't any smaller than the joy of her father when she war born. Them words went right through me. I was standing over the i'nin' board, an' Mary was opposite to me, but all of a sudden, instead of her, I seemed to see my husband's face, that had been dead ten year, an' him a-leanin' down over our little baby, that only lived two weeks, the only one I ever had. Seemed to me I couldn't get over it, when that baby died. An' I seemed to see my husband smilin' down at it, an' it lyin' there, all soft and white—she was a white little baby, such a pretty baby!—an' before I knew it, I was droppin' tears all over the starched clothes, an' I turned round an' went an' put another penny in that box, for the look on my husband's face when he held her that time. . . . An' before I went to bed I went out in the dinin' room, an' I put in a little bright three-

penny-piece for my baby, because I couldn't bear to count her jest like everythin' else, and I found myself crying because I hadn't enough money jest then to
spare anythin' bigger.

That night Mrs. Pickett dreams about her mother and father and their love
for her, and wakes up crying "Oh Lord, I am a wicked, ungrateful woman!"
From then on she can't find enough pennies with which to count all her
blessings, until the box is full and she decides to take it to the missionary
meeting herself. Where, of course, "there was singing' an' everythin', jest as
there always is, only it was all new to me, an' everyone seemed as glad to see
me as if I'd been as rich as any of 'em." Mrs. Pickett testifies before all to her
changed heart, whereupon the ladies put their arms around each other, cry
and praise God.

Audiences of poor and working people assembled in missionary institutions were being admonished in foreign missionary propaganda such as this to
forgive the wealth and admire the philanthropy of the social and political
elites who represented the missionary movement on its home front. But also,
and perhaps even more importantly, they were being invited to join the community of missionary philanthropists by supporting foreign missions themselves. It is this invitation that distinguishes the political thrust of missionary
interventions at the end of the period covered in this chapter from that of
previous generations. Power was no longer to be produced in the relationships established *between* communities, as it continued to be in the colonies.
Power would increasingly be produced *within* the community of organized
religion and the nation beyond.[140]

Foreign missions figured in this home missionary project in a different
way than they had in its previous incarnation. As you will recall from chapter 3, the preeminence of foreign missions among evangelical philanthropies
during the early nineteenth century was registered in the frequent and usually deferential reference to the foreign mission field in home missionary discourse. Home missionaries sought to justify their operations by comparing
the heathen classes in Britain to the heathen races in foreign lands. It was
then, in other words, because of what working-class and colonized peoples
had in common, that home missions found their rationale; racial difference
figures in this discourse little if at all.

These kinds of arguments do not, of course, disappear. But they are encountered less frequently during the second half of the nineteenth century.
And when they are invoked it is usually not to describe the working classes
as a whole, but to refer to a degenerate minority therein, what contemporaries referred to as the "residuum."[141] Missionary discourse, home and foreign, now tends instead to emphasize the differences that distinguish the

working classes from the colonized. It is now foreign missions that increasingly solicit support by relating their efforts to the home mission agenda, promoting their operations abroad as a means to the home missionary end of incorporating the working classes within the religious community.

This quintessential liberal incorporation of the British working class was thus predicated upon the racial exclusion of the beneficiaries of missionary operations abroad.[142] The very precondition of home missionary interventions was that working-class Britons were in many instances heathen themselves. This left little except their race to justify their collective assumption of the posture of power implicit in missionary benevolence. And it was, conversely, their racial brotherhood and sisterhood with the evangelical middle class that made possible their inclusion in foreign missions' metropolitan community of support.

Conclusion

In chapter 3 I argued that the foreign missionary auxiliary within organized religion was a crucial site of middle-class formation, providing both the institutional ground on which a middle-class community cohered and the ideological material for contesting the cultural as well as the political hegemony of the upper governing classes. Within this middle-class culture, however, women played a central role. The responsibility for propagating religion within the middle-class family was deemed to be the ultimate expression of a respectable woman's nature. And this construction of femininity enabled pious women to assign themselves increasingly important roles in the missionary agencies that propagated religion in British society and in the world at large.

I have tried to suggest here that the gendered attributes of middle-class respectability encouraged the telescopic predilections of mid-Victorian Congregationalism (that is to say the preference of foreign over home missions during the first two-thirds of the nineteenth century) *and* informed the foreign missionary movement's "social imperial" adjustment to its eventual displacement at the pinnacle of evangelical affections. With regard to the first development, I have argued that evangelical women preferred foreign over domestic missionary involvement because of a central contradiction of evangelical femininity. While their pious nature rendered women the logical agents of spiritual nurture if not of religious proselytization (which was reserved for men throughout the nineteenth century), middle-class women's respectability depended upon their social seclusion from contaminating contacts with the unrespectable, as the lower classes were deemed to be. Seen from this perspective, the foreign field represented a safer outlet than did its home counterpart; geographical distance as well as race protected middle-class women from the kinds of infection that were risked in contacts with the unrespectable classes at home.

The resulting feminization of foreign missionary philanthropy over the course of the nineteenth century both reflected and reinforced the "socialization" of missionary philanthropy in the second half of the nineteenth century. The anticivilizing missionary emphasis of early LMS discourse was displaced during the middle decades of the nineteenth century by an emphasis on creating environments conducive to Christianity or, conversely, on removing environmental obstacles in the way. This had at least two contradictory political consequences. On the one hand, foreign missionaries' growing attentiveness to health, education, and welfare brought them into closer accord with especially British colonial governments, whose expansion foreign missionaries were increasingly inclined to encourage and whose political objectives were facilitated in many ways by missionary contacts with the colonized. At the same time, the social ministrations of foreign missionaries brought them into conflict with other Europeans in the colonies whose interests were threatened by the nature of the civilization that missionaries sought to bring about. And it was these other interests that increasingly predominated in the British public's image of an ever more popular empire; soldiers, explorers, adventurers, businessmen, and starry-eyed expansionists were the embodiment of the martial and masculine imperial ideals being propagated on the British Empire's home front.

Missionary critics of empire were increasingly portrayed, by contrast, as effeminate thorns in the side of the very imperial project they had done so much to bring about. And it was from this position of political vulnerability that foreign missionary advocates confronted the competition of evangelicalism's resurgent home mission, a cause rendered all the more urgent by the intensification of class conflict during the 1860s and 1870s. The convergence of these imperial and domestic developments resulted in an effective reversal of the relative priority of home and foreign missions in the evangelical lobby's larger war aims. Home missions were no longer forced to justify their operations to a suspicious public as means to foreign ends. Foreign missions were now the ones forced to stake their claims to evangelical support on the home benefits that would ensue, chief among which was the domestic object of attaching the metropolitan working class to the supraclass community of organized religion, and by extension, to the imperial nation state.

Foreign missionary outreach to working-class Britons was, in this regard, a variant of the "social imperial" strategies of rule that accompanied the "new imperial" phase of European expansion at the nineteenth century's end. German historians coined the phrase to describe Bismarck's deliberate use of colonial policy to distract the German public's attention, and especially that of the organized working class, away from divisive domestic issues.[143] Drawing on this work, Freda Harcourt has similarly argued that Benjamin Disraeli initiated the "scramble" for colonies that ushered in the new imperialism as an antidote to class struggle, a way of containing the forces of democratization on the empire's metropolitan home front.[144]

The foreign mission field functioned in a similar manner with respect to the British working class. Class differences were purportedly diminished by a shared missionary agenda. Underlying this broad similarity in structure, however, lay important differences in function. Whereas Disraeli's imperial exploits appealed to a plebian masculinity's capacity to identify with the martial exploits of British soldiers, explorers, and other adventurers abroad, missionary imperialism focused on the morals of the working-class child. And its agents at home, as well as abroad, were more and more often middle-class women. Moreover, the missionary cause behind which working and middle-class evangelicals united emphasized the reforming uplift of their colonized beneficiaries rather than their military subjugation.

Missions were, then, a feminized variant of the social imperial agenda. And agendas are, thus far, all that is on our analytical table. For as Geoff Eley has reminded us, social imperial policies rarely produced the results their makers intended.[145] As we shall see, this was no less true in the case of our British missionaries than it was in the case of Eley's German elite. This chapter has attended to the transformation in missionary strategies of rule at home and abroad, a transformation I have depicted in terms of a shift from a telescopic to a social imperial mode of philanthropy. The consequences of this shift have yet to be determined. It is to the popular response to this revised missionary agenda that we will now turn.

CHAPTER 5

Pride and Prejudice: The Social Relations of Missionary Philanthropy, 1867–1914

The bourgeoisie has more in common with every other nation of the earth than with the workers in whose midst it lives. The workers speak other dialects, have other thoughts and ideals, other customs and moral principles, a different religion and other politics than those of the bourgeoisie.
　—Friedrich Engels, *The Condition of the Working Class in England*

We must either Christianize heathenism, or it will heathenize us, and heathenism is a matter of social life just as much as religion.
　—Frank Lenwood, *Social Problems and the East: A Point of Honour*

The poor, habituated to their irrevocable station, have often been made accessories, through their own good nature, to their own oppression.
　—E. P. Thompson, "Patrician Society, Plebian Culture"

During the second half of the nineteenth century, foreign missions were more and more often promoted as a means of rendering organized religion attractive to the English working classes. This social imperial mission had as much to do with middle-class concerns about the social and especially the political consequences of working-class irreligion as it did with working people's spiritual well-being. Like its missionary counterpart abroad, it was, in short, as much about preserving power in this world as about eternal salvation. More important for our purposes, however, is the extent to which the meanings of home and foreign missions, and especially the constructions of their beneficiaries, remained intertwined while changing over time.

The actual content of this meaning was not determined solely by the middle-class leadership of the missionary movement. Intentions and consequences, in other words, never fully coincide, although they are invariably related. In this chapter I will turn to the question of just how successful the social imperial missionary campaign described in chapter 4 was at mobilizing working-class constituencies in support of the foreign mission cause. My efforts to engage this question are admittedly limited by the scarcity of working-class voices in missionary records.[1] Although their social reach extended quite far down the social scale, foreign missionary institutions at the local as well as the national level were effectively controlled by middle-class individuals throughout the period examined in this study. There were, however, suggestive exceptions to this pattern of control, and their number increased near the nineteenth century's end as a result of the home missionary initiatives described above. This accounts for the chronological placement of this chapter. As we have seen, working people were involved in the missionary campaign from its outset; my sources, unfortunately, are concentrated disproportionately in this later period.

The fact that middle-class people controlled the institutions through which nineteenth-century Congregationalism speaks to the present does not mean that working-class people were not mobilized by or, at the very least, exposed to missionary propaganda in large numbers. As argued above, the Victorian churches through which foreign missionary societies disseminated their ideological wares were far more successful in attracting popular audiences than has often been acknowledged. Sunday schools alone can be credited with exposing virtually every working-class child to missionary propaganda and to the social relations of philanthropy that will be described in more detail below.[2]

What it does mean, however, is that the significance of popular participation in these institutions remains elusive. The records show, in other words, that working people came to church, attended missionary meetings, and read missionary literature; but the fact that they consumed missionary material does not in itself reveal the consequences of their so doing. Evidence pertaining to working-class reactions to the missionary message is scattered and indirect. We can gain from it, however, a sense of the wide range of working-class reactions to the missionary imperial vision. This diversity underscores the complexity of popular subjectivity, and, hence, the impossibility of anything so limiting as a unitary popular response, much less a singular working-class consciousness. At the same time, these responses also attest to the necessity of reading missionary propaganda with reference to the social relations of philanthropy on the local ground, where class tensions are very much in evidence. These tensions were not necessarily obviated with the embrace of the mission cause. To the contrary, organized religion's very success in assimilating a substantial working-class following placed new difficulties in the way of social harmony. When working people supported missions, it was not necessarily on the terms intended by the Congregational middle class. Conversely, many of the latter found themselves unable to deliver on the missionary movement's democratic promise, a failure that disrupted from the opposite social direction the community that missionary activists were trying to construct.

This chapter will argue, then, that the social tensions between the churched and the unchurched classes were not so much resolved by as reproduced when the working class was admitted into the missionary imperial fold. Moreover, both these axes of struggle (between the churched and the unchurched and between working and middle-class Congregationalists) were affected by and refracted in the LMS's fortunes in the decades that bracketed the twentieth century's turn. As key metaphor and practical means whereby the working classes were invited into the religious community, the foreign missionary cause was also a critical site at which the social fissures and ideological contradictions in the incorporationist project of English Congregationalism were particularly exposed to view.

Working-Class Pride and Popular Racism

The LMS enjoyed its greatest success in mobilizing working-class support in the Sunday schools. It is estimated that by 1907 the LMS was receiving about 15 percent of its total income from Sunday schools.[3] In 1908, the Congregational Union estimated that about 80 percent of its Sunday schools took a "practical interest" in the LMS: "With very few exceptions, all but our smallest schools, and some in the poorest neighbourhoods" do something for missions.[4] Given the poverty of working-class children, it is not surprising that much of the money attributed to the schools was collected by the scholars rather than contributed out of their own pockets. But it was more likely than not collected from within the working-class community. Children, in fact, were considered the most effective agents for this purpose, as their youthful innocence could shame even the poorest into giving for the heathen.[5] A treatise on home support for missions written in 1878 acknowledges the debt of the missionary movement to these scholar-collectors:

> The real strength of the work rests on the hundreds of quiet, unassuming collectors of small sums, who go on with their humble labours year after year without any taking count of them. The Sunday-school children with their missionary-boxes, and the cards with the labouriously gathered shillings and sixpences—these are the real main support of our great societies.[6]

The Society's organizers judged children to be particularly susceptible to supporting what were called "special objects"—such as sponsoring a native teacher or supporting a cot in a particular hospital.[7] Among the other entice-

ments aimed at children were the opportunities to dress up for public performances in the costumes of the mission field. A juvenile rally held at Salem
Chapel in Leeds in 1910 included "a well arranged pageant . . . in which
representatives of five Congregational Sunday schools participated in costume. In chorus and recitation each company gave a brief description of one
of the great Heathen religious systems and practices associated with it."
Speakers at children's meetings were also requested to wear costumes to illustrate their talks.[8] The programs distributed at children's meetings were
amply illustrated with drawings and photographs of the exoticized peoples of
the mission field in their native dress. Sunday scholars were also visually
stimulated by magic lantern lectures: the society's agent in Scotland reported
of his magic lantern presentations in 1885 that "in all cases we had large audiences both of Sunday Scholars and adults, in nearly [every] case the church
or hall was crowded."[9]

Music figured prominently at children's meetings. Children were encouraged to perform special missionary services of song. In 1886, Agent W. J.
Wilkins highly recommended musical services for their popular appeal: "In
country towns, even large as Leeds, I frequently see 'Services of Song' advertised, and am told they invariably draw large audiences. A twofold purpose
would be served by a good 'Service of Song'; interest in Missions would be
quickened, and funds would be raised."[10] LMS services at Marshall Street, a
working-class chapel in Leeds, were only "moderately attended" in 1888, for
example; all enthusiasm in the press report went to the afternoon services for
young people, which were attended by a "large gathering" of scholars from
several Sunday schools who were "greatly interested" in the missionary deputation's lecture on the South Seas, and who performed "specially printed
hymns."[11]

A number of historians have recently called attention to the significance
of hymn singing as a working-class religious practice. Singing hymns was
and perhaps still is conducive to the expression of what historians refer to as
the diffusive Christianity adhered to by the bulk of the British population
in this period, characterized by a rather vague belief in God and an afterlife,
in which an ethic of neighborliness, generosity, and fair play loom large.[12]
Singing hymns is an undogmatic and communal act, and the LMS sought to
capitalize on the popular appeal of this practice, especially among working-
class Sunday scholars, on behalf of the missionary cause.[13] By 1890, Agent
Wilkins was attributing very successful meetings in the north to hymn
singing. In Rotherham, for example, 900 people from a single church attended a weeknight missionary meeting. They were attracted, in part,
Wilkins claims, by the choir and Sunday schools' performance of hymns:

"The result is that the people anticipate the Missionary Meeting much in the same way as they look forward to their School meetings, and come out in numbers."[14]

As this latter quotation suggests, Sunday schools also provided the missionary movement some access to working-class adults. Missionary publications were "supplied for the benefit of the children and their parents."[15] The minister at Headingley Hill Congregational Chapel in Leeds saw the provision of written propaganda for scholars as the "missing link" between the home and Sunday school, recounting the following scene as typifying the influence of Sunday schools in the working-class home. "One of our members, a little girl, reads the 'daily portion' to her father (he explaining) at tea-time, when his day's work is over."[16] Parents and other adult friends were invited to Sunday school Demonstrations and other missionary meetings.[17] That adults did attend such meetings is suggested by an LMS agent's report that "In one large and most promising Sunday School 80 adults stayed to our . . . meeting at the close of which 24 joined the Watcher's Band; it had lapsed here."[18]

We know less about the motivations of missions' working-class supporters than about those of the many working-class radicals who rejected, by and large, the missionary message. Like the literary critics of missions described in chapter 4, this rejection often took disturbingly racist forms. Foreign missions were implicated, for example, in the popular radical indictment of the antislavery movement. As the reader will recall from chapter 3, foreign missions enjoyed close ties with the antislavery movement, in the eyes of their enemies as well as of their friends. Although the antislavery movement, like its foreign missionary counterpart, enjoyed considerable working-class support, many radicals were incensed by the apparent contrast between the bourgeois Christians' sympathy for slaves and their support for the reform of the Poor Law, which effectively abolished outdoor relief for Britain's poor. Here, too, domestic social policy and imperial developments were experienced in relation to one another.

That popular radicals would resent the same missionary movement's intrusions into the working-class community should come as no surprise. Emma Martin, an Owenite socialist, was forcibly ejected from the annual meeting of the LMS's Manchester Auxiliary in 1844, after which she gave a public lecture on "The crimes and follies of Christian Missions." Complaining bitterly that the supporters of Christian missions "grind the faces of the poor to propagate God's truth," Martin painted a haunting image of the missionary movement's telescopic philanthropy. She instructed her audience to picture "the philanthropic lady, who weeps in the most approved style . . . at

The National Archives
Bookshop
Kew
Richmond

VAT No. GD 182   Date 06/1

------------CASH SALE------------
State Secrets: Behind the scenes 20t
            1 @   7.99
Bargain Book
            1 @   .99

Exchange

            NETT   :   1
            VAT   :

            TOTAL   :   1

            CASH   :   1

            CHANGE :

Staff Name STAFF   Time 1
Receipt No. 292470   Till N

The National Archives
Bookshop
Kew
Richmond

VAT No. GD 182   Date 07/11/06

-----------CASH SALE-----------

NP6 - Gunpowder plot postcard
            1 @   0.50   0.50

NETT   :   0.43
VAT   :   0.07

TOTAL   :   0.50

CASH   :   0.50

CHANGE   :   0.00

Staff Name STAFF
Receipt No. 292685   Time 17:53
                                  Till No. 1

the dreadful tale of Chinese ignorance of God," while wearing "a splendid dress over which the weaver's curse has been poured:—over which the sigh of the poor girl expired in its making has been expended."[19]

Such righteous resentments often found expression in easily racialized outcries on behalf of the audacity of middle-class philanthropists' daring to compare free-born Englishmen of however humble a station to the heathen savages of the empire. William Cobbett was perhaps the best known and certainly the most popular of the popular radicals who juxtaposed working-class interests and the duplicitous and hypocritical machinations of Exeter Hall.[20] Breaking up antislavery meetings became "a statement of class consciousness by working-class radicals," who, according to historian Patricia Hollis, believed that "the exploitation of factory children financed the very philanthropy of their masters, their subscriptions to Bible Societies, to anti-slavery societies and to chapel building." In addition to Cobbett, Hollis singles out Richard Oastler, the Tory paternalist who led the campaign for factory reform, and Bronterre O'Brien, the Chartist journalist, as similarly vociferous in their antipathy toward those missionary philanthropists who "preferred their objects of benevolence at a distance and possessing 'a black hide, thick lips and a wooley head.'"[21] In 1840, a group of Norwich Chartists broke up a meeting of the African Civilization Society (which included prominent supporters of evangelical missions), shouting, "Emancipate the white slaves before you think of the black" and "Look to the slavery and misery of the New Poor Law."[22]

In the aftermath of the home missionary initiatives described above, childhood displaced slavery, white or black, as the primary trope in the radical critique of missionary philanthropy. Organized religion's success in mobilizing popular support for missions is indicted as a betrayal of childhood's innocence. The missionary movement's targeting of working-class children shaped the terms on which many working-class adults expressed their disaffection. They were, in effect, looking back with considerable anger at the social relations established between missionary philanthropists and working-class children.

The social relations of missionary philanthropy figure prominently in one of the most widely used sources in the history of popular religion in this period, Robert Tressell's novel about Edwardian house painters, *The Ragged Trousered Philanthropists*. While certainly not a transparent reflection of social reality in this period, fiction is widely regarded as an invaluable point of entry into the elusive world of popular piety.[23] Unlike most authors, moreover, Tressell was writing about a world with which he was intimately acquainted; he was himself a house painter. Robert Noonan, who wrote under the name of Tressell, was born in 1870; he died in 1911, before his novel, written in 1906, had found a publisher. While he was presumably not from an evangelical background himself (Noonan was of Irish extraction), the novel acknowledges in its effort to disrupt the extraordinary reach of organized religion in the working-class family even at this late date. Since its eventual publication in 1914, *The Ragged Trousered Philanthropists* has sold over 500,000 copies, and it is frequently cited by historians for its insights into the nature and extent of popular religiosity and secularism alike in this period.[24] While we might be skeptical with regard to Tressell's analysis of the motives of the working-class Christians he so obviously despises, the novel does document a self-designated socialist's critique of middle-class missionary outreach to the poor, and the place of foreign missions therein.

The picture drawn of poorly dressed, ill-fed, and sickly children being exhorted by their fathers' wealthy employers to self-denial on behalf of foreign missions is a key image in Tressell's indictment of British capitalism. For Tressell, the clergy embodied the evil of the social relations of philanthropy:

> He was arrayed in a long garment of costly black cloth, a sort of frock coat, and by the rotundity of his figure he seemed to be one of those accustomed to sit in the chief places at feasts. This was the Rev. Mr. Belcher, minister of the Shining Light Chapel. His short, thick neck was surrounded by a collarless stud . . . being fastened in some mysterious way known only to himself, and he showed no shirt front. The long garment before-mentioned was unbuttoned and through the opening there protruded a vast expanse of waistcoat and trousers, distended almost to bursting by the huge globe of flesh they contained. A gold watch-chain with a locket extended partly across the visible portion of the envelope of the globe. He had very large feet which were carefully encased in soft calfskin boots. If he had removed the long garment, this individual would have resembled a balloon: the feet representing the car and the small head that surmounted the globe, the safety valve; as it was it did actually serve the purpose of a safety valve, the owner being, in consequence of gross overfeeding and lack of natural exercise, afflicted with chronic flatulence, which manifested itself in frequent belchings forth through the mouth of the foul gases generated in the stomach by the decomposition of the foods with which it was generally located. But as the Rev. Mr. Belcher had never been seen with his coat off, no one ever noticed the resemblance. It was not necessary for him to take his coat off; his part in life was not to help to produce, but to help to devour the produce of the labour of others.[25]

Tressell's imputation that the Rev. Mr. Belchers of the world were getting on quite nicely was not far off the mark. The salaries collected by the leading ministers of Congregationalism were often very high indeed. Rev. C. S. Horne was hired by Kensington Chapel in London at an annual salary of between £600 and £700 in 1888.[26] The minister's salary at Headingley Hill Congregational Chapel in Leeds was £500 per year in 1898.[27] The minister at St. James' Congregational Chapel was regarded as "the best-dressed man in Newcastle"; his successor's "chief relaxation consisted in visits to the Continent."[28] By way of contrast, regularly employed working men could expect to earn about £72 per year in 1906, with clerks averaging £80. The London School Board paid its male teachers £105–£165 per year during the 1890s.[29]

Nor was Tressell alone in his disgust at the social contrasts displayed within the religious community. The correspondence columns of the *Leeds Mercury*, for example, printed regular attacks on religion via the privileges enjoyed by its professional representatives. The following is from a letter printed in 1893:

> Our ministers are not blind to their own interests. They devote the most time to what pays best . . . and want as big a salary as they can get. This cannot be got from the slums of our towns. . . . Leave out the slums, and only go down as low as the artisan, or the poor, struggling shopkeeper—those who can only drop a penny or a three-penny piece into the collection box. Are our ministers familiar with this class of their own congregations? Let anyone ask them, and it will be found that they are ignorant of this class also. Many a true Christian never sees his minister inside his door. His minister is not his friend and counsellor, but merely a sleek, well-dressed stranger, to be admired from a distance.[30]

Henry Snell, a Labour MP and eventual member of the House of Lords, regretted his childhood involvement in the foreign mission cause. Snell grew up in an isolated agricultural community in Nottinghamshire during the 1870s, the child of agricultural laborers, who, like most of their counterparts, "felt spiritually more at home" in one of the Nonconformist chapels (they were Baptists) than in the local parish church. Even, if not especially, in such isolated rural enclaves, the missionary vision occupied a considerable cultural space:

> The intellectual torpor of an English village sixty years ago may be illustrated by the fact that until I left the one in which I was born I never saw a copy of The Pilgrim's Progress, or any of the works of Charles Dickens, and I never heard any one mention the names of Lincoln, Wilberforce, or Lloyd Garrison. But many precious pennies were coaxed from my usually empty pocket for the needs of missionaries to the "heathen."

These "precious pennies" symbolized to Snell's adult mind the fundamental immorality of a professedly Christian society allowing its children to live, much less exhorting them to give, in such poverty as he'd endured:

It was under conditions such as these that the children of rural England then served the richest and most pious nation on the earth. . . . British employers managed somehow to tolerate these conditions, while at the same time believing that "Who so shall offend one of these little ones . . . it were better for him that a millstone were hanged about his neck, and that he were drowned in the depths of the sea."[31]

The poverty of working-class children traumatized even middle-class observers in the mid-Victorian to late Victorian period.[32] The children to whom the LMS and other missionary societies were pitching their appeals were often "so poor as to have no clothes in which they care to be seen at the Sunday services, and thus it is only through these week-night meetings that we are able to influence them for good."[33] The LMS occasionally evinced some awareness that soliciting from such constituencies posed particular responsibilities, as, for example, in this rather nervous apologia in 1851 for a recently uncovered scandal at one of the society's missions: "But although it must be deeply regretted that in a single instance, any portion of the funds, derived, to some extent, from the hard-earned offerings of the poor, should be expended on Agents incompetent or disqualified, yet such occurrences are happily very infrequent."[34]

For the most part, however, the society's representatives saw poverty as an organizational challenge, something to be countered by a hard sell. As one agent argued in 1887, "From what I have seen myself in a very large number of our Churches were we to relax our efforts to raise money our income would certainly decline considerably. It is only by means of constant and persistent effort that we can keep the work of our Society before the minds of our Congregation and thus lead them to think of it, and assist in its support."[35] This same logic was applied to the working-class children of the Sunday schools. The LMS's Boys Brigades (suborganizations in the Sunday schools) were exhorted in 1920, for example, to increase their contributions in order to help offset the postwar price inflation that was crippling field operations: "It is a good thing you boys are earning good wages; so that when I suggest to you that each of you might reasonably try to do a bit more than in the past, I know I am not squeezing a dry sponge!"[36]

Sunday Scholars were frequently chided for not giving enough. In 1886, Agent Wilkins, the society's northern agent, complained that

I am anything but satisfied with the work of our immensely large Sunday Schools in Lancashire and Yorkshire. A large proportion of the Scholars are in the receipt of good wages, and yet from most of these institutions we receive very little aid. . . . The scholars give largely to their own Sunday School expenses and etc.; but I fear in many cases they have not been encouraged to give towards Mission work.[37]

Two years later, this same agent was still finding it "lamentable to see how largely our work is neglected amongst the young; for not only do we lose the substantial help they could now give, but the next generation not having been interested in our work, or taught to form habits of self-denial whilst they are young, will not easily learn this lesson in later years."[38]

Such complaints say as much about the LMS's expectations as they do about the level of Sunday school support. The LMS typically received at least a quarter of the funds raised in most Congregational Sunday schools. Fish Street Sunday School in Hull, for example, raised a total of £2,240 in anniversary collections starting upon its founding in 1815 and ending in 1899. Of this, £1,000 went to the LMS, £500 to the Benevolent Society, and the remaining £740 to the support of the school and chapel.[39] The 400 scholars of one Sunday school in Newcastle contributed £40 per year to the society.[40] The Sunday school at Headingley Hill Congregational Chapel in Leeds donated half the proceeds of its annual exhibition to the LMS.[41] The Congregational Sunday School in Roundhay (a suburb of Leeds) contributed over £14 to the LMS and just under £7 to home missions in 1907, while spending almost £27 on its own expenses (prizes, hymn sheets, a summer treat, and hospitality for the ministers who spoke at its anniversary).[42] Contributions from the scholars at Beeston Hill, a working-class chapel, accounted for about half of the chapel's contributions to the LMS in 1894.[43] At least one of the society's own agents defended even the Lancashire schools against her predecessor's charges of selfishness, saying they were giving as much to missions as they possibly could, which was, even here, about a fourth of the funds raised; the remainder of their collections were needed for the support of their Sunday school and chapel. In her report to the LMS's Funds and Agency Committee on December 19, 1905, Clara Benham, LMS organizing agent, doubted that scholars could give any more than their current levels of support: "in many of the Lancashire and Yorkshire Sunday-schools, scholars give regularly every week towards the support of their own school and chapel. Some have yearly collections and some quarterly, and in many cases the teachers say they cannot institute collections oftener than monthly."[44]

In urging working-class children to ever greater contributions, the society was not unaware of the sacrifices this might entail. To the contrary, "self-denial" was the very essence of the foreign missionary gift. One Sunday school booklet published by the LMS held up the ideal to scholars of "Two poor Sunday-school girls who worked at a mill raised 15s. for the ship by giving up their dinner-hour for several days and selling a loaf of bread which they needed for themselves. For the same object some boys earned a shilling each, after labouring through the day by working all night in a coal-pit."[45]

The virtues of sacrifice and service were considered essential to training the children of the poor: "you cannot implant the principle of 'giving' too early. . . . In that child's mind [who has just dropped his penny in the missionary box] others' wants and woes have been thought of; there has been a looking beyond personal comfort and pleasure; an upward lift has been given to that child's character."[46] Scholars therefore required incessant encouragement of philanthropy as a lesson in kindly consideration for the needs of others over one's own:

> To encourage the growth of altruism—"the other regarding faculty", should ever be thought of as a spiritual privilege. . . . To direct this growth into right channels is a part of religious education. . . . It is not the financial result of this larger vision which is of the first moment—in many cases this would necessarily be small—but the inculcation of the principle of intelligent giving. This should be invaluable in after years.[47]

This lesson was sufficiently important to override any concerns that contributions to missions might come out of the necessaries of the donor's life, although LMS representatives took care that their own personal pockets would not be affected. Supporters in Edinburgh in 1895, for example, lobbied the society to change the date of their anniversary meetings so that scholars would not be precluded from contributing by their rent or other bills coming due around the same time. According to the society's Scottish agent: "The real crux this year, I fancy is, as follows:—Mr. M'Corquodale is a house agent, and employed by Mr. Mack, in collecting rents and etc., he is also our Juvenile secretary, and doubtless did find the two duties clash somewhat, I think it is he who is moving to have the dates changed."[48]

Kindness was not always the first word to the minds of contemporaries when discussing working-class children's contributions to the foreign mission cause.[49] Embittered diatribes against the social relations of foreign missionary philanthropy were as central to the socialist critique of bourgeois society as philanthropy itself was to the bourgeois defense of capitalist forms of accumulation and free labor. For many working-class children, coming of age appears to have been marked by a moment of disillusion with foreign missions, representing, perhaps, a step along that political and intellectual trajectory by which working men moved from Nonconformist chapels into trade union activities or socialist political involvement. LMS agents referred nervously on occasion to "anti-mission prejudices" in young men's Sunday school classes, suggesting that older scholars' drift out of the church involved, at least in part, a recoil from the foreign mission cause.[50] There are scattered references to lack of cooperation from Sunday school teachers, many of whom were probably Sunday school graduates, particularly in the North. A questionnaire returned by 75 percent of the Congregational Sunday schools in England and Wales in 1908 reported that only one in fifteen Sunday school teachers were day-school teachers, whereas a very negligible number were of the "leisured" classes. As for the rest, the report cites somewhat vague answers, such as "nearly all our teachers work hard during the week." A London school reported that "most of our teachers are engaged in hard manual work"; while from Essex, "we cannot get teachers from among day school masters and teachers, or from the richer classes who have all the week to prepare, but from among the poor, and those who have to slave for a living." The report itself concludes that "the main source from which teachers are obtained is the school itself."[51]

The social gulf between (working-class) school and (middle-class) chapel was greatest in the north of England, where it was often the case that "not only is there an almost total lack of any control, but also of any official knowledge of those appointed." Although "large manufacturers, successful businessmen, active citizens" taught on occasion or served as school superintendents, all too often, according to the authors of this report, even superintendents were appointed by the teachers, circumventing the chapel altogether.[52] The LMS's organizing agents found this state of affairs clearly to their disadvantage. Some teachers frowned upon prizes for collectors, looking upon them as a form of bribery, whereas others were critical of scholars collecting money for missions at all, arguing that it was "making the children beg."[53] The superintendent in one such Sunday school in Shipley (a suburb of Bradford in the West Riding of Yorkshire) refused to promote LMS appeals at all in his school because he didn't believe in missions.[54] LMS agents repeatedly alleged that whereas the scholars were willing and interested in the mission cause, their leaders were often apathetic: "Some of the Lancashire places are particularly hard to move, and repeated visits are necessary there and in Yorkshire, and often long waiting before promises are fulfilled and better efforts made. The scholars are generally ready enough, but the difficulty is to find the right leader."[55]

Just as foreign missionary propaganda juxtaposed missionary self-denial and the selfishness of socialism, so the socialist critique of missionaryism informed at least one section of the working class's rejection of organized religion. LMS Foreign Secretary R. W. Thompson complained in 1908 about the rising popularity of "painfully anti-Christian" socialism within the working class, whereas one of the society's agents assessed missionary prospects in Blackburn and Darwen in 1897: "At neither place was there any strong missionary feeling, at least I failed to notice it. Socialism and not Missionaryism seemed to be the dominant factor."[56] In 1912, Rev. W. H. Green complained at an LMS Exhibition in Leeds about the city's "indifference" to the missionary cause, claiming that Leeds was "one of the meanest, if not the meanest, large town in England in regard to foreign missions."[57] These remarks sparked off an irate correspondence. One "Isis" took particular offense at the fact that the very ministers who pushed for contributions themselves lived

> in a sumptuous dwelling, far away from the habitudes of the children of poverty and eld, they to whom a mite from this "beggarly £10,000" [Leeds' contribution to missions that year] would mean a new lease on life. What hypocrisy! This money for converting the heathen! What to? Christianity? My dear, reverend friend, go into Leeds market any Saturday night, and see children with the baby light still in their eyes, side by side with the old, palsied, mumbling woman, searching amongst the discarded garbage for the wherewithal to feed them. Go into the slums, and see the crumbling hovels. And this, sir, is the Christianity you have in store for the heathen, the child of nature, who lives better and purer and dies happier than a great many in this Christian country.[58]

Such social resentments of the wealthy representatives of the foreign missionary cause occasionally slid in the direction of hostility toward the beneficiaries of foreign missionary outreach. One "layman" responded to Green's challenge by arguing that home needs should have absolute priority over such foreign concerns:

> Think of that £10,000 gone away to a foreign country, to be used for the conversion of foreigners, when thousands at home require conversion. Perhaps 'tis not spiritual conversion they all need, but undoubtedly they, many of them, would welcome bodily and material conversion. . . . It is a sin and a crime to send money, even £10,000, out abroad to convert the heathen, who know nothing of Christianity as yet, when thousands of poor civilised Christians are destitute and starving at home.[59]

The missionary project obviously failed at home as well as abroad to resolve the social tensions against which it was directed by its middle-class promoters—indeed, in the instances cited above it provided fuel for their fire. On the other hand, the terms on which it was predicated tempted many of those who sought to resist the missionary connection between Britain and its colonies to shift their attacks from the middle-class promoters of missions to the foreign targets of their beneficence. In this way were the class struggles that swirled around the missionary project contained in many instances within the ideological parameters of white supremacy, on the basis of which the empire's continuance and expansion would be justified.[60]

Prejudice

Certainly not all Sunday scholars moved from the juvenile missionary auxiliaries of Britain's Sunday schools to an "anti-missionary" socialism. In fact, most working people, whether or not they were themselves actively involved in the religious community, continued to send their children to Sunday school with pennies for the missionary collection. And a significant minority therein was more actively involved in regular chapel life. It was individuals such as these, from lower-middle and largely upper-working-class backgrounds, who comprised the majority of the members of most Nonconformist chapels. And it was from this plebian constituency that Congregationalism recruited the vast majority of its foreign missionary emissaries.

That foreign missions "were probably the most adept at getting the cooperation of the poor" of all the bourgeois philanthropies that plied their wares in the working-class community attests to their influence in bringing working-class people into supraclass communion.[61] The foreign mission cause made real in a more immediate way than did virtually any other Congregational institution the possibility of community across the class divide. The widow's mite was as vital to foreign missionary success as was the middle-class fortune, and it was only by working together that these diverse constituencies could succeed in bringing all the world to Christ.

The entry of large numbers of working-class people into Victorian Congregational institutions did not resolve class tensions, however, so much as transfer them to the institutional terrain of chapel life itself. The community created in Congregational institutions did not, in other words, preclude class struggles; to the contrary, it was their contested and unstable product. This had in large part to do with the middle class's inability to play the role assigned it in the social gospel script. Even the communion of saints, when it took place across the class divide, was more than many if not most middle-class Congregationalists were able or at least willing to take part in.

The social gospel invited working-class people to join and by their joining to create republics of Christians, in which all stood equal in the church as before God. This dream would seem to have been realized at the Rev. J. Guinness Rogers' chapel in Ashton-under-Lyme:

> The church was composed mainly of working people, but there was a considerable element of their employers, and a still larger infusion of what may be regarded as the middle class. I was anxious that the three should all have their place in the councils of the church and before long succeeded in securing my object. Let me say here that while there were two or three magistrates of the highest standing among the deacons, no one secured more attention in our deliberations than those who were working men and who were treated by all their colleagues as Christian gentlemen.[62]

The fact that working-class deacons seemed worthy of comment (despite their being a majority of the members) suggests that even the limited representation celebrated in Rogers's church was a somewhat unusual state of affairs. Indeed, Congregational practice typically fell well short of its increasingly egalitarian prescriptions. And given the unequal distribution of material resources within the Congregational community, one would be surprised if this were not the case. Nonconformist chapels received no government support, which meant that individual Congregational chapels had to be almost entirely self-supporting for most of our period. This meant that building costs, ministers' salaries, chapel maintenance, and all other expenses of worship had to be paid for by each chapel's members themselves.

It is easy to imagine the financial logic of political influence that prevailed within a socially diverse chapel community. Those who contributed the most money would invariably call the shots. The LMS's own treasurer, Albert Spicer, was notorious for bringing his favorite ministers with him on his family's holidays; the local incumbent would be unceremoniously "requested" to take a break. One of Spicer's children recalled with some embarrassment that, "the arrangement worked admirably—for us. Such a system, however, was symptomatic of an abuse of the Nonconformist system. . . . It was not uncommon to find chapels which were entirely dependent on the contributions of one man."[63]

The working class's increasing numerical preponderance was not sufficient to offset the middle-class's fiscal power. It was economics rather than demographics, in other words, that ensured that Congregational "preaching, buildings, ministers, manners, notions, and practices bore the air and impress of English middle-class life."[64] Within this context of unequal social power, Christian community would not surprisingly mean different things to Congregationalism's different constituencies. These differences, however, were partially protected from direct encounters with one another by the institutional boundaries between Congregationalism's diverse social constituencies. Residential segregation ensured that chapels replicated the social complexion of their immediate neighborhoods (although when neighborhoods changed, the city center chapels were often attended by suburban commuters). In any case, the decentralized nature of the Congregational denomination meant that such socially distinct chapels enjoyed little contact with one another.[65]

The one exception proved this rule. Middle-class Congregationalists were institutionally connected to working-class congregations they supported as home missions. Even here, however, there was little social interaction. The relationship between parent chapels and their mission branches was typically formal and limited to administrative concerns, that is, representatives were sent to the mission's chapel and Sunday school teachers' meetings, missionaries were sent from the mother church to work in the mission branch or, more often, proxies (e.g., bible women) were hired; but rarely if ever were there joint meetings of the memberships on any sort of equal basis as coworshipers of Christ. All of this ensured that the worlds inhabited by individual Congregationalists were socially homogeneous. Even within chapels, social boundaries were marked by the spatial segregation of scholars and the poor to free seats in the gallery, separated off from those able to afford the dues of church membership and the rental of a pew.[66] Otherwise, the working-class Sunday schools remained quite apart from the chapels that supported them.[67]

The social geography of Nonconformity in the early to mid-nineteenth century was such that the wealthiest chapels were typically concentrated in urban-industrial areas, and the very poorest in rural-agricultural areas. St. James' Chapel, for example, was situated at the pinnacle of the social hierarchy of Congregational chapels in the northeastern city of Newcastle, a center of English shipbuilding and coalmining. A journalist described the atmosphere of the chapel after a visit in 1881:

> A glance round will suffice to learn that St. James's is a wealthy congregation. There is an ex-Mayor. Here is a Town Councillor, there is an Alderman, and two or three pews off a well-known local merchant and a shipowner. In short, it may be called a fashionable congregation. The black hat with the luxurious black feather immediately in front are worthy of admiration. So are the golden coins which hang from the pearly shell-like ears, while the wonderful combination of material which composes the wearer's dolman could never be made in a Bradford loom. Exquisite little bonnets with abundance of feathers seem in vogue; so do large hats. . . . If the chapel is suggestive of a large jewel box, the ladies seated on delightfully soft cushions and clad in luxuriant furs, set it off to the best advantage.[68]

In contrast to the opulence of a St. James, Congregational chapels in rural areas were usually dominated by laboring families and the poor, who "felt spiritually more at home" in Nonconformist chapels than in the parish church, as the former were "run by their own class and calling."[69] In 1903, an Essex minister reported to the Congregational Home Missionary Society of the "depressing poverty" of his church's members, "so poor . . . that their wives had to do tailoring work to keep the house going. . . . The most strenuous opponent he had was the representative of the State Church. . . . 'To him I am a heathen. We Dissenters are almost lepers.'"[70]

There were equally significant social divisions between the chapels of urban Congregationalism.[71] Leeds, a woolen textile manufacturing city in the West Riding of Yorkshire, is instructive in this regard. Leeds had its equivalents to St. James, for example, in Queen Street, East Parade, and Headingley Hill Congregational chapels. Headingley Hill was built in 1864, designed by the same architect who worked on the city's town hall and corn exchange.[72] It was surely chapels such as these that lent Congregationalism its middle-class reputation. As residence patterns shifted, however, the social composition of chapels usually changed accordingly. Leeds' Salem Chapel, for example, underwent a continuous social decline after the 1870s. According to the chapel's historian the 1860s had been

> days when worshippers came to Salem in "carriage and pair." But times had changed. South Leeds had become rapidly industrialized. Salem was surrounded by the homes of people whose bread and butter was earned in the engineering workshops of Hunslet. The old "carriage and pair" congregation drifted away to the north of the city, and the new workers were not drawn in. The church declined as congregations decreased and debt increased.[73]

Salem was saved from the auction block by the efforts of its ministers, Bertram Smith and Francis Wrigley, who came to the chapel in 1891. They were young advocates of the progressive social gospel out to prove "that the reflection of the class structure of society in organized religion is due only to lack of understanding, imagination, and boldness in the existing church."[74] They instituted a wide range of ancillary programs to draw in the surrounding community, and they were very successful. Leeds's Belgrave Chapel Congregational Church underwent a similar experience. The chapel's church minutes record a steady drop in membership in the early years of this century, and in 1904 there was even talk of selling the chapel. Belgrave was rescued by the Leeds Congregational Council, which agreed to contribute to the chapel's support on condition that the church be run on "forward movement" lines, which meant organizing Pleasant Sunday Afternoons to attract working-class men and women from the surrounding neighborhoods.[75]

Leeds's working-class chapels more typically originated as Sunday schools and missions, constructed in poor neighborhoods, far away from the chapels that sponsored them. These included Marshall Street (1836), North Hall (1872), Beeston Hill (1858), Woodsley Road (1870), Kirkstall (1886), Nether Green (1888), Sheepscar (1860), Accommodation Road (1868), and Oak Road (1866), all of which were founded as missions by Leeds's major chapels and intended primarily for working-class constituencies. These intentions appear to have been realized, at least insofar as the chapels' reaching the upper stratum of the working classes. Beeston Hill's church records, for example, list the occupations of 24 of the 118 individuals who joined the chapel between 1866 and 1869 (most of those with no occupation designated were women, and 41 of these new members were men). These were largely people in skilled working-class occupations.[76] The minister's stipend at Beeston Hill was only £160 a year in 1887, whereas the chapel's register of collections indicates that most of the funds were appropriated for "the poor members of the church."

Contemporaries were acutely aware of a chapel's social profile. Prominent Congregational minister Alexander Raleigh regretfully declined an invitation to preside at Beeston Hill's opening ceremony with a self-conscious reference to its humble social claims: "I would come to your opening with great pleasure if I could—far more readily in fact than if your chapel had more of architectural pretension, and were intended for a higher class."[77] The ties that bound these mission chapels to their more prosperous benefactors combined social/spatial distance with administrative/political power, not unlike the ties that bound Britain and its empire, Headingley Hill's minister Rev. James Legge astutely observed:

> Any loosening of the bonds between these branches and the mother Church, is to be greatly deprecated. It would be reckoned a great disaster for England, should her magnificent colonies in Australasia, Africa, and Canada drift away from her, because of indifference to them on England's part, or because of decreasing loyalty and kindly feeling on their part. Though it may seem to be comparing small things with great, I do regard these Mission Stations as holding a somewhat analogous relationship to us, that her colonies hold to England. And I believe it would be a calamity to us as a Church, were anything to cause a diminution of sympathy with these useful and promising Missions. *They* still need our aid, both in personal service, and in pecuniary support. Nor less do *we* need them as spheres of active labour, as channels through which our Christian love may flow forth to bless the world.[78]

The administrative relationship between mother chapels and their branches appears to have been much as Rev. Legge suggests—an imperial democracy. It was democratic only in the sense that the middle classes who financed chapels and their missions actively sought to involve working-class people in religion; it was imperial in the sense that this involvement did not mean that they would work alongside one another, nor would working people control the institutions to which they were assigned.[79] The autonomy of mission chapels, for example, was limited by the fact that major offices of mission chapels were often held by members of the founding chapel rather than by the mission itself. This was particularly true with regard to trustees, who were in charge of their chapel's expenditure and thereby exerted a critical influence over the chapel's policies.[80]

The LMS assumes particular significance in this context of the social segregation between the chapels that made up Congregationalism at the local level. For the LMS was the primary institutional site of regular contact between the members of the independent chapels of Congregationalism for most of the nineteenth century.[81] As one of the few occasions on which Congregationalists from different chapels met together on an ostensibly equal basis as cosupporters of foreign missions, the LMS Auxiliary displayed to an unusually public degree the imperial relations that prevailed within the Congregational Republic. The auxiliary's presence in the local community highlighted the contradictions in the attitudes and aspirations of Congregational elites, particularly between their desire to Christianize the working classes and their feelings of moral and social revulsion toward the poor. Such contradictions undermined the cohesiveness of the missionary community. Far from providing an egalitarian haven to those who suffered from inequalities in their economic or political lives, the religious community replicated and reinforced these inequalities.

The social structure of local Congregationalism, for example, was reproduced in the auxiliary committees of the LMS. To be sure, the "best men" of each chapel were nominated to the LMS Auxiliary Committee, as they were to most other chapel offices. Nevertheless, chapels varied significantly in the relative social stature of their most prominent members. The wealthiest chapels in a village, town, or district were invariably represented by leading local notables; chapels whose members were of a more modest social station would, correspondingly, be represented by humbler sorts of people. The Leeds Auxiliary of the LMS was typically diverse in its social composition. The city's largest and wealthiest chapels were represented on the auxiliary committee by wealthy merchants and manufacturers, by men such as George J. Cockburn, who represented Headingley Hill Congregational Chapel on the auxiliary during the decades that bracketed the twentieth century's turn. Cockburn retired in 1880 on a fortune amassed as an East India merchant, after which he engaged in a range of public services, including spending six years on the Leeds Board of Guardians, chairing the Leeds School Board, and serving as a city magistrate for a total of 33 years.[82] T. R. Leuty was another active member of the auxiliary from Headingley Hill. Leuty headed T. R. Leuty and Co., which manufactured heavy linens. Leuty was also a Sunday school teacher and superintendent, but his "special care" was said to be the Congregational Domestic Mission and the LMS. In addition to his business and church-related activities, Leuty was heavily involved in local and national Liberal politics; he was chairman of the Leeds Liberal Federation, and he was elected to the Leeds City Council in 1882, served as the city's mayor in 1893, and was the Liberal member of Parliament from East Leeds from 1895 until he was thrown out in the khaki election of 1900. Leuty's various activities—chapel, work, and politics—were pieces of one cloth, which missions helped weave together. The Rev. A. Holden Byles, longtime minister at Headingley Hill, said in the course of the sermon he delivered at Leuty's funeral in 1911 that Leuty's last words to him were "what is England going to do with the opium traffic?" demonstrating, in Byles' words, "the keen interest he had in all that made for righteousness." Leuty's employees, appropriately enough, were reported to have encircled the grave.[83]

At the other end of the spectrum, Marshall Street's representatives between 1870 and 1920 included a leather merchant, a chemist, a corporation gas collector, a joiner, and two grocers. Beeston Hill was represented by an accountant (whose neighbors were clerks, which I presume means he was of a similar status), an examining officer of customs, the proprietor of an accounting firm, a foreman, a clerk, a joiner, another foreman, the manager of a co-op, a reporter, a blacksmith, and an electrical engineer. Further down the social ladder were the representatives of Headingley Hills's two missions at Kirkstall and Nether Green: two salesmen, a warehouseman, a woolen "manufacturer" (whose neighbors were a porter and a salesman), another woolen manufacturer (whose neighbors were a furniture broker and a music teacher), a caretaker, and a gardener's daughter.[84]

The officers of the LMS Auxiliary Committee were drawn almost entirely from the city's most prestigious chapels for most of our period. The Dodgshun family, prominent woolen manufacturers who worshipped at Queen Street Chapel, controlled the critical office of treasurer throughout the century.[85] The office of secretary had a higher turnover rate, but its occupants before 1900 similarly tended to be prominent men from Queen Street, Headingley Hill, or East Parade. John Mather, of Mather Brothers Woolen Merchants and East Parade Chapel, was the auxiliary's treasurer in 1871. Mather was succeeded by W. H. Rinder of W. H. Rinder and Co. Woolen Manufacturers, who served from 1872 until 1880. George J. Cockburn of Headingley Hill assumed the post until 1892, when he resigned to devote more attention to his duties as chairman of the Leeds School Board. John T. Barker, a corn merchant from East Parade Chapel, was the auxiliary's secretary from 1892 until 1903.

In other words, the fit and proper classes of Congregationalism predominated in the offices of the LMS Auxiliary as on the platforms of its public meetings. The coexistence of such patrician controls during the very period of heightened outreach to the working classes suggests the ambivalence at the heart of the missionary ideology of brotherhood and of Liberal Nonconformity's related embrace of democracy. Neither intended that the working class would serve on governing bodies; what they had in mind was government in the interest of the working class, but run by their betters. So explained Huddersfield's Nonconformist MP, Edward Leatham, who, when queried as to why only two working men had been elected to Parliament as late as 1885, responded that this was simply proof of the system's success. Thanks to the "rare discretion" of the working class, "we have arrived at the vigour of Democracy, without experiencing what I may term the shock of its brute force." This, according to Leatham, was "the very meaning of election." "We elect, not the random elements, which in their infinite variety are to be found scattered everywhere upon the surface, but what is best and soundest; and it is only on this grand hypothesis that this House is honourable, or that it is any honour to sit in it."[86] These were the same principles by which the religious institutions of Nonconformity, such as the LMS, were governed; in the words of Clyde Binfield, "there is room . . . for radicalism, pragmatism, and flexibility but not for democracy; its concept of respect and responsibility is too great for true democracy.[87]

Actual personal contact, in fact, proved to be more democracy than many Congregationalists were willing to stomach. Even for its most ardent advocates, the home missionary prescription of cross-class association required struggling with a natural repulsion. A missionary pamphlet of 1878 directs home supporters' attentions to their own attitudes toward the poor to calm their impatience for detailed news from abroad about individual converts: "how many, do you think, of the children in your . . . [Sunday] schools . . . for instance, would furnish matter for an interesting story?" Stressing that poverty makes its victims mentally dull as well as physically repulsive abroad as at home, the narrator explains that "it was an effort not to shrink from them, though of course such a feeling would never be yielded to." Enlightened by this analogy, a member of her audience asks "how could any one love such creatures?" The answer reflects the ambivalence at the heart of missionary philanthropy in this period: "not in the sense of personal liking of course . . . at least at first; but with the love of compassion, and the longing to bring these poor neglected little ones into the Saviour's fold."[88]

The incorporationist logic of the social gospel was continually betrayed by middle-class reluctance to practice the uplifting virtues of social contact their denominational leaders preached. That the majority of Sunday school teachers and superintendents, for example, were working people themselves was a state of affairs at least partly the consequence of a shortage of missionary labor from the more leisured classes. Francis Wrigley of Salem Chapel in Leeds complained about the lack of interest in Sunday school work among the "more cultured class in our congregation," and warned that

> it is of vital importance that the best energy and the most skilled labour in our churches should be brought to act upon the children. One cannot contemplate a gathering of our Sunday school teachers with equanimity. . . . Let us admit at once the devotion and self-sacrifice of many who have stood in the breach when

workers were few and hard to get. Still the question is, "Can we afford to continue to use 'unskilled labour' in this the most delicate of all operations?"[89]

Part of the attraction of the home mission project to middle-class Christians was that it provided the social benefits of a Christian working class while keeping distasteful social contact to a minimum. Within chapels, social diversity was managed by scheduling separate services for poor and working-class listeners, for, as one London minister put it, "if these people were to come to the ordinary Sunday services, the respectable congregation would be frightened away."[90] Many of the members at both Belgrave and Salem considered selling their chapels and relocating elsewhere to be preferable to canvassing for members in the declining neighborhoods of their chapels. One Belgrave deacon complained in 1903 about a widespread "spirit of criticism" in the chapel, mentioning in particular the "attitude of regular worshippers towards strangers and . . . the importance of giving a warm welcome to all who came to the services."[91] It was only the combined pressures from their ministers and the Yorkshire Congregational Union that saved these chapels for their communities.[92]

The prejudices that erupted at moments of social change were always just below the surface in the local organization of the LMS, as a result of its uniquely integrated character. United meetings (meetings attended by members of more than one chapel) often proved difficult to organize. In 1908, for example, a Newcastle minister warned that a proposed interchurch "Missionary Parliament" would "court disaster."[93] A committee formed to organize the biennial bazaar on behalf of the LMS in Leeds dissolved in 1916 when "the appointment of Secretaries proved a difficulty."[94] One Congregationalist complained of such problems in organizing missionary meetings in 1879: "Are we so independent of each other that we cannot at any time combine for any special object?"[95]

The social logic at the root of much of this independence is most evident in relation to children. As we have seen, children were at the center of the revised home missionary agenda, a critical point of entry into the working-class community. This shift in missionary practice registered the social transformation of the working-class child "from a component of the labour force into a subject of education."[96] On the one hand, this constituted childhood as prior to class as well as to race; the child was pure potential, education (the civilizing mission waged by adults against children), the means of its realization. But as Carolyn Steedman has argued, there were considerable "ambiguities that attached to the 'sacralisation of child life' when it was the children of the unskilled labouring poor who were under consideration."[97] Many would-be organizers for the LMS seem to have hesitated at the prospect of approaching working-class Sunday schools on the society's behalf. E. A. Shalders of Rochester, for example, complained to the society in 1866 that

> the levelling character of our Sunday School institution, as it affects the teachers in their corporate capacity, hinders many from undertaking Christian work who ought to be foremost in it. I only notice it as a fact that many of our best educated young people are kept back from Christian work lest they should form undesirable connexions.[98]

Shalders's evident desire that the society allow its respectable supporters on the local level to avoid contact with the Sunday schools was shared by others in LMS ranks. Charles Phillips, one of the Society's missionaries to Samoa, confronted similar concerns when touring provincial auxiliaries in 1888. The Society's supporters in Kent were bitterly divided by a wealthy contributor's insistence that middle- and working-class children attend separate missionary services. Phillips worried about the "complications and difficulties" likely to ensue. Although he assured the Society that he would follow its instructions, he made it clear that he had "no sympathy with Miss Unwin's desire for a special 'service at home so as to avoid meeting the Sunday School children,'" and warned that other of the society's supporters would be naturally aggrieved by "Miss Unwin's refusal to take part or allow any of the pupils to take part in the bazaar in aid of the chapel which is going on this week."[99]

Contact was especially problematic where middle-class children were concerned. These latter were organized on behalf of the LMS separately from Sunday school juvenile auxiliaries in what were called Children's Missionary Bands (their "object being specifically to gain the interest and support of children not in the habit of attending Sunday Schools").[100] As late as 1919, supporters in Leeds were reluctant to hold united meetings of these two sets of youthful missionary supporters.[101] Leeds Roundhay Chapel's Sunday school was exceptional in that its scholars were apparently the children of the members of this very prosperous suburban chapel.[102] This was probably the reason that Roundhay teachers were reluctant that their school participate in the united meetings associated with the Leeds chapter of the LMS Juvenile Auxiliary. In 1904, Roundhay teachers voted to "reply in the negative as to whether we should be in favour of a Children's Demonstration in connection with the next Annual Missionary Meetings." In 1911, the teachers softened a bit, deciding "that, after communication with Mr. Hall to find out exactly what was wanted, we should send some children to sing if it did not mean their having to attend rehearsals."[103]

What is surprising, given the extent of middle-class prejudice, is that more working people were not sufficiently offended by the power relations imprinted on missionary institutions to reject the missionary invitation into the fold of organized religion. Many working-class Christians appear to have taken the social gospel at its word, accepting rhetorical avowals of spiritual equality as fair exchange for their material subordination in the world outside their chapel republics. This is not in itself evidence of deference; working-class Christians' tolerance of the indignities embedded in the social relations of the religious community could well have been a preeminently practical reflection of their financial dependence on middle-class contributions to their institutions.

Ironically, however, their acceptance of these terms exposed one of the central contradictions within missionary ideology, the contradiction between the prejudice that justified the missionary middle classes' imperial relations with their missionized beneficiaries at home as well as abroad *and* the egalitarian promise of inclusion on which conversion was predicated. This contradiction gave rise to at least two unintended yet interrelated consequences. On the one hand, the inevitably pejorative nature of missionary constructions of heathenism tempted working-class recruits to try to distance themselves from the Otherized position of object of missionary benevolence by embracing full membership in the cross-class Christian community. This was, at one level, the realization of the missionary movement's social imperial aim. But, and not surprisingly, given all that we have seen, the incorporation of the working classes into mainstream chapel life created signficant problems for their middle-class hosts.

That participation in missionary relations carried with it tainting associations with foreign heathenism is suggested by the determination of working-class converts to distance themselves from missionary associations as quickly as possible. Working-class chapels, for example, seem to have been embarrassed by their mission origins. The introduction of a centenary history of Marshall Street Chapel in Leeds pointedly defined its mission status as meaning that it was "a Church with something to do."[104] Salem Chapel's historian was similarly defensive:

> Those who only knew Salem by reputation often seriously mistook its nature. Salem has always rejected the conventional title of "A Mission Church." Many a noted preacher has failed on a visit to Salem through assuming that he had to deal with "the usual mission crowd"—whatever that might be—and preaching down to an audience which he thought wanted to be amused. . . . Smith and Wrigley respected their audience. . . . This notion of a "Mission Church" raises other questions. It is steeped in the atmosphere of class consciousness. Has Christianity only got a "mission" to those who are economically below the level of the comfortable middle classes? Is a Mission and a Church a different thing, and does one section of the community have churches and the other missions?[105]

This recoil from the mission label was also manifested within the working classes; it provided a language with which the respectable distinguished themselves from their nonrespectable counterparts. Gwen Davies, whose father was a relatively prosperous and deeply religious tinworker in the south of Wales, described the "hooligans" who tormented her in childhood as "terrible": "They thought you were a class above and they liked to have their revenge on you, coming in gangs and run after you. . . . They were from very poor homes, you see, very poor, very dirty homes. They were children you wouldn't mix with. They weren't very sweet-smelling. . . . Oh it was heathenish, it was heathenish. Beyond."[106]

An obvious way of protecting oneself from such debilitating distinctions was to apply for membership at the parent chapel with which one's mission was associated. In 1888, for example, the deacons of New Court Congregational Chapel in London received with great consternation applications for membership from one of their mission chapels. They did, albeit reluctantly, approve these applications upon the applicants forgoing their right to vote at or attend church member meetings.[107] Sunday scholars and their teachers similarly requested permission to attend church services. The deacons of Edmonton and Tottenham Chapel in London refused such a request in 1875 on the grounds of insufficient room. The deacons at New Court Congregational Chapel proved somewhat more reasonable in 1895, when they agreed to allow scholars to sit in the gallery during the morning services on the day of the school anniversary; they even went so far as to grant the scholars' request to perform a hymn on the occasion, "it being understood that this concession would not lead to larger requests another year."[108]

There is indirect evidence that working-class Christians were dissatisfied with the disproportionate influence of their middle-class counterparts in institutions such as the LMS. The society's agents reported widespread complaints that auxiliaries did not distribute the honor of missionary deputations fairly, allowing wealthy chapels to monopolize their talents.[109] Salem Chapel's representatives led the protest against such policies on the committee of the Leeds Auxiliary. On November 13, 1901, the auxiliary's executive committee promised to allocate missionaries to every church. Apparently these promises were not fulfilled. In September 1903 the Leeds Auxiliary's minutes show that

> Rev. Bertram Smith raised the question of the allocation of the missionaries making strong comments on the assumed fact that three of the churches claimed to have a missionary every year, holding that the allocation should be conducted on a democratic basis whereby in regular rotation all the churches should be visited by a missionary independent of financial considerations. These

remarks led to a discussion which showed that opinions differed considerably as to the mode of arranging the Anniversary services altogether.[110]

These democratic initiatives from below were supported at the national level. The LMS's officials and agents began pressuring provincial auxiliaries in the mid-1880s to broaden the constituencies to which they appealed for donations and to make their auxiliary committees more representative. Auxiliaries were reminded that "some of our noblest leaders in the field have sprung from the smallest and poorest rural churches. And to argue as though the missionary interest were only worth cultivating in a community capable of substantial contributions, is to turn a spiritual into a material undertaking, and to leave out its divine side."[111] The Bradford Auxiliary was commended in 1885 for enlarging its membership to represent all the churches of the district.[112] The Fylde Missionary Council was reorganized in 1894 on a "more representative" basis.[113] In 1902, the Sheffield Auxiliary Committee was "broadened so as to allow a better representation of its growing constituency."[114] The Newcastle Auxiliary, which had long enjoyed a reputation for being virtually self-elected, reorganized along more democratic lines in 1905.[115] And the Nottinghamshire Auxiliary was democratized in 1912.[116]

Such initiatives from on high were frequently resisted on the bourgeois-dominated ground. In 1912 the LMS's organizing secretary urged the Leeds Auxiliary to organize a missionary committee in each of the city's chapels that "should be more representative than it usually is"; the auxiliary committee was also admonished to reorganize itself in order that it be "thoroughly representative."[117] As late as 1916, complaints were voiced in Leeds about a lack of "charity in our judgements of others and their gifts," and the auxiliary's attentions were directed to the "necessity of spreading the net wider and making the mesh smaller" when collecting on the society's behalf.[118]

Over time, however, the increasingly liberal leadership of the LMS apparently succeeded in encouraging where possible, and forcing where necessary, its democratizing initiatives at the local level. By the turn of this century, we begin to see the officers of the Leeds' Auxiliary being selected from the city's lesser chapels. The Dodgshuns of Queen Street remained in control of the treasury, but in 1903, James Bointon, a solicitor from Belgrave Chapel Congregational Church(which became a supported mission chapel of the Yorkshire Congregational Union the following year) was elected secretary. Bointon was replaced the next year by Newton Park's John Scott, a district manager of the national telephone company, who served until he was transferred to Manchester in 1905. Scott was succeeded by George Hudson, an advertising manager from Burmantoft Chapel. In social terms, control of the auxiliary seems to have been shifting away from an entrepreneurial elite (the woolen master class) in favor of lower-middle-class representatives of churches whose members were from even humbler backgrounds.

In the long run, however, this capture of the missionary auxiliary executive would prove a Pyrrhic victory. Democratization precipitated a middle-class flight from missionary institutions, which further exacerbated the latter's fiscal decline. It would appear that the middle-class advocates of foreign missions on the local level were not sufficiently careful in composing their wish that the working classes would join the missionary community. Their wish came true: working people accepted invitations to join Sunday schools, mission chapels, and Brotherhood meetings, and they gave their time, prayers, and pennies to the missionary coffer. The language of brotherhood in which these invitations were cast, however, had a democratic momentum that did not sit well with local notables, who had come to identify responsible government with their own personal rule and respectable association with social segregation.

These difficulties were what the Rev. James Legge of Leeds was alluding to when he stated that while he was "glad to think that the movements now in operation to ameliorate the condition of the working people and poorer ranks of society will have the heartiest sympathy of our Churches," he thought that the advocates of social reform should proceed with caution lest they exacerbate misguided social antagonisms:

> there is, indeed, great need for care not to do injustice to one class in the desire to benefit another. The speaker who embitters the relations of men by denouncing the rich or flattering the poor, is a most unwise friend of the cause he champions. But to insist that the Christian principles of justice, love, and brotherhood should be applied to the solution of these difficult social problems, is both a duty and a privilege which I trust Christian ministers will never abandon. . . . I believe that in Christ and His teaching that the world will find the key to unlock these difficulties, and that the world's hope lies in the spirit of Christ becoming dominant in all its social relations.[119]

Where ministers were not so careful to avoid "flattering the poor," they risked alienating the middle-class minority who paid their chapels' bills. The entire diaconate of Lightcliffe Congregational Chapel near Halifax, Yorkshire, resigned in 1883 when their chapel's members refused to dismiss a minister who delivered a series of provocative sermons, the titles of which included "A Workman's Life," "Women's Work in the World," and "Christ and Art."[120] These deacons must have felt affirmed in their action by their former chapel's trajectory in subsequent years. By the end of the 1880s, this same chapel boasted a Brotherhood of 800 members and a Sisterhood of 1,000. In 1911, the chapel's minister could publicly argue that

Temperance, thrift, education, patriotism—these things are all possible to citizens whose material circumstances are above the line of penury. To those who live below that line they are impossible. And it is surely the first business of the State to give the citizens "a chance" by progressive and cumulative legislation that will help them to cross the line.[121]

Scattered testimonials suggest that the fit and proper founders and financial backers of the missionary project deserted the communities transformed by their mission. As early as 1892, local advocates were complaining that "experience has taught us that it is useless for us to ask gentlemen" to participate in local missionary functions, in stark contrast to the support that local notables had showered upon missions in past years. The Rev. Wickham Tozer of Ipswich complained to the society that overture "almost always ends in failure, loss of time and patience. Three years since we wrote to one after the other and failed with all of them."[122] The Edinburgh Auxiliary was similarly unable to find a "suitable" replacement for its treasurer in 1898, having "approached many gentlemen of position and influence, but they all declined. . . . Finally we nominated Mr. A. D. Stewart—a good man—but not holding the social position which former treasurers have held."[123]

The society's organizing agents confirmed that men of prominent position were increasingly less likely to involve themselves in any sort of personal way, a withdrawal reflected in the level of their contributions as well. Agent Wilkins reported in 1887 that

In comparing the income of our Society today with that of a generation back, another fact has to be taken into account. We had then a considerable number of the most generous givers whose means were large. A Congregational collection at a church in Manchester used to be about £500 or thereabouts for many years; but three gentlemen gave £400 of this amount, leaving out £100 for a large Congregation to make up. Either we have not men as wealthy as their predecessors, or they have not acquired the willingness to give. My impression is that money is not so easily gathered as it was, and further that our people live more extravagantly than was the fashion a generation back. Considerations of this kind partly explain why it is that contributions have not steadily increased year by year with the increasing demand for our efforts in heathen lands.[124]

Agent Wilkins located the society's financial difficulties in the cold shoulders of the well-to-do, who had apparently rejected the stewardly values and missionary loyalties of their forefathers, "Were the hearts of many of our more wealthy members in full sympathy with this great work, our income could be easily doubled. It is most saddening to see Christians living in a princely style content to give a guinea a year towards the world's conversion."[125]

Many of these reluctant stewards appear to have withdrawn completely from the Congregational community in favor of the Established Church, or to have abandoned organized religion altogether. The society's agent in Scotland reported in 1886 that "the class of people attending our churches appears to be changing and their capacity for giving is less."[126] Rev. Samuel Macfarlane, a former missionary to Papua, New Guinea, who served as the society's organizing agent in the Midlands, reported in 1890 that

> My district is chiefly an agricultural one, and the majority of the churches are, as regards *numbers* and *funds* decidedly on the "Down grade." Congregationalism is suffering greatly in small towns and villages. Some have left our churches on account of Agricultural depressions. Some have gone to the Established Church on account of social position. Others on account of church squabbles, and some because it is cheaper. With many of our churches, it is a struggle for existence, and so they are unable to do much for Foreign Missions. Still, on the whole, they do remarkably well for our Society. As well, indeed, as can be reasonably expected amidst so many other claims.[127]

Agent Wilkins reported a similar social decline in the north, citing specific examples of Hornsea, Driffield, Barnard Castle, Whorlton, and Cotherstone, whose people are described as "deeply interested" in missions but too poor to give much money. Lincolnshire is said to be hopeless simply because of the state of agriculture, whereas Wigan's churches are too caught up in "struggling for existence" to have much left over for outside causes. Manchester city churches are weak and their stronger (i. e., richer) suburban counterparts are absorbed in new building schemes. Stockport alone seems promising. Agent Wilkins concluded that

> When I undertook this Agency nearly two years ago, I was astonished to find that the gifts of the churches for Mission work were little larger than they were 30 years ago, although the number of congregations was greater, and the people attending the Churches appeared to be more wealthy. But a larger knowledge has shown me that I was wrong in the estimate I had formed of the growth of the Congregational Churches in the North of England during this generation. Slowly the conviction has been forced upon me that with a few exceptions we are not much, if at all, stronger than we were 30 years ago: whilst in many places the expenses connected with our worship have increased considerably, thus leaving the people with less money to devote to work away from their own immediate neighbourhood. In the Agricultural Districts it is most painful to hear the stories of the struggles our churches have to make to preserve their existence. People, who would give largely to the support of our work if it were possible, have told me that they have to give nearly all they can spare to keep their own churches from collapse; and further, that knowing the financial difficulties of their neighbours, they cannot ask them for money as they have done in former times. In our towns there are many churches which have been for-

saken by those well able to assist them, these having gone away to reside in the suburbs.[128]

The withdrawal of Congregationalism's propertied elite, be it to the suburbs or out of the religious community altogether, left their former chapels in financially straitened circumstances, with less and less to spare for outside concerns like the LMS. In Manchester, for example, Agent Wilkins found that

> whilst it is perfectly true that they [the churches] are more numerous than they were 25 years ago, there are more poor and struggling ones than there were then. And it seems to be a rule with few exceptions that a young church considers its chief and almost sole duty is to care for itself; Mission work being disregarded until their own wants are fully satisfied. One result of this selfish action follows:—the desire to help others is lost, and is with great difficulty recovered.[129]

Conclusion

This narrative would seem to confirm Stephen Yeo's findings in Reading. Rather than the inevitable consequence of sociological modernization or cultural secularization, the decline of organized religion in Britain had specific ideological and institutional origins. Popular support did not just drift away in secular boredom, stomp off in intellectual enlightenment, or otherwise disappear into the sociological dustbin of modernity's forward march. To the contrary, it was the middle classes that first jumped the ship of organized religion when its social complexion became distasteful to them. It was only then that these ships began to sink, not through want of numbers, but as a result of the financial weight of institutional expenses on an increasingly impoverished constituency.

The social tensions that disrupted support for missions at the local level were vital preconditions of the remaking of an imperial culture in Britain during the closing decades of the nineteenth century. The so-called scramble for colonies during the 1880s and 1890s was accompanied by a shift in colonial policy, away from efforts to create colonial markets (in which missions were among the agencies deployed to create civilized consumer demand) to the making of a disciplined working class. The civilizing ambitions of the mid-Victorian imperialism of free trade was displaced at the nineteenth century's end by a "new imperialism," centered around a more Machiavellian praxis of control.[130] These shifts in high colonial policy were refracted in imperial culture at home in the replacement of the missionary hero in colonial iconography with the soldier, the adventurer, the explorer, and other personifications of the nationalist who conquered rather than of the benefactor who saved.[131] Humanitarianism more generally and its missionary embodiment in particular were increasingly suspected of sapping the "national character, emasculating its virility."[132]

The missionary events narrated above may have contributed to this process at a number of different levels. Its finances and morale at low ebb, the missionary lobby could ill afford to contest the competing imperial ideals that were increasingly allowed to enjoy the ideological upper hand. Indeed, the LMS seems to have abandoned all efforts to do so at the popular level. In an apparent attempt to translate the growing popularity of increasingly conservative visions of empire into missionary contributions, LMS propaganda produced for popular consumption, such as the *Juvenile Missionary Magazine* (renamed *The Juvenile: A Magazine for the Young* in 1888), which was distributed in Congregational Sunday schools, began to reverse its priorities, to promote the mission cause as a means to imperial ends. Articles more and more often represented missionaries as imperial functionaries, praised by imperial proconsuls for their service to the nation, while the empire itself was increasingly represented in unproblematically positive terms.

In this and other regards, the missionary movement sowed ideological seeds of a political crop that its enemies would be best positioned to reap in the social and imperial circumstances at the twentieth century's turn. Popular radicals' social critique of missionary philanthropy may have contributed to making this key constituency available to the more conservative imperial and racial identifications being promoted in this period. Similarly, if for diametrically opposed social reasons, was the evangelical middle class positioned to embrace conservative alternatives to a missionary imperialism that went too far abroad, as it had at home. Even those who remained within the mission community would have been influenced in more conservative directions by the society's ideological capitulation—in its popular literature if not in its colonial practice—to its opponents' imperial goals. Thus did imperial and social developments converge to muffle the missionary alternative to the conservative imperial ideals that held sway on the eve of World War I and beyond.

CHAPTER 6

The Strange Death of Missionary
Imperialism, 1895–1925

Foreign policy may not be so self-generating and self-subsistent as it
sometimes appears, and not quite so divorced from the rest of social
and political life. The ambassador and the machine minder may after all
share a common world.
> —Bernard Porter, "British Foreign Policy"

The problem of the twentieth century is the problem of the color line.
> —W. E. B. Dubois, *Souls of Black Folk*

In the politics of the world the Colour problem is the one thing that
matters.
> —Edward Shillito, "The Race Problem"

The overall thrust of this book has been to argue that the empire mattered to the course of British history as well as to that British public in whose
name it was defended. The representation of British political culture in insular terms has been assailed at one of the sociopolitical sites where its claims
would presumably be the strongest. This is the site of the local as well as the
national cultures of English Congregationalism, one of the central pillars of
the influential Nonconformist wing of the British Liberal Party. Their missionary involvement focused Congregationalists' attention on the empire on
a regular and passionate basis. In turn, the missionary movement provided
the empire with one of its more enduring ideological legitimations and far-
reaching sources of metropolitan popular support.

The missionary perspective on empire was ambiguous, to say the least. It
changed significantly over the long nineteenth century surveyed here. Orig-
inating in the humanitarian critique of slavery and other physically coercive
forms of authority, evangelical missionaries, and particularly the Dissenters
among them, consistently portrayed themselves as enlightened liberal alternatives to the ancien regime, at home as well as abroad. This often put missionaries in direct opposition to conservative colonial administrations.

Even at their most antagonistic, however, Victorian missionaries seldom questioned the moral validity of Europe's imperial domination of the non-European world. In fact, their argument was often that missionary modes of control were more effective guarantees of European power in the colonies than were those of the soldier or slaveowner. Only rarely did missionaries and their home supporters construe the targets of their mission as subjects who might be better left to control themselves. But it was their relative autonomy from direct material interest in the colonies—a distance less real than imagined in some cases—that lent the missionary movement its power to validate. It was, in other words, because they were so critical of colonial policy and so innocent of direct material interest that missionary legitimations of the imperial ideal carried so much ideological weight.

And by the middle decades of the nineteenth century, missionaries began to display a more positive view of colonial officialdom, a measure of the evangelical middle class's incorporation in the British political nation after 1832. State support was increasingly deemed necessary to develop the infrastructural conditions for free labor and consensual political practice in the foreign fields of heathendom that existed in Britain. There were, no doubt, many exceptions, missionaries who rightly feared that an overly close association with the British political establishment would jeopardize their local standing. But missionaries were generally in favor of the extension of British rule, particularly in areas threatened by other European rivals or by the European settler regimes to which the British government was bent on devolving power. During the middle decades of the nineteenth century, missions can be seen as a voluntarist offshoot of the "imperialism of free trade"; at a time when many conservatives were opposed to colonial entanglements, the missionary movement was at the vanguard of expansionist sentiment.[1]

During the second half of the nineteenth century, the missionary movement would be placed on the defensive by the very processes that brought its imperial dreams to fruition. Britain's rapid scramble for colonies during the 1870s and 1880s created as many problems for evangelical missionaries as it had been meant to solve. The influx of competing European interests into the mission field forced missionaries to befriend the natives if they were to have a constituency left to proselytize. Missionaries' difficulties with other Europeans in the colonies often drew them into conflict with colonial officialdom as well. But, again, missionaries' criticisms of colonial authorities were usually couched in terms of practice falling short of imperial ideals, rather than imperial ideals themselves being called into question. And ironically, missionaries' lament that the empire was falling short of its divine mission helped to generate and to reinforce one of British imperialism's most enduring rationales.

In this, missionaries were not simply men and women of their times, as missionary apologists would have it. Missionaries and their metropolitan supporters helped to create a political culture in which imperialism was rendered effectively unassailable. This most liberal sector of the British public not only explicitly and repeatedly embraced the empire as a divinely ordained means to sacred ends; the missionary movement also carried its imperial dreams to British society's furthest reaches. Even the most isolated rural villages encountered the colonies on a regular basis through the local institutions of organized religion; even the children of the very poorest classes were enlisted in an imperial project via the missionary box, Sunday school lesson, and juvenile missionary auxiliary.

The empire represented in missionary propaganda was interjected into British political culture by means such as these at the most local of levels. And the ideological work it accomplished there was of crucial social as well as imperial importance. The missionary project provided one of the primary languages through which community was imagined amidst the diversity that characterized the Victorian social landscape. The existence of such communities calls into question the scholarly presumption that these were social lives lived apart or separate gender spheres; working-class and middle-class men and women joined forces on behalf of the missionary imperial cause, occupying shared institutional space, embracing the same ideological agenda.[2]

Class and gender differences were not displaced, however, by competing missionary claims. To the contrary, this study has argued that the missionary movement contributed considerably to the very making of class and gender identities. Its institutions, its opportunities, and its ambitions, as well as the frustration of these ambitions, were the material out of which local and immediate concerns found their imaginative expression. That the contradictory interests of Congregationalism's diverse constituencies found expression in a singular missionary imperial language was a hegemonic achievement. But it was not one that precluded conflict; to the contrary, the missionary project itself became a terrain of class and gender as well as racial struggle.

Congregational attachments to the empire accrued much of their ideological power from the missionary movement's influence on social relations at the local level. We know far more about the sort of community middle-class Nonconformists used missions to imagine than about the sort of communities imagined by their working-class counterparts. Middle-class contributions were more crucial to the foreign missionary project's financial survival and were, apparently, more vulnerable to offense—hence the care taken in missionary sources to compliment and cultivate the middle-class contributor and to articulate the foreign missionary agenda in terms of middle-class aims. The

missionary movement's success in this regard calls into question recent asser-
tions that the imperial ideal "never embraced Birmingham or Manchester."[3]
I have tried to suggest here that the piety for which middle-class Congregationalists were renowned was predicated on a near obsession with foreign
missions that was readily extended to though never entirely coterminous
with the imperial contexts in which foreign missions operated.

That said, the LMS mobilized support from a much broader social constituency than the Congregational middle class. The widow's mite was critical to missionary operations, and working-class people predominated within
the missionary audience. LMS agents testified over and over again that the
warmest support for the society came from those quarters least able to afford
it. Organizing Agent Macfarlane reported from the Midlands in 1890 that

> Everywhere I meet with the greatest kindness, and often with most encourag-
> ing devotedness to our cause, although it is generally those who are least able to
> help us who appear most anxious to do so. In many of the small struggling
> churches may be found those who are amongst the best supporters of our Soci-
> ety. They take a deep interest in foreign missions, and although their gifts may
> be comparatively small their prayers surely help on the good work.[4]

"Many of the Churches in Cornwall are very poor and small, the enthusiasm
often manifested was very pleasing," reported another agent in 1885. "In most
of the small and struggling churches, many in lonely villages, the feeling of
love for the London Missionary Society is specially tender," concluded a report submitted in 1915.[5]

A fuller understanding of the meanings invested in the empire in such
quarters will require probing beyond the primarily institutional sources of the
LMS examined here. From this vantage point, however, popular complicity
in the foreign missionary project sometimes involved the kind of deference
associated with "incorporation."[6] Working-class missionary supporters gave
money in response to propaganda that valorized altruism in the face of ad-
versity, compassion as a response to oppression, and spirituality as solace for
material deprivation—none of which challenged their earthly subordination.
At least some working-class people, in short, bought into a missionary pack-
age that offered spiritual equality as the primary concession for their acceptance of social and political inequality.

At the same time, the longings represented in this settlement can be understood very much in relation to the circumstances of the social subordination of the working class. The seemingly irrational act of giving away one's
"precious pennies" forged a spiritual terrain that enabled poor and working-
class Congregationalists to affirm their moral dignity against the manifold
humiliations that characterize daily existence in a class society. The respect

and affection for God mean most, perhaps, to those who can expect least of these affirmations in virtually every other part of their lives. As one poor woman confessed to a Congregational minister: "I go up into the free seats in the gallery near the door, and slip out as soon as the service is over, for I am not in a dress fit to be seen, and nobody knows me; but the Lord knows me and that is enough."[7]

Remarks such as these suggest that feelings of shame were prominent in the structure of feeling that drew many working people to seek their haven in the missionary imperial community. Evangelical Christianity, in particular, spoke to perhaps universal longings for recognition and inclusion. At the same time, its gift of acceptance was conveyed via institutions and functionaries whose own pretensions to respectability were predicated on working-class people's requiring conversion, uplift, and civilization. Hence perhaps the resonance of the conversion experience's emphasis on sin and redemption for the working-class convert. Herein also lay the incorporating capacity of organized religion, at least as it was sociologically constituted in this place and time. The shame voiced in conversion, embodied in joining a chapel run by your social superiors, ultimately conceded the legitimacy of the judgments of those who possessed the institutional power to exclude—you slip out the door, for only God could view your degradation with compassion and understanding.

The logic of working-class support for missions, no less than that of the middle classes, was moral rather than material. It did, nevertheless, voice needs and desires generated out of the circumstances of class. Working-class support for missions also appears to have been gendered. The social gospel's concentration upon men, manifested in the emphasis on the Brotherhood movement, was an anxious commentary upon the apparent fact that working-class women were far more likely to remain attached to the institutions of organized religion than were working-class men.[8] Some of the tensions identified above, between the bitter indictment and the embrace of the social relations of missionary philanthropy, were fought out within families. The incident in North Meols described in chapter 1, in which a miner berates his wife for participating in missionary meetings, may not have been as uncommon as was its outcome, which took the form of the miner's contrite conversion. The first annual report of the London Female Mission, published in 1836, laid the blame for working-class irreligion squarely at the feet of working men:

In several instances, by remonstrating with fathers who were professed deists, she has so far prevailed as to induce them to suffer their wives and children to attend on public worship, and has received for her interference the grateful acknowledgements of some of the parties, who have apparently been rescued from ignorance and misery and placed in the path which leads to knowledge and happiness.[9]

Twenty years later, the London City Mission similarly complained about a self-described atheist's unfortunate influence:

The missionary says for three years I have called upon Mr.—he is a shoemaker, and when I have spoken to him he has often replied to me in a very obscene manner in the presence of his wife and daughter (a young woman). His wife and daughter are well-disposed toward religious duties; each of them has had much opposition from him, in consequence of their attending a place of worship; he has waited for their return in a state of intoxication to curse and scold them, but they still continue to go.[10]

Paul Thompson quotes at length an Essex farmworker's son, angered by the way his mother was treated at their local parish church:

And when people left the church, although as I said he was a nice old kindly vicar, he didn't seem to have any time for the lower classes. Mother and her friends would pass out of the church door, the vicar would stand near the church door, and he would just nod and smile, perhaps not that, even. But when the higher class people came out he would shake hands and beam to every one of them as if they was somebody far superior to my mother. . . . And I didn't like that. I thought my mother was worth a handshake as well as the rich. . . . I used to discuss this sort of thing with my mother. . . . I said it wasn't right, it wasn't proper. I said she shouldn't go to church. She said, "Nothing will ever stop me from going to my church."[11]

We need to know much more about why such women continued to participate in an institutional culture in which they were regularly subjected to insults that drove many of their husbands and sons away. It is possible that the working-class community did not provide the same associational opportunities or moral support to women as it did to men. It is also possible that middle-class missionary interventions within the working-class community affected men and women in significantly different ways. If women were isolated in working-class homes in which they exerted little control, perhaps they would not have been as negatively affected by missionary intrusions therein; these were an attack on their husband's domestic prerogatives rather than on their own.[12] Such appears to be the thrust of the Rev. G. W. Kitchin's analysis of working-class alienation from the churches. Note that it is the female gender of the missionary to which he attends, the working-class wife being invisible in an exchange that is obviously about the working-class man.

The excellent well-meaning wives of us all offend more or less unconsciously in two ways: they are either patronising Lady Bountifuls, or they meddle with domestic matters, till the man's castle seems to be in the hands of the enemy. Their very virtues offend: people are up in arms if rebuked for dirt and lack of fresh air, and so on. For the working man feels, probably wrongly, that his independence is attacked; his home should be inviolate for him.[13]

There is certainly a level on which evangelicalism's valorization of the least of these—a theme on which missionary propaganda laid great emphasis—must have resonated with working women erased from all sides. The missionary movement conceded the humanity and dignity of all its supporters, offering a fleeting moment in the moral sun, in which the last sat alongside the first. Missionary collectors and agents received working-class widows' mites, whether pennies or prayers, with a public show of reverence; these gifts were all the more precious because of the sacrifice they represented. Missionary fund-raisers may well have been more interested in using the poor as a foil to shame propertied donors into higher standards of giving. But in supporting missions, working-class Congregationalists were striving, I think, to demonstrate that human worth was not a function of social standing but of one's capacity to care for others; the more distant these others, or, perhaps, the more abstract the gift relationship, the better such gifts served to demonstrate the point.

That working people embraced missionary philanthropy for its egalitarian implications is suggested by their efforts to reshape the missionary community along more democratic lines. Working people took the missionary movement at its democratic word when they joined missionary auxiliaries, volunteered to host visiting missionaries, and came forward to serve as officers and to take their places in other ways alongside their middle-class brethren on behalf of the mission cause. In the end, it was the middle classes who seem to have sacrificed their piety to the golden calf of social prejudice, a somewhat ironic reversal of the rather simpleminded materialism usually attributed to working people.

The social tensions identified in this book ultimately resulted in the virtually complete rout of missionary imperialism during the period between the two world wars. On the most obvious level, the decline of organized religion in these years resulted in the decline of the missionary movement for financial reasons alone—fewer and poorer practicing Christians in Britain inevitably translated into financial crisis for increasingly expensive missionary operations abroad.[14] Diminishing support on their home front, in turn, pushed missionaries to look increasingly to the mission field for support, prompting a reassessment of the missionary's relation to the colonial state. The imperial identifications of the LMS's pioneers were steadily eroded if not fully jettisoned in postwar efforts to secure the missionary movement's legitimacy in the eyes of more and more popular and powerful colonial nationalist movements.[15]

Missionaries' often desperate efforts to ingratiate themselves with potential convert populations led them to abandon much of what was distinctively Christian in their mission. In 1921, for example, the LMS was rocked by scandal, when two missionaries in Bangalore, India, omitted Jesus' name from local publications so as not to offend Hindu sensibilities. The society's Foreign Secretary, Rev. Frank Lenwood, joined H. T. Spencer, chairman of the LMS Board's India Committee, in recommending that the board "trust in those who are facing the problem and doing the work." The board initially agreed, with only two directors dissenting, expressing its confidence in "the evangelistic purpose" of the missionaries concerned and "leaving them freedom to use the method of evangelism they thought most helpful."[16] This resulted in a wave of protest from provincial supporters, however, especially in those country districts that had formerly been most ardent in their support for the mission cause.[17] The divisions exposed by the Bangalore affair were primarily theological and generational. The Bangalore missionaries' critics were of the more old-fashioned evangelical persuasion; their defenders were more open to theological modernism and biblical criticism. One observer interestingly attributed the dispute to the "high strung and overwrought condition of the theological mind, one of the reactions of the war period, I presume."[18]

Although the society's upper administration was dominated by theological (as well as political) liberals, they began to reconsider their position in light of widespread fears at the local level that the society's finances would be adversely affected. In December 1921, the board rescinded its June resolutions of support and referred the question to a deputation dispatched to investigate conditions in the field. The deputation issued two reports. The majority (led by Lenwood) obtusely acknowledged the "legitimacy" of the Bangalore method without endorsing it; the minority disapproved, though it recognized the two missionaries involved to be good Christians.[19] The board of directors split the difference, affirming its commitment to the relative autonomy of its operatives in the foreign mission field, while urging upon them "the constant remembrance of the evangelistic aim of the LMS educational work, namely, the bringing of every pupil to Jesus Christ as Saviour."[20] In a telling postscript, Frank Lenwood was forced to resign as the LMS's foreign secretary after publishing a book entitled *Jesus: Lord or Leader?*, which questioned the divinity of Christ. Lenwood resumed his ministerial career at a missionary post in London's East End.[21]

The narrative of the missionary movement's decline also overlaps with the "strange death" of the British Liberal Party. The Liberal Party was in office for 38 of the 54 years between 1832 and 1885, an electoral ascendancy dependent in part upon a particular denominational configuration of political allegiance. The religious community was split almost evenly between the Church of England and the chapels of Nonconformity. Anglicans, however, were not nearly as united in their conservatism as Nonconformists were in their liberalism. Whereas Conservatives outnumbered Liberals in the Church of England by between two and a half and four to one, between eight and twelve Nonconformists voted Liberal for every one who voted Conservative.[22]

The configuration of political allegiances that had favored the Liberal Party began to unravel after 1885, and imperial issues figured large in the circumstances that brought this about. The Conservative Party was elected in 1886 when the Liberals' leader, William Gladstone, came out in favor of Irish Home Rule. The Conservatives remained in power for the next 20 years, except for the brief interlude of the Gladstone-Rosebery government of 1892–1895. The Liberal Party recovered temporarily in 1906, governing until the wartime Coalition of 1915, which ruled until the Conservatives were returned in 1922. The Liberal Party, however, now found itself displaced by Labour as the party of opposition, a politically marginal position from which it never recovered.

The disintegration of Nonconformity as a cohesive political bloc was a crucial factor in liberalism's electoral decline. The social tensions that divided the chapel community were replicated on the political level. The missionary impulse that was transforming the social organization of the chapel community had its concommitant in a social gospel that embraced the new liberalism at home as well as the trusteeship state abroad. Both these political sides of the missionary coin undermined the heretofore solidly Liberal front of Nonconformity. According to his biographers, Robert F. Horton's "outspoken utterances on social questions" alienated many of the wealthy members of his Hampstead church. Horton, an ardent supporter of foreign missions as well as of domestic social reform, complained bitterly about some of his members' opposition to his electioneering activities during the 1880 Liberal campaign: "My ministerial work is almost suspended; people don't like it. 'We had rather a minister did not take part in politics'! Hypocrites!" Horton was unmoved by such opposition, continuing his activities on behalf of what he termed advanced Liberalism.[23] David Livingstone's daughter was outraged that the LMS selected Rev. C. S. Horne to write her father's biography. The society stood by its decision and by Rev. Horne, the foreign secretary replying: "I am sorry you feel so strongly about my friend, Mr. Silvester Horne. He is a Liberal. Probably he would describe himself as a Radical. I was not aware that he was a Socialist. But he is an earnest Christian minister and intensely interested in mission work."[24]

Liberal foreign policy proved equally if not more divisive in Nonconformist ranks. In fact, it was a foreign affair that first disturbed the close association of religion and political affiliation that had characterized mid-Victorian political culture. Congregational loyalties to the Liberal Party, for example, suffered their first substantial jolts during the Home Rule crisis of 1886. Most Congregationalists remained loyal to Gladstone, although a prominent few, such as Birmingham's R. W. Dale, joined the Unionist secession. Congregationalism's official historian, R. Tudur Jones, notes that "politics became a sore point" in denominational circles in the years following. "When a speaker at the autumn meeting of the [Congregational] Union in 1888 sought to animadvert upon Dale's Unionism, Dale left the Assembly never to return except to say a word in memory of Alexander Hannay."[25] Rev. J. D. Jones found that political tensions among his chapel's members heightened significantly after 1886. Jones himself remained within the Liberal Party but curtailed his political activities to avoid alienating the Unionists in his congregation, who included "some of my best men . . . though the Church was predominantly Liberal."[26]

The "rift which had first appeared in English Nonconformity with the Irish Home Rule dispute in 1886" widened significantly during the Boer War. Feelings within the denomination ran high against those who criticized the war. Congregationalists were "miserably divided," and those who criticized the government were "shamefully treated by their fellow denominationalists."[27] The Conservative Party's political labor can be credited for much of Liberalism's misery on this issue. Conservative vilification of their opponents as traitors to the empire reached its height during the war. Liberal critics of Britain's war strategy (which included burning Boer farms and incarcerating Boer civilians in concentration camps) were viciously harassed in and out of Parliament. In the words of historians Robert McKenzie and Allan Silver, "few democratic political parties can have so systematically and ruthlessly called into question the integrity, the devotion to the institutions of the country, and the patriotism of its opponents."[28]

Congregational loyalties were pulled in conflicting directions by the South African war. Missionaries long-standing hostility to the Afrikaaner community overrode their traditional reservations about conservative colonial policies. They rallied for the most part behind the government's war aims.[29] The Congregational Union of South Africa and the native churches formerly affiliated with the LMS passed resolutions in support of British policy. J. S.

Moffat, former LMS missionary, son of Robert Moffat, and David Living-stone's brother-in-law, urged support for Britain on the grounds of native and missionary interest, which he felt would be imperiled by a Boer victory. "There is no exaggeration in speaking of the native question as one of the principal causes which have led to the present war."[30]

According to Moffat, the war had resulted from the fundamental incompatibility of the racial ideologies embodied in the so-called native policies of the Cape and the Transvaal. Moffat's description of the constitution governing the Cape clearly linked its native policy to the Victorian liberal tradition:

> Its spirit is noble, it gives to every man, whatever the colour of his face, the right to be a free citizen, and a chance to attain any position in the community which is open to honest intelligence and industry. And whence did that spirit come? . . . It came from the old country which was just then awakening to a larger conception of true civil and political freedom.[31]

Afrikaaner attitudes toward Africans, by contrast, were "narrow," "reactionary," and "ignorant": "The British notion of the aboriginal man as a man with all human rights has been a standing occasion of offence to the Boer ever since the Union Jack has floated in South Africa. The Boer looks upon the Black as a 'schepsel,' not as a man. He may have a right to kindly treatment, like a horse, but legal rights as a human being, No!"[32] Moffat concludes his attack on Afrikaanerdom with a discussion of the situation of missions in the Transvaal:

> That there are many missionary stations there is true enough. The missionary is tolerated and looked down upon as belonging to an inferior order of clerics. He must be discreet, he must teach his flock to be submissive to their superiors and contented with that state of life in which it has pleased Providence to place them. There are some missionary societies to which the air of the Transvaal is unfavourable. These are they who believe that it is right to teach the native that he is a free man, who ought to learn to stand on his own feet, and to become fitted to exercise the rights of a human being, the door of which should stand open to him. We are justified in believing that what holds good of the Transvaal in such matters would have held good in the Cape colony also, were it under Boer domination, and not under the rule of Great Britain.

In this quotation the missionary cause is identified with the humane treatment of the native peoples of South Africa, and both are identified with British victory over the Boers. This brings our story of missionary imperialism full circle, but to a very different political conclusion. Moffat is here deploying the familiar missionary argument in support of an imperial vision premised on a London-ruled empire with minimal settler autonomy. His liberal critique of Afrikaaner racism, however, is directed against that pro-Boer

faction within the Liberal Party, which included a number of prominent LMS
supporters such as Rev. C. S. Horne and Rev. J. Guinness Rogers, and in
support of the colonial policies of a Conservative regime:

> Let those who are contending for what they call the "independence of the Boer
> Republics" remember the following facts. We cannot ignore the Black man as
> one of the chief factors in the future of South Africa. On the subject of the Black
> Man the Boer regime and that of Great Britain are irreconcilable. Two dominant
> systems so vitally different co-exist side by side. The predominance of the Boer
> is out of the question, that of Great Britain the only possible alternative.[33]

The pro-Boers, in turn, defended their loyalty to the empire by reference
to the same liberal "mode of power" that had long inspired missionary cri-
tiques of colonial policy. It was in liberalism's capacity to produce consent
that Britain's imperial greatness lay; hence the true imperialist, according to
the Rev. Andrew Martin Fairbairn, must oppose the war.

> The expansion of what it is the fashion to call "our Empire" has been due to the
> action of Liberal ideas, and is in the main the achievement of Liberal policy. Any
> decrease, therefore, in their energy or in the strength with which they are held,
> and the force and the faith with which they are applied, can only mean distaste
> to our people and State. No Empire—if we must call the reign of our people
> by so unsuitable a name—was ever so much the creation of a race and so little
> the product of anything that can be called by any name implying either cen-
> tralised or individualised power, either military force or military ambition. It has
> been due throughout to the wholesome and natural action of great ideas work-
> ing through the plastic medium of resolute yet susceptible men.[34]

Again, it was not imperialism per se that was being challenged by these critics of the South African war, but rather an un-Christian version of it. As Rev.
Horne warned his congregation in 1901:

> God fashions His instruments, and if they fail Him, he breaks them and fashions
> others. . . . The proudest empire on which God's sun ever rose or set must hold
> its authority simply on these terms. . . . I am not aware that this is ever an ex-
> actly popular line to take. It is not the sort of greasey patriotism that sustains an
> easy existence on the wine-cup and a brass band. But it is the higher patriotism.
> Jeremiah did earnestly and tearfully desire that his nation should prove fit to be
> a chosen vessel, for use and not for rejection. . . . God's will, he pleaded, is
> greater than any mere human prosperity.[35]

Contradictions within the missionary imperial project of the Livingstone
era erupted to the political surface under the pressures of the new imperial
expansion, one result of which was a political disintegration of Nonconformity paralleling the centripetal pressures on its social cohesion. Rev. Horne

complained of feeling "very much alone" in Congregational circles as a result of his criticisms of Britain's conduct of the Boer War.[36] The LMS board was so divided over the war that the society was unable to come to any official position, according to the society's *Annual Report* for 1900:

> There has been a very marked and painful divergence of feeling and opinion even among Christian men as to the justice and expediency of the position our country has taken in this quarrel, and not a few of the Society's friends and supporters have been disposed to demand that it should—as having a direct and important part in the evangelization of South Africa—publicly connect itself with the party which condemns the war as unrighteous. The Directors have not considered it to be their duty to introduce the discussion of what is confessedly a very complicated political question into their deliberations on mission work, or to attempt to arrive at a common judgement upon a matter which is so entirely outside the range of their missionary operations as the relation of Great Britain to other civilized states.[37]

In other words, the society had to avoid offending its pro-Boer supporters at home without compromising the position of its missions in the field.

By the end of the war, that almost unassailable association of the Conservative Party with the empire had been established in the popular imagination. The Liberal Party was the loser in these domestic realignments of the empire and its mission, its political cohesion sacrificed on an imperial alter that missionary principles had done so much to build. To be sure, the empire was a mixed blessing for the Conservatives as well. They were swept out of office in the Liberal landslide of 1906 in large part because of the Party's promotion of imperial protection and because of Liberal objections to the use of Chinese labor in South Africa. The political legacies of empire were, then, highly ambiguous and contingent on immediate circumstances on all sides.[38]

But the Liberal Party would not repeat its tremendous success of 1906; after the war the new Labour Party displaced it as the party of opposition. Missionary imperialism, however, like liberal ideology more generally, survived the Liberal Party's Parliamentary demise, providing an enormously powerful language of trusteeship and development through which British people across the political and social spectrum had learned to talk about colonial relations of power. Around these precepts were constructed what seems to have confronted contemporaries as a virtually impregnable rationale for the British Empire's preservation. Critics were few enough, while true enemies of imperialism were rare within British political culture.

This book has explored the popularization of only one of the many imperialisms to which British audiences were exposed; it has also attempted to locate the appeal of this imperialism in the social relations, political struggles, and often righteous discontents that informed religious philanthropy at the local level.[39] This picture would no doubt look quite different if I had focused on other sites at which Victorians encountered the colonies. British politicians and officials, soldiers and seamen, emigrants and travelers, social scientists, health and other professionals, engineers, trade unionists, and consumers were all connected to the colonies by personal experience as well as by institutions, and these connections left imperialist marks upon British political culture that were no doubt distinctive one from the other. I suspect this story would also have turned out differently in subtle as well as not-so-subtle ways if it had been about another of Britain's numerous and diverse missionary organizations. The Church Missionary Society at one extreme and the Primitive Methodist Missionary Society at another mobilized very different social constituencies and no doubt bound them to the empire by different kinds of cultural and ideological ties, with different political outcomes at home as well as abroad, than did the LMS, on which I have focused.

Thus, while the language of empire and race may invoke a fairly narrow repertory of ideological themes, the considerable diversity below its social surface ensured that its meanings were multiple, often internally contradictory, and always complex. Even within the single institutional community established in relation to the LMS, the ideological work accomplished by missionary invocations of nation, race, and empire varied enormously by gender as well as by social class. Women were affected differently by their involvement in the mission cause than were men, and the rich were affected differently than were the poor. A closer look at missionary republics at home as well as abroad reveals Christian empires that were no less imperial for being under attack, and Christian republics that were no less liberating for those who managed entry because of their construction on the basis of racial privilege.

That popular support for missionary—or any other—imperialism can be understood in relation to the circumstances of deprivation and the politics of resistance in no way minimizes its implications for subordinate populations in the empire. As Barbara Fields has reminded us, popular longings may take the form of "fungus as well as flower."[40] And the fungus in this case, as in Fields's American South, was race. But as this narrative has demonstrated, race is just the point at which historical analysis begins. Racism is not a unified or cohesive ideology. Racial identifications take many and distinctive forms depending upon the social as well as the cultural and political context. Racial consciousness, moreover, did not diminish over the period surveyed in this book; to the contrary, racial attachments fluctuated in their intensity rather dramatically over the course of the nineteenth century, increasing if anything at the twentieth century's approach. In the missionary movement's early days, racial categories were more fluid than they would later be; the targets of missionary operations at home and abroad were not viewed as culturally much less biologically distinct. This is not, of course, to say that social hierarchy did not exist; the poor and colonized were alike viewed as damned, their salvation dependent on others' influence if not control. But the rationale for heathen subordination was not articulated, at least not primarily, in explicitly racial terms.

Racial distinctions between the targets of missionary outreach at home and abroad become more apparent during the second half of the nineteenth century. The missionary movement's embrace of civilization during the century's middle decades made possible the sort of cultural racism that Catherine Hall, among others, has argued distinguished missionary constructions of their non-European beneficiaries from other more biologically fixed racialisms then in circulation.[41] Also important was the shift to more incorporationist strategies of social control with respect to the working classes at home. The British nation was increasingly conceived of in terms that encompassed British society as a whole, which was both cause and consequence of the extension of the franchise in 1867 and, again, in 1884. While by no means viewed as equal, working people were acknowledged for the first time in the franchise to be of a kindred nationality.[42]

And it is race that functions as an important marker of and means by which working-class incorporation into this more inclusive nation was achieved.[43] Working-class inadequacies were more and more frequently framed as a racial disease threatening to infect the entire social body rather than as something outside, which the body politic could control.[44] And colonized peoples increasingly constituted the nation's racial boundaries. With respect to the missionary variation on this theme, it was by uniting in missionary outreach to the colonized that rich and poor Congregationalists combined to form a national community on the basis of a shared capacity to bestow the gift of foreign missions, a capacity that was explicitly denied to the racialized convert in the colonies.

Support for missions almost invariably assumed the missionary philanthropists' superiority to his or her beneficiary in the mission field—a "deformation of the gift" reflected in many working-class Christians' aversion to the mission label at home. There were, no doubt, exceptions, Christian Britons whose professions of brotherhood across the colonial divide reflected a genuine solidarity. (And these exceptions would become more common as the twentieth century progressed.) But the influence of hierarchical and often racist formulations of the missionary agenda was pervasive, encompassing even those who sought to resist the logic of missionary texts. Plebian radicals and socialists often defended the working class against missionary aspersions by claiming the fixed, if not the biological, otherness of those colonized peoples positioned by missionary discourse as working-class Britons' moral and social rivals. Here again, the critique of missions finds expression in a more conservative imperial vision than the missionary options being criticized. This is not, of course, because working-class people were inherently more racist than were the middle-class promoters of missions, nor because working-class people were easily duped. Rather, the ideological options available to working people were constrained within discursive parameters established by more powerful interests, whose control of institutions established a field of debate, outside of which it was extremely difficult, though not impossible, to venture. And herein lies the tragedy of this story for the British nation's imperialist working class as well as for the empire's subject races. By embracing the nation and especially race as a language of class struggle, missionary supporters and their critics alike helped keep the workers of the world divided.

Reference Matter

Notes

Chapter 1: Introduction

1. Nightingale, 37.   2. Alexander, 182.

3. Nightingale, 37.   4. Ibid., 19.

5. Thompson, *The Making of the English Working Class*, 219.

6. Himmelfarb, *The Idea of Poverty*, 307–70; and Jones, *Outcast London*, especially Part 3: "Middle-Class London and the Casual Poor."

7. Cited in McCord, *British History 1815–1906*, 225.

8. Quoted in McLaughlin, 103. See also Nord.

9. Pioneering exceptions include Davin; Hall; Walkowitz; Burton; and Mackenzie.

10. Such assumptions would account, at any rate, for that scholarly asymmetry about which Dipesh Chakrabarty has complained: while Third World scholars typically find it necessary to familiarize themselves with European historiography's method as well as with its content, European histories are generally void of references to colonialism or to contemporary Third World scholarship. Mary Pratt, too, criticizes precisely this "imperial tendency to see European culture emanating out to the colonial periphery from a self-generating center," a tendency that "has obscured the constant movement of people and ideas in the other direction" (90). Complaints to this effect have multiplied in recent years. See Mackenzie, *Imperialism and Popular Culture*, 1–16; Marks; Burton, "Rules of Thumb"; and Gregg and Kale.

11. See Thompson, *Alien Homage*. George Orwell, for example, attributed his conversion to socialism to his observations of the workings of colonial power while he was serving in the Burmese police. See *Road to Wigan Pier*, 173–85. Eric Hobsbawm, born in Alexandria, Egypt, was also formed at the crossroads of empire; see Kaye, 132.

12. Although as Shula Marks reminds us (114), Thompson makes suggestive reference to the colonial prefiguring of metropolitan labor relations in *Writing by Candlelight*. Thompson's failure to integrate imperial developments into the bulk of his social history in a more systematic manner was not a function of indifference to colonial exploitation. His father was an active supporter of Indian nationalism, and Thompson grew up in an atmosphere steeped in south Asian culture and anticolonial politics. That Thompson's father and possibly Thompson himself, like many European fellow travelers of colonial nationalist movements, failed to transcend the white-supremacist assumptions of their own intellectual and political formation is of crucial importance for understanding the limits of, as well as the limits imposed by, his work (Gregg and Kale). However, Thompson's own unwavering opposition to the British colonial project and to neocolonial development policies must also be acknowledged; note, for example, his indictment of western development strategies in "Time, Work-Discipline and Industrial Capitalism." I would add that Thompson's social historical work provides us with the methodological capacity to explore the linkages his critics chastise him for ignoring; I thank Fred Cooper for reminding me of my debt to Thompson here.

13. On the continued insularism of the social historical project, see Eley's "Playing It Safe." E. J. Hobsbawm (*Industry and Empire*) and Victor Kiernan (*Imperialism and Its Contradictions*) have been exceptional in this as in so many other regards.

14. For more or less explicit denials of imperialism's influence on popular and working-class culture, see Pelling; Price, *An Imperial War*; and G. S. Jones, "Working-Class Culture and Working-Class Politics in London, 1870–1900."

15. See, for example, Cain and Hopkins.

16. The quote is from Innes, 171–72; a wrenching indictment of this gloss on popular culture is found in Steedman, *Landscape for a Good Woman: A Story of Two Lives*.

17. J. C. D. Clark, 42.

18. This point is made in Richard Price's important critique of the narrowing thrust of recent revisionist historiography, "Languages of Revisionism," 245. My thanks to Professor Price for allowing me to read this article prior to its publication.

19. The exception that proves this rule is J. G. A. Pocock's recent call for a broadening of the national subject in imperial directions. Pocock explicitly excludes from the colonies to be included in his larger Britain those not populated by "British" cultural stock; this would exclude most of the people governed by the British Empire during the nineteenth century (319, 330). The geographical boundaries of the British historical subject are being stretched in what I consider more productive ways. Kearney, for example, takes seriously subnational variations within the United Kingdom. British historians are also increasingly attentive to their nineteenth-century subjects' interest in and identification with developments on the continent; see, for example, Biagini; Finn; and O'Connor.

20. Colley, "The Imperial Embrace," 97–98. I am not sure how to square Colley's sentiments in this article with those expressed in "Britishness and Otherness," in which she argues that "the consequences of this imperial episode [the acquisition of the so-called second British Empire after 1783] in terms of the forging of a British identity were extensive, though as yet they have hardly begun to be explored" (324).

For skepticism about the empire's importance in British political culture, see also M. Taylor, "John Bull," 94, and "Patriotism, History and the Left in Twentieth Century Britain," 987.

21. The impact of empire, in other words, need not have been fatal nor all-determining in order to be of sufficient significance to warrant systematic study; see Marshall, "No fatal impact?" 8–10.

22. For two early and influential studies of colonialism's reverberations within metropolitan Europe, see the works cited by anthropologist Eric Wolf and by anthropologist Sidney Mintz.

23. We need more detailed knowledge about the numbers of British people who experienced the empire directly and about the impact of that experience on their political and social attitudes. Of these personal or direct connections between Europe and its colonies, only travel writing has, to my knowledge, been examined in any systematic way; see, for example, Pratt; see also John M. Mackenzie's "Studies in Imperialism" series with Manchester University Press; Temperley; Drescher; Midgley; Cameron; and Semmel, *Imperialism and Social Reform*.

24. See Tabili; Faith Lois Smith; and Burton, *At the Heart of the Empire*.

25. The Society for the Propagation of the Gospel (SPG) had been founded almost a century before in 1701, but it ministered primarily in and around European settlements rather than targeting the "heathen" populations beyond.

26. I am quoting here from a sermon by the Rev. Arthur Tidman, delivered at the annual meetings of the LMS in May of 1845. Tidman's remarks are quoted in Lovett, 2:675.

27. Seed, "Unitarianism, Political Economy and the Antinomies of Liberal Culture in Manchester, 1830–1850," 2–3.

28. Olive Anderson, 467. According to J. F. C. Harrison, "The churches were still the great arbiters of public attitudes towards social issues" as late as the 1870s (133).

29. For a compelling evaluation of the persisting influence of organized religion in Britain throughout the nineteenth century, see McLeod, "New Perspectives," 31–49; see also Laqueur.

30. Bebbington, *Evangelicalism*, ix, 105.

31. Jemima Thompson, xiii–xiv.

32. The home organizational apparatus of British foreign missionary societies is described in Prochaska's important article, "Little Vessels," 103–18; and in Brian Stanley, "Home Support for Overseas Missions."

33. See Moffat, *Lives of Robert and Mary Moffat*, 4.

34. These were the sentiments of Robert F. Horton, who ministered at the very prestigious Congregational chapel in Hampstead. In his autobiography, Horton insisted that being a missionary was "the greatest thing a man can do upon earth," and that those on the home front "can only make up for our inferiority by frankly owning which order comes first, and by using all our opportunities and powers to send and to support the pioneers" (68, 233, 349).

35. Illustrations of missionary boxes and traveling caravans are plentiful in the archives of the LMS.

36. *London Quarterly Review* 7 (1856), 239; quoted in Cecil Peter Williams, "The Recruitment and Training of Overseas Missionaries," chap. 1, n. 25.

37. See Brian Stanley, *The Bible and the Flag*, 61, and "Home Support for Overseas Missions," 280. See also Frederic Stuart Piggin, "The Social Background, Motivation, and Training of British Protestant Missionaries," preface.

38. Andrew Walls, "British Missions," 164.

39. Piggin, "The Social Background, Motivation, and Training of British Protestant Missionaries."

40. See Mary Turner, *Slaves and Missionaries*; John Comaroff; and Langmore.

41. See Beidelman; Langmore; John Comaroff; and da Costa.

42. I thank John Cell for pressing me on this point.

43. Andrew Porter, "'Commerce and Christianity,'" 620; see also Andrew Porter, "Religion and Empire."

44. The most famous example being the LMS's Rev. John Smith, who was sentenced to death by an angry planter legislature convinced of his complicity in a slave rebellion (see da Costa). Charles Abel, another LMS missionary, had to travel in Papua, New Guinea, with an armed escort to protect himself from white settlers' outrage over his efforts to bring to justice the European murderers of three unarmed Papuans (Langmore, 222). See also Catherine Hall, "The Economy of Intellectual Prestige."

45. Robert Strayer, "Mission History in Africa"; and Jean and John Comaroff. See Landau for a dissenting view.

46. Cited in Nemer, 134.

47. Leeds' millionaire Robert Arthington contributed £5,000 to the LMS in 1859 for "the moral conquest of Africa"; see Horne, *The Story of the LMS, 1795–1895*, 259.

48. These statements are from Livingstone's obituaries in *Dublin University Magazine*, 83 (Apr. 1874), 464; and *Geographical Magazine* 1, (May 1874), 46.

49. According to John M. Mackenzie, Livingstone was "the greatest heroic myth of the [nineteenth] century"; see "Heroic Myths of Empire," in *Popular Imperialism and the Military: 1850–1950*, 114.

50. *Dublin University Magazine*, 51 (Jan. 1858), 61, 63.

51. J. A. Ross, "How Missions Prevent War." Reginald Thompson similarly expressed satisfaction over the fact that "in all the tribes where the Livingstonia missions preceded Government, no military expedition was necessary." See Reginald Thompson, 94.

52. See, for example, the correspondence between W. M. Onslow-Carleton and R. W. Thompson about compulsory labor practices at the LMS mission in Matabeleland, July 13, 1910, Incoming Letters, Home, LMS Archives. See also Thomas C. Holt's discussion of liberal resort to force in Jamaica in *The Problem of Freedom*; Saunders; and Northrup.

53. Missionary reports from Central Africa, for example, complain about the "considerable difficulty with them [student converts] at first because of conceit and an inclination to show themselves superior to their usual tasks and to discipline. This trouble is constantly before the Livingstonia authorities and ourselves and we are all do-

ing our best to cope with it. Is it not incident with all transition stages?" See Dr. W. McFarlane to R. W. Thompson, Apr. 20, 1909, Incoming Letters, Home, LMS Archives; see also William Govan Robertson to R. W. Thompson, May 18, 1909, Incoming Letters, Home, LMS Archives.

54. I want to thank Njoroge Wainaina and the Rev. Shane Benjamin of Good Shepherd United Methodist Church, Durham, N.C., for pressing this point in conversation. See also Hamid; Jean Comaroff; and Landau.

55. Karen E. Fields.

56. Peter Marshall suggests as much in "Imperial Britain," 381.

57. Viswanathan, 12.

58. The secondary literature on British missions in their foreign fields of operation is massive; I am most familiar with the African material. In addition to the works already cited, see Ajayi; Ayandele; Ekechi; Etherington; Kooiman; Ranger and Weller; Rotberg; and Mary Turner.

59. Brian Stanley, "Home Support for Overseas Missions"; Prochaska, "Little Vessels"; Laqueur.

60. Missions functioned to legitimize and even encourage imperial interventions in much the same way that Weber has suggested Protestantism more generally helped to incite capitalism; see Max Weber, *The Protestant Ethic*.

61. For a penetrating survey of this historiographical sleight of hand, see Burton, "Rules of Thumb."

62. See Mackenzie, "Introduction," *Imperialism and Popular Culture*, 1–16.

63. See Paul Gilroy, *"There Ain't No Black in the Union Jack"*, especially chap. 2.

64. This literature has mushroomed in recent years, and to survey it here is beyond my ability. I have been influenced most by Said, *Orientalism*, and *Culture and Imperialism*; Viswanathan; Suleri; and by the work of John M. Mackenzie, including the works published under his editorial auspices in Manchester University Press's "Studies in Imperialism" series.

65. Marks, 115.

66. Ibid, 114.

67. Or, as Nicholas Thomas has put it, "Only localized theories and historically specific accounts can provide much insight into the varied articulations of colonizing and counter-colonial representations and practices" (ix).

68. The Irish, the Welsh, and especially the Scottish contribution to British foreign missions was considerable. But it was also, and I think more importantly, distinctive in ways that require systematic local study on a scale and in languages I am unequipped to deal with here. Issues of subnationality as well as ethnicity will no doubt generate different outcomes than those I recount here. See, for example, Hempton, "Women and Evangelical Religion in Ireland;" Mackenzie, "David Livingstone."

69. Clyde Binfield is exceptional in this regard. See his *So Down to Prayers*; *George Williams and the Y. M. C. A.*; and "Asquith."

70. McLeod, *Religion and Society in England, 1850–1914*, 28.

71. From undated/untitled news clipping found in the records of the Market Harborough Congregational Church, Leicester Record Office, DE 3190/122.

72. Thorne, 74–75.

73. On the continuities across the denominational spectrum of Victorian Evangelicalism, see Mark Smith, 4.

74. My concerns about the revisionist retreat from class analysis are developed more fully in Mayfield and Thorne.

75. This is the general thrust of the argument in Mackenzie, *Imperialism and Popular Culture*, and many of the other volumes in the "Studies in Imperialism" series published by Manchester University Press. Tabili is exceptional in this regard.

76. Contrast Anna Davin's integration of class and race, and of social and imperial histories, to the retreat from class analysis in preference for race announced in Michelle Barratt's introduction to the revised edition of *Women's Oppression Today*.

77. Although see Louise Tilly's important admonishment to European historians to engage these connections between class formation in Europe and its colonies.

78. See Beidelman, especially chap. 3; and Comaroff and Comaroff, especially chap. 2.

79. Douglas Lorimer argues that class was the prototype for racial thinking in Britain as well.

80. See Ann Laura Stoler, "Rethinking Colonial Categories."

81. Briggs, "The Language of 'Class' in Early Nineteenth-Century England." The *Oxford English Dictionary* claims that the first reference to "class" as a sociological grouping is in Josiah Hanway's 1772 pamphlet, *Observations on the Causes of the Dissoluteness which reigns among the lower classes of people*.

82. Or as Catherine Hall has recently put it, "In the England of the 1830s and 1840s religion provided one of the key discursive terrains for the articulation . . . class, gender and ethnicity as axes of power"; see "Missionary Stories: Gender and Ethnicity in England in the 1830s and 1840s," in *White, Male and Middle Class*, 207.

83. Laqueur; R. Tudur Jones.

84. Lovegrove.

85. Howsam.

86. Seed, "Unitarianism, Political Economy and the Antinomies of Liberal Culture in Manchester"; Kidd.

87. Although see Ann Stoler's admonition that we not treat "bourgeois 'civilizing missions' in metropole and colony as though they were independent projects"; *Race and the Education of Desire*, 15.

88. See Thorne, "Protestant Ethics and the Spirit of Imperialism," especially chaps. 1 and 2.

89. Alexander, 194.

90. *Social imperialism* is a term coined by German historians to describe Bismarck's attempt to use colonial policy to the domestic political end of diverting public attention away from controversial domestic issues. See Eley, "Social Imperialism"; and Harcourt.

91. Important recent examples include Stoler, *Race and the Education of Desire*; and McClintock.

92. Davin; Catherine Hall, *White, Male and Middle Class*; Midgley; Ware; Burton, *Burdens of History*.

93. See especially Vicinus, 250–51; Rendall, especially chap. 3; and Levine, *Victorian Feminism 1850–1900*, chap. 4.

94. I am not trying to suggest that these denominations' engagement with the empire is less interesting than is that of my Congregationalists; I am simply pointing out that their institutional, social, and political differences probably rendered the meaning and impact of missionary imperialism different within their ranks.

95. Bebbington, *The Nonconformist Conscience*, and "Nonconformity and Electoral Sociology, 1867–1918."

96. Even when liberal or progressive support for imperialism is acknowledged, it is usually understood as an inconsistent reaction to a national emergency—e.g. Nonconformists' "conversion" to imperialism during the jingo hysteria of the 1890s and 1900s. See Bebbington, *The Nonconformist Conscience*, 106.

97. Opportunistic in the sense that they accepted imperialism as an evil that was necessary to finance progressive ends at home, a formulation that retains the conception of imperialism and reform as antagonistic political principles, their coincidence an "unnatural" union of contradictory commitments. See, for example, Semmel, *Imperialism and Social Reform*; Searle, *The Quest for National Efficiency*; and Price, *An Imperial War*, especially 71–80.

98. Paul.

99. Snell was secretary of the Labor Commonwealth Group of members of the Parliamentary Labor Party for seven years. He was insulted by South African suspicions of his imperial loyalties as a socialist while he was touring Britain's southern African territories with a delegation of the Empire Parliamentary Association. However, while Snell was more than willing to continue Conservative Party policies of censoring films shown to African audiences of all reference to "sex-disloyalty" or drunkenness among Europeans, he did resign from his position as parliamentary undersecretary in 1931, fearing "that under a Government which was predominantly Tory in composition I might find myself associated with acts of repression in India which I could not have defended." See Henry Snell, *Men, Movements and Myself*, 5, 211, 219, 235, 253.

100. Cited in Darwin.

101. Cox, 170–71. Cox's study is one of the few that acknowledges the evangelical contribution to progressive politics and social reform. See also Fraser, especially 115–23.

102. See Cox, 171.

103. Stead, 301.

104. Ibid., 142, 154. Henry Snell similarly invoked imperial legitimation of his socialism. Referring, for example, to the extreme exploitation of agricultural laborers in Britain, Snell ridiculed only the hypocrisy and not the principle behind Great Britain's claims to be "engaged in the breeding of a proud imperial people." See *Men, Movements and Myself*, 5.

105. For a general survey of this period, see Stuart Hall, "The Rise of the Representative/Interventionist State."

106. See Matthew Price, "A Moral Consensus for Reform: Progressive Politics and the Social Gospel in Britain and the U.S., 1890–1920," paper presented at the Social Science History annual meeting, New Orleans, November 1996.

107. Holt, "Marking," 7. Within this space, it must be said, the empire was not the only determinant of an emergent racial consciousness, nor was color its only coordinate. See, for example, David Feldman, *Englishmen and Jews*.

Chapter 2: The Birth of Modern Missions

1. Jemima Thompson, xiv–xv.

2. See Latourette, vol. 2; see also Alden.

3. Neill, *A History of Christian Missions*, 220–22; and Bebbington, *Evangelicalism*, 40–41.

4. For a concise account of these developments, see Brian Stanley, *The Bible and the Flag*, 56–57.

5. Murray; Dharmarah.

6. Brian Stanley, *The Bible and the Flag*, 61; see also Piggin, "Halévy Revisited."

7. I have borrowed this suggestive term from Lawrence Goodwyn.

8. Expression borrowed from Hobsbawm's classic *Age of Revolution*.

9. John Wesley, quoted in North, 18.   10. Armstrong.

11. R. Tudur Jones, 109.   12. Watts, 450–64.

13. Rupp, 112.   14. Ibid., 259.

15. Owen, 11–16.   16. Andrew.

17. Andrew Porter, *Atlas of British Overseas Expansion*, 124. See also Neill, *A History of Christian Missions*, 226; and Latourette, 3: 49.

18. Stevenson.   19. Armstrong, 60.

20. Quoted in Heitzenrater, 58.   21. Heitzenrater, 67; Armstrong, 60.

22. Missionary hostility toward those whose souls they served to save was particularly in evidence at the LMS's mission stations in Matabeleland; see Carnegie.

23. Quoted in North, 18.

24. Wesley's disgrace went far beyond the failure of his Indian ministry; he was effectively run out of Savannah by angry colonists who were incensed by his refusal of communion to a woman he had courted and the new husband to whom he'd lost her; see Heitzenrate, 69–71.

25. Quoted in Heitzenrater, 80.   26. Watts, 394.

27. Ibid., 396–97.   28. Ibid., 440–45.

29. R. Tudur Jones, 109. It was the Welsh revivalist, Howell Harris, who professed to these desires after his conversion in 1735; see Watts, 396.

30. See Watts, 450–56.

31. Gilbert, 32–36. Gilbert cites incidence of chapel registration as proof of the marked decline in Congregational numbers after 1710.

32. R. Tudur Jones, 147–48.

33. And, according to North, early Methodist philanthropy continued to emphasize the importance of works (See North, 13).

34. This trajectory was perhaps unique to Great Britain. With the single exception of Spain, no other major colonial power looked to colonies for the purposes of large-scale settlement, as had the British in North America, which was the unrivaled jewel in the eighteenth-century colonial crown. (Except for Quebec, French intentions in North America, like Dutch involvement in the East Indies, had more to do with trade than with settlement.) As Ann Stoler has pointed out to me, the considerable European settlement, which did subsequently take place elsewhere, succeeded and was always subordinate to conquest.

35. Valenze, "Charity, Custom, and Humanity," 59–78.

36. The following discussion, is heavily indebted to Andrew, especially chaps. 5 and 6.

37. Owen, especially Part 1: "Philanthropy in the Age of Benevolence (1660s–1780s)."

38. This was not immediately made apparent. The problem of governance would remain on the back burner in India, for example, for thirty odd years after British dominance was guaranteed; extraction continued to be the dominant modus operandi here as in North America, as evidenced in the vast nabob fortunes accumulated after 1763. Curbing these abuses was the purpose of the reforms enacted by Cornwallis during the 1790s. See Bayly, *Indian Society*, 65.

39. Crafts, 44–59.

40. See K. D. M. Snell, chap. 4. This period would also see the beginnings of a new variant of settler colonialism, with Australia and New Zealand being developed to absorb Britain's "surplus" (unemployed and/or criminal as well as radical) population. It seems to me that these colonies were positioned in relation to Britain very differently than was their North American predecessor; they were valued less for economic reasons than as political and demographic safety valves.

41. Boyer, especially chap. 2.

42. According to K. D. M. Snell, poverty and unemployment were the cause rather than the consequence of the increased birthrate in this period. The decline in arrangements whereby agricultural laborers lived in with their employers coupled with the drastic drop in the availability of agricultural opportunities for women forced women and allowed men to marry earlier, and this resulted in married couples producing more children (157–63).

43. Wilks, 8, 12–13.

44. Ibid.

45. On the connections between Anglican and largely Tory evangelicals and Poor Law reform, see Hilton; see also Mandler, "Tories and Paupers."

46. To be sure, "the English had always considered Asians and Africans inferior," but, as Christopher Bayly has argued, "these attitudes had rarely been codified or rigid and they had only limited effect on the political hierarchies of colonial territories which perforce had included indigenous rulers and merchants" (*Imperial Meridian*, 3–8). See also Linda Colley, "Britishness and Otherness."

47. These remarks were uttered in a sermon given in 1792, quoted in Morison, 192.

48. Colley, *Britons*.

49. Blackburn, 11.

50. James, "The Attractions of the Cross."

51. Perham, *African Apprenticeship: An Autobiographical Journey in Southern Africa 1929* (New York: Africana Publishing Co., 1974), 27–8; cited in Strobel, 44.

52. Conservative proconsul, Lord Curzon, quoted in McCord, *British History*, 426.

53. The nature of the relationship between the middle class and the industrial fraction therein and the landed elite has been the subject of considerable debate. Important interventions include J. C. D. Clark; Langford; Cain and Hopkins; Daunton, 137–40; Andrew Porter, "'Gentlemanly Capitalism' and Empire;" Berg and Hudson, 43–44; and Seed, "From 'Middling Sort' to Middle Class," 128–29.

54. On the political influence of middle-class Dissent at the local level, see Watts, 482–83; and Perry.

55. Obelkevich, *Religion and Rural Society*.

56. As Anthony Howe and Patrick Joyce, among others, have pointed out, entrepreneurial vitality found expression across the denominational spectrum. The majority of cotton manufacturers, to take the most representative industrial and entrepreneurial fraction within British capital, were not Dissenters at all but Anglicans, and their number included many High Churchmen.

57. Such ties were facilitated by the presence in business circles of many younger sons of the landed elite; conversely, the landed classes replenished their finances by marrying their sons to the richly endowed daughters of Britain's increasingly wealthy bourgeoisie. See Perkin; though for a contrary view, see Stone and Stone.

58. By rational dissent I refer here to the Unitarians, who were even more likely than their evangelical counterparts to resort to explicitly radical challenges to the ruling practices of the landed elite. But their disinterest in missions ensured that their opposition would never find the mass support that might render it truly dangerous. See Seed, "Gentlemen Dissenters" and "Theologies of Power."

59. According to Hugh McLeod, "from 1789 on, the attack on the power and influence of the official churches was an integral part of any attack on the existing political order, and the demand for religious freedom and equality became an essential part of any programme of liberal reform"; see *Religion and the People of Western Europe 1789–1970*, v.

60. On the seriousness of Catholic threat, see Colley, "Britishness and Otherness," 316–23.

61. This cooperation was also a reflection of the "powerful controls of clientage" by which the middle class continued to be rendered dependent upon the Establishment. See E. P. Thompson, *Customs in Common*, 89; and Brewer, "English Radicalism," 339.

62. Seed, "Gentlemen Dissenters," 300; see also Phillips, especially 286–305.

63. O'Gorman, 159.

64. See Bayly, *Imperial Meridian*.

65. Colley, *Britons*; Bayly, *Imperial Meridian*. See also P. J. Marshall's distinction be-

tween the libertarian imperialism of the eighteenth century and its authoritarian successor against which missionary imperialists rebelled; 8–10.

66. From an untitled sermon by the Rev. David Bogue delivered in 1705, quoted in Morison, 187.

67. Wilcox, 84.

68. Griffin, 19–20.

69. Quoted in Mason.

70. Cited in Warne.

71. Cited in Mearns, 11.

72. Dale, 604.

73. Cunningham, "The Language of Patriotism"; see also E. P. Thompson, "The Patricians and the Plebs," reprinted in *Customs in Common*, 92–93.

74. Kiernan, "Evangelicalism and the French Revolution," 53. Kiernan suggests that this was primarily the position of diehard High Churchmen, which he contrasts with the forward-looking vision of Wilberforce, More, et al.

75. Quoted in James Ross, 44.

76. Morison, 185. The following discussion of Bogue is taken from Morison.

77. While unsuccessful, the repeal campaign was but the opening round in British radicalism's initial response to the revolutionary fervor in France. Corresponding committees were convened throughout the country, sympathetic manifestos were issued, and debate was hotly entered. See Bradley.

78. I thank John Seed for reminding me that this claim does not apply to the empire or to Ireland, where repression many times before and since far exceeded in ferocity the reprisals directed against radicals in England in this period.

79. John Bowles in *The Anti-Jacobin* (October 1800), 87; quoted in Ford K. Brown, 169.

80. On the establishment's adjustment of radical forms—namely mass mobilization—to conservative political ends, see Philp; also see Hilton. The battle between missionary and more traditional modes of authority was fought within the church as well as between it and evangelical Dissent. More faced considerable opposition from within the Anglican community to her campaign to educate the poor. See Kiernan's juxtaposition of the forward-looking nature of the evangelicalism of the Clapham Sect to diehard High Churchmen's opposition to all forms of popular mobilization; "Evangelicalism and the French Revolution," 53.

81. See E. P. Thompson, *The Making of the English Working Class*, 56–57.

82. Rev. David Bogue was still described in an Anglican obituary published 50 years later as a "bitter and somewhat revolutionary political Dissenter"; see Morison, 180.

83. Morison, 187–88; and Calder, 2–3.

84. Norman, 31; Lovegrove, chaps. 6 and 7; and E. P. Thompson, *The Making of the English Working Class*, especially chap. 5.

85. At least this is what the establishment's evangelical competition triumphantly claimed a generation later. In a sermon delivered before the LMS's directors in 1826, the Rev. John Griffin argued that "The horrid deeds of massacre and blood, perpetrated in Paris, terrified the friends of order and justice of every station and rank in the kingdom. The great infidels and the infidel great were terrified at their own shadows. The rulers, and the upper ranks of society, began to acknowledge that

Christianity was the only effectual barrier that could oppose the demoralizing and destructive career of atheism. Facts had taught the superior orders, that religion, and the religious, were the best friends to the well-being of the state" (19–20).

86. Wicks, "Bristol's Heathen Neighbors," 21.

87. This according to Burls, 25.   88. See Pope, 105.

89. Lovegrove, 157–60.   90. Inglis, 11.

91. Lovegrove, 135–37; Penelope Carson. For a contrary view, see Stanley, *The History of the Baptist Missionary Society 1792–1992*, 26.

92. See Halévy; Semmel, *The Methodist Revolution*.

93. Or as Bayly has put it, the divide "between dissenting evangelicals and conservative Anglicans, which bulked large in England, often dissolved in the colonial context;" see *Imperial Meridian*, 137.

94. It was only in the face of a groundswell of resistance to these initiatives from below—on the parts of slaves, Irish peasants, and native Indians—that their initial enthusiasm for independence turned, and very quickly, into its opposite. The Crown's protection was sought out, and British officialdom's way left clear, to institute a dramatic round of colonial reforms that resulted in a far more centralized and authoritarian colonial state than had heretofore governed a colony on Great Britain's behalf. Bayly, *Imperial Meridian*, 5–6.

95. See, for example, John L. Comaroff.

96. See da Costa; see also Mary Turner.

97. Holt, *The Problem of Freedom*.

98. Etherington; Ajayi; Ayandele.

99. Bayly, *Imperial Meridian*, 144. See Antoinette Burton, *Burdens of History*.

100. This is one of many points in this narrative at which the agency of colonized peoples makes itself felt. But the sources of this agency—the aspirations that shaped indigenous peoples' embrace, appropriation, or rejection of the missionary message—have not been the subject of my archival inquiry. For studies specifically devoted to colonized people's response to missions, see Jean Comaroff; Kooiman; Dharmarah; and da Costa.

101. Mary Turner argues, for example, that many missionaries were not at the outset opposed to slavery, but that they were subject nonetheless to extreme forms of abuse by a suspicious planter elite; see especially chap. 1.

102. Wilcox, 79.

103. Langmore, 222; and da Costa.

104. Piggin, *Making Evangelical Missionaries*.

105. John Comaroff.

106. Latourette, 3: 49; Andrew Porter, *Atlas of British Overseas Expansion*, 124–27.

Chapter 3: "Congregationalism's Special Mission"

1. Binney, 9.

2. By none other than Matthew Arnold himself, who is quoted in Kay, 82.

3. For an important local study of this influential stratum, see Hennock, *Fit and Proper Persons*.

4. This quote is from Warne, 93; see also Howe, 68–69, 279; and Howkins, 180.

5. While "religious congregations in the towns and cities of early nineteenth-century England were rarely in any straightforward sense 'middle class' nevertheless the middle class were *overwhelmingly* affiliated to organized religion." Seed, "From 'Middling sort' to Middle Class," 130–31.

6. Salter, 2. According to Salter, "as the Industrial Revolution proceeded many Dissenters attained to considerable wealth as manufacturers and businessmen and the social level of the Dissenting communities was correspondingly raised."

7. McCord, *The Anti-Corn Law League 1838–1946*, 26–27.

8. McHugh.

9. See also Binfield, "Thomas Binney and Congregationalism's 'Special Mission.'"

10. The connections between religion and middle-class formation have long interested sociologists and social historians. See especially, Weber; Tawney; and, more recently, Seed, "The Role of Unitarianism in the Formation of Liberal Culture 1775–1851"; Davidoff and Hall; and R. J. Morris, *Class, Sect and Party*. Organized religion was not, of course, the only site of middle-class formation; see Nicholas Rogers, "Introduction," 299–304; and Money.

11. According to Koditschek, a consciousness of class was not manifested in Bradford until the 1810s (78); Briggs dates it slightly earlier, but notes, and Koditschek confirms, that evangelicals played a critical role in its articulation (10).

12. R. J. Morris, "Voluntary Societies and British Urban Elites," 101; and, most recently, *Class, Sect and Party*.

13. For information about the political mobilization of especially evangelical Dissent, see Binfield, *So Down to Prayers*; Bebbington, *The Nonconformist Conscience*; Brian Harrison; Hennock, *Fit and Proper Persons*; McHugh.

14. Which is not to say that missions were the only site at which the middle-class public engaged colonial questions or encountered colonized peoples. Commercial relationships, military and colonial service, and more inchoate connections established by the consumption of material goods, artifacts, and literature from or about the empire were all important. I do think, however, that missions mobilized more people on a more regular and emotionally charged basis than did any other of these media.

15. Comparative national statistics on Victorian philanthropy are notoriously hard to come by; for cautionary remarks see Owen, 169. I have sampled the records of Congregational chapels throughout England and have found few exceptions to the rule that foreign missions were the single largest beneficiary of Congregational collections for "outside" purposes; this is also asserted in passing by Obelkevich, *Religion and Rural Society*, 207–8; Howe, 273–79; Lovegrove, 219, n. 58; and Howsam, 187–88.

16. Quoted in Lovett, 2: 675. Despite missions' enormous popularity, historians of the middle class have only recently begun to explore the missionary movement's influence on middle-class formation in nineteenth-century England; see, for example, Catherine Hall, "Missionary Stories: Gender and Ethnicity in England in the 1830s and 1840s," in *White, Male and Middle Class*.

17. See for example Obelkevich, *Religion and Rural Society*, 207–8: "The trio of anniversaries—chapel, Sunday school and missionary—were great money makers as

well as popular festivals. It is remarkable that the Wesleyan Missionary Society, the most remote of these causes, held if anything, a greater appeal than any of the others."

18. See, especially, Catherine Hall, "Missionary Stories," in *White, Male and Middle Class*; see also Twells, "So Distant and Wild a Scene."

19. This, at any rate, is the thrust of Brian Stanley, "'Commerce and Christianity.'"

20. Although Catherine Hall's work is exceptional in this as in so many regards; see, for example, "Rethinking Imperial Histories"; see also Stoler, *Race and the Education of Desire*; and Mehta, "Liberal Strategies of Exclusion."

21. Cain and Hopkins, 132–33. This book takes issue with Cain and Hopkins' assumption that the only vital connection between Britons and the empire was that established at the sociological level of the gentlemanly capitalist classes. The importance of their work is reflected in the considerable critical commentary it has generated. Fieldhouse, for example, has argued that the City had no interests in Africa (which was, by contrast, an area of great interest to the provincial middle classes so prominent within evangelical Dissent). See also Andrew Porter, "'Gentlemanly Capitalism' and Empire"; Berg and Hudson, 43–44; and Daunton, 137–40.

22. "I do not see class as a 'structure', nor even as a 'category', but as something which in fact happens (and can be shown to have happened) in human relationships" (9); "Class is a relationship, and not a thing" (11).

23. See also Reddy, 24–25.

24. Or as Catherine Hall, summing up her own work with Leonore Davidoff, as well as the work of R. J. Morris, has put it: "In this context the establishment of arenas of public prestige which might enable them to build an alternative power base to that of the established aristocracy and gentry was vital. Voluntary associations provided just such an arena, and the period after 1780 was marked by the proliferation of scores of voluntary associations, based initially in the towns but moving out into the countryside with an extraordinary variety of aims and objectives." See "The Economy of Intellectual Prestige," 171.

25. Briggs, 13.

26. London Congregationalists were generally more receptive to centralizing initiatives (from which they were likely to benefit proportionally, being located in the center, as it were). In 1727, in connection with Baptist and Presbyterian ministers, they formed the General Body of Protestant Dissenting Ministers of the three denominations residing in and about the cities of London and Westminster. Selbie, *Congregationalism*, 115.

27. On Congregational resistance to the Methodist Revolution, see R. Tudur Jones, 160–61.

28. By old Dissent I mean those groups that cohered around the ministers ejected from the Church of England in 1662: Presbyterians, Baptists, Quakers, and Independents or, as the latter would be increasingly often referred to during the nineteenth century, on which this book focuses, Congregationalists. To these denominations we must add during the second half of the eighteenth century a small but influential body of Unitarians, most of whom had originated in secession from English Presbyterian chapels.

29. Bebbington, *Evangelicalism*, chap. 2. On the Wesleyan origins of most of the Congregational chapels in the West Riding of Yorkshire, see also Trigg, 5.

30. Or so intoned Philip David, a Congregational minister in Monmouthshire in 1775; quoted in R. Tudur Jones, 161.

31. R. Tudur Jones, 162–63.

32. The chapel opened in 1761; Whitefield died in 1770; see David Jones, 7. Given these stakes, the intensely critical self-scrutiny in the diaries of early Victorian Congregationalists comes as no surprise. See, for example, the diary (1828–1845) of Esther Morris, an earnest member of the Tabernacle Congregational Church in Lewes, East Sussex Record Office. My thanks to Christopher Whittick for drawing my attention to this family's records.

33. I borrow this phrase from R. Tudur Jones; see 162.

34. Like its counterparts elsewhere, the Congregational community in early Victorian Lewes was largely self-enclosed, and it is doubtful that Wille kept such views to himself. See Charles Wille the younger, Diaries, East Sussex Record Office.

35. Thomas Morgan, a Congregational minister at Morley, was an early critic of the Revival on just these grounds, complaining in a letter written in 1765 about the "unhappy *Divisions* almost in all the Congregations in the Kingdom chiefly occasion'd by *Methodistical Delusions*" (emphasis his). Quoted in R. Tudur Jones, 161.

36. Gilbert, 61.

37. McLeod, *Class and Religion*, 33; McLeod, *Religion and the Working Class*, 13–15; Gilbert, 63; and Laqueur.

38. McLeod, *Religion and the Working Class*; and "New Perspectives on Victorian Class Religion."

39. McLeod, *Religion and the Working Class*, 13. See also Laqueur; Obelkevich, *Religion and Rural Society*; and Valenze, *Prophetic Sons and Daughters*.

40. As discussed in chapter 2, the LMS's Anglican and Methodist supporters were effectively lost to the establishment of these denomination's own missionary institutions in the decades after the founding of the LMS.

41. Lovett, 1: 56.

42. The society was called into being at massively attended meetings in London on Sept. 22, 23, and 24, 1795.

43. Lovett, 1: 128–29.

44. According to the society's official historian, the "spiritual enthusiasm" of the society's founders was irrational in the extreme, inspiring the "advocacy by ardent friends of almost every kind of possible and impossible missionary enterprise." Many of the missions established in the society's early years (including those in Canada, South America, Malta, Mauritius, and on the continent) would have to be abandoned. See Lovett, 1: 65, 79, 92–97, 101, 105, 127; and 2: chap. 27.

45. That such marriages were fairly common in this early period is in stark contrast to the repugnance with which they were viewed in the closing decades of the nineteenth century, by which time a more biologically grounded racial discourse would all but preclude them.

46. Lovett, 1: 62–65.

47. Ibid., 1: 127.

48. So argued Rev. David Bogue, who professed to "higher ideas of the qualifications of missionaries" than others of his generation. The second party purportedly became "clamorous for money" upon the return to London—again a clear allusion to the base motivations attributed to the poor who were recruited to do the LMS's bidding. This was cited by the likes of Rev. Bogue as further indictment of the society's "hasty methods of selection." See Lovett, 1: 56–63.

49. The Rev. Bogue was one of the most prominent and influential Congregational ministers during this period; he was the minister of the Congregational chapel in Gosport from 1777 until his death in 1825, and he was also one of the principal figures involved in the founding of the LMS in 1795. See Lovett, 1: 60–62, 127.

50. Lovett, 1: 68–70. On the policies that followed thereafter, see Piggin, "The Social Background, Motivation, and Training of British Protestant Missionaries"; and Williams, "The Recruitment and Training of Overseas Missionaries."

51. Lovett, 1: 81.

52. "The traditional nonconformist conviction that all Christian work must be firmly based in the gathered congregation of Christ's people . . . was now being challenged by the impact of the new world of evangelical philanthropy, a world in which those who held the purse-strings would increasingly hold the power." Brian Stanley, *The History of the Baptist Missionary Society*, 28.

53. Joseph Hardcastle, who served as the society's treasurer from 1795 to 1817, was the "beau ideal of a great city merchant," who allowed if not insisted that the society's directors meet at his place of business at Old Swan Stairs, where he also helped to found the British and Foreign Bible Society (BFBS) as well as the Religious Tract Society (RTS). See Morison, 47–131.

54. Lovett, 2: 655–56.

55. Ibid., 2: 656.

56. Brian Stanley, *The History of the Baptist Missionary Society*, 27–28; Binfield, *George Williams and the Y. M. C. A.*, 41.

57. Lovett, 1: 81.

58. The LMS posted missionaries outside the formal boundaries of the empire as well, in places like China, Madagascar, and the South Pacific, but in these areas too European imperial influence was an ever-present concern.

59. Jim Obelkevich's description of the special resonance of missionary anniversaries in rural areas (where most Victorians lived) applies to many urban areas as well, at least during the first half of the nineteenth century. According to Obelkevich, the "respectable concourse and temperate conviviality . . . were very real attractions to villagers whose traditional fairs and feasts had come under attack from parsons and magistrates; but they were attractions that presupposed specific, and temporary, social conditions . . . the economic prosperity, the relaxation of class tensions, the sober and orderly behaviour of crowds; they also depended on the cult of preachers and on the continuing scarcity of respectable means of secular entertainment." See *Religion and Rural Society*, 210–13.

60. During the first half of the nineteenth century, however, the celebrity enjoyed

by foreign missionaries was almost unique. The royal family was extremely unpopular well into Victoria's reign, and the military's public standing plummeted after Waterloo and would not fully recover public support until the century's closing decades. See Cannadine. On the eventual displacement of the missionary hero by more muscular military and official figures, see Dunnae.

61. Moffat, *Lives of Robert and Mary Moffat*, 223. The demands on Moffat's time and energy during his so-called furlough from mission work were intense: "He was hurried from town to town with scant opportunity for a moment's rest." Moffat was finally taken ill, at which point he was allowed some respite.

62. Mackenzie, *Popular Imperialism and the Military*, 114. It was not until the closing decades of the nineteenth century that the British imperial tradition was recast in ways that associated it with monarchism and the military. Key turning points in this transformation of the British imperial ideal would include Victoria's investiture as Empress of India in 1877 and Gordon's ignominious defeat cum martyrdom at Khartoum in 1885.

63. Jan. 28, 1857, Incoming Letters, Home, LMS Archives. Barrett had served as a missionary in the West Indies from 1834 until 1848, whereupon he returned to England to a pastorate in Royston, Hertfordshire, from 1848 to 1855. Barrett (1812–1865) served as the society's Manchester District secretary (or organizing agent, as his successors would be called) from 1855 until 1859. Prout (1802–1871) served in a succession of pastorates in England, and for a brief spell was an itinerant minister in Ireland, before serving as the secretary in charge of the society's home organization from 1852 until 1865.

64. Quoted in Burton, "Fearful Bodies," 559.

65. Sibree, 70.

66. Ibid. The evidence I have examined testifies only to what my native British subjects believed these "native deputations" to have said. Whether or not these latter actually believed the words ascribed to them or even expressed themselves in the manner reported is a different matter altogether. Converts were carefully vetted before being brought to England and were coached upon their arrival as to what they should say, and many of them spoke, moreover, through the missionary translator who accompanied them. Even so, the society viewed their presence as a dangerous risk, and over the course of the nineteenth and early twentieth century it more and more often rebuffed the very frequent applications from its auxiliaries to make more "native deputations" available to home audiences. See, for example, LMS Archives, Board Minutes, Sept. 12, 1881; Apr. 9 1888; Apr. 23, 1888; and Feb. 28, 1905. See also Rev. E. A. Wareham's expression of relief that one Mr. Chatterji's speaking tour had not resulted as yet in "calamity"; LMS Archives, District Secretaries Reports, Sept. 16, 1904, Home, Odds, Box 16.

67. See Twells, "The Heathen at Home and Overseas."

68. A typical example is the diary of Esther Morris, East Sussex Record Office; see especially entry for Wednesday, May 14, 1828.

69. Quoted in Driver, 15.

70. The Essex Auxiliary of the LMS described one such ordination as "a sight

which the Committee trust elicited from their [the congregation's] hearts some sparks of that missionary flame which beams so brightly in the breasts of those who thus dedicate their labours and lives to the Redeemer's cause . . . a scene which they still hold in sweet remembrance." See Essex Auxiliary of the LMS, "The Second Report of the Essex Auxiliary Missionary Society, September 12, 1816," 7.

71. Moffat, *Lives of Robert and Mary Moffat*, 224.

72. Theddingworth Congregational Chapel, Minute Book of the Church Meetings, Leicester Record Office. The reference to Popery reminds us of the intense antipathy toward Catholicism that fueled evangelical missionary aspirations for most of the nineteenth century. British Protestantism's Catholic foil in the south Pacific was, of course, France. Closer to home it was the Irish, in England and Scotland as well as in Ireland, who were the Catholic subjects, or rather objects, of British Protestant missionary outreach. I thank Catherine Peyroux for reminding me that home and foreign missionary practice and their accompanying ideologies of class and race converged in missions to the Irish; for an excellent recent study, see Hickman.

73. Both reported in David Jones, 39–40.

74. Moffat, *Lives of Robert and Mary Moffat*, 237. One of those roused by Moffat's deputation tour was David Livingstone, who would eventually become Moffat's son-in-law and the LMS's most famous missionary. See Horne, *Story of the LMS*, 88.

75. Moffat, *Lives of Robert and Mary Moffat*, 237.

76. Ibid., 4–7; Jeal; Lovett, 1:238.

77. Seven of the ten were women, which required the congregation to resolve in 1837 that "since it had happened and may again happen, owing to our peculiar circumstances, that at our public prayer meetings there are no men present or not sufficient to conduct a prayer meeting, in future the female friends present shall conduct the meeting, and shall not retire without accomplishing the purpose for which they assemble. But this resolution is not to be acted upon when there is a sufficient number of men present to conduct the meeting." Theddingworth Congregational Chapel, Minute Book of Church Meetings; see especially the first entry and that for June 15, 1837.

78. See, for example, Beidelman, 50–51; and Comaroff and Comaroff, 73–75, 81.

79. Pratt.

80. Although he was not particularly sinful, Robert Moffat was set on his missionary course by William Roby, the minister at one of Manchester's most patrician chapels. John Williams was similarly rescued by his master's wife and her minister, Matthew Wilks. See Lovett, 1:239; and Moffat, *Lives of Robert and Mary Moffat*, chap. 1. This, as Catherine Peyroux has reminded me, is typical of the Samuel Smiles narratives so popular in this period.

81. These are the terms that Albert Spicer's daughter used to underscore the significance of his willingness to entertain missionaries in his home; see *Albert Spicer 1847–1934*, 26.

82. James, "The Attractions of the Cross," 29.

83. As late as 1900, the society was still refusing to allow its missionaries to sit on its board in a voting capacity. See LMS Archives, Board Minutes, Mar. 27, 1900.

84. Lovett, 1: 70–71. It was in this sense, of instilling self-denial and repressing any self-promoting propensity to challenge one's subordinate status, that missionary service represented what historian C. P. Williams refers to as a "bridge to the middle-class establishment and its values." see C. P. Williams, "'Not quite Gentlemen.'"

85. Macfadyen, 100.

86. Shalders to Rev. Arthur Tidman, LMS Foreign Secretary (1839–68), Apr. 19, 1866, LMS Archives, Home, Incoming Letters, Box 12.

87. This is a quote from a description of the annual meeting of the Leeds Auxiliary in the *Leeds Mercury*, Oct. 14, 1895, p. 4, but the sociology it observes was in play from the auxiliary's beginnings. According to Anthony Howe, "The cotton lord was a familiar figure at the Quarterly Meetings of Missionary Societies, which also benefited from sizeable bequests" (68–69, 279).

88. The element of display involved in the crowding of local notables onto missionary platforms was parodied in the personal correspondence of a missionary activist in Leeds in 1864: "J. D. Baines ought I think to be invited as representative of the Baineses, Mr. Yates and Mr. Conyers will no doubt—expect—a little say and then we shall have the grand army of whitechokers. . . . With 500 speakers we might get through the business of the meeting in 5000 minutes or 84 hours." Beeston Hill Congregational Church Records, Acc 2074, Item 41, Leeds Archives Department, Leeds. Baines, Yates, Conyers and the local whitechokers were all members of the Leeds Auxiliary of the LMS.

89. Brian Stanley makes much the same point with reference to the Baptists; the centralized administration, auxiliary system, and large public meetings violated the "traditional nonconformist conviction that all Christian work must be firmly based in the gathered congregation of Christ's people." See Brian Stanley, *History of the Baptist Missionary Society*, 28.

90. Or so claims Basil Matthews in his biography *Dr. Ralph Wardlaw Thompson*, 95.

91. See Thorne, 203–8.

92. Thomas Simpson to Prout, Nov. 12, 1859, LMS Archives, Home, Incoming Letters, Box 11, Folder 7.

93. The Leeds Auxiliary, for example, devoted a great deal of its energies to extending invitations to chair annual meetings to some of the most prominent men in the denomination and beyond—men such as Stephen Massie of Manchester, Mark Oldroyd, MP for Dewsbury, Sir Malcolm Didsworth of Harrogate, Edward Crossley of Halifax, and Wright Mellon, a JP from Huddersfield. Thorne, 211–12.

94. Wicks, "The Bristol Missionary Society," 28, LMS Archives. See also Chadwick, 401.

95. Brian Harrison; and Hollis, *Pressure from Without*.

96. Elie Halévy was one of the first historians to argue that foreign missions helped to deflect the potentially revolutionary energy of an emergent middle class away from the volatile British home front, thus providing a safety valve for tensions that might otherwise have found expression in more direct challenges to the ruling regime. See Elie Halèvy's influential *The Birth of Methodism in England*; see also Bernard Semmel's *The Methodist Revolution*. For an argument contrary to both Halévy's

and mine, see Piggin, "Halévy Revisited." Piggin denies that the Methodists supported foreign missions at the expense of their counterparts at home. My evidence suggests otherwise, at least where Congregationalists are concerned.

97. Davidoff and Hall, 21; and Catherine Hall, "The Economy of Intellectual Prestige," 169.

98. Cain and Hopkins, chap. 2.

99. James, "Attractions of the Cross," 6, emphasis his.

100. Borrows, 6–7.

101. Andrew Porter attributes the relative egalitarianism of missionary constructions of the heathen targets in this period to the fact that there was still relatively little opportunity to change one's status in British society during this period, hence even middle-class audiences were not likely to equate virtue with power or even with great wealth; see "Commerce and Christianity." According to Mary Pratt, British conceptions of West Africans became more respectful across the board in the closing decades of the eighteenth century as British interests in Africa shifted from slaves to markets; See Pratt, 71.

102. Johnston, 13.

103. Steven, 66.

104. Clayton, 4.

105. The missionary movement's antipathy to slavery would appear to be a social exception to this rule. However, as Mary Turner has argued (see chaps. 1 and 3), missionaries' objections to slavery were more a pragmatic response to planter obstruction than a social critique of the institution. And they had mainly to do with its legal interference in the free exercise of worship rather than with its social consequences.

106. Steven, 71.

107. Johnston, 17.

108. James, "The Attractions of the Cross," 20.

109. Pratt.

110. Johnston, 19.

111. Quoted in E. P. Thompson, *The Making of the English Working Class*, 42–43.

112. James, "Attractions of the Cross," 10.

113. John Pye Smith, 15.

114. See Brian Stanley, "Commerce and Christianity."

115. Harris, 25.

116. James, "The Attractions of the Cross," 12.

117. In fact, as Andrew Porter has pointed out, early missionary advocates went to great lengths to protect their missions from too close an association with trade or commerce as well as from political involvement. See "Commerce and Christianity," 601.

118. James, "Attractions of the Cross," 8.

119. See Scott. This privileging of rationality, and a rather functionalist variant at that, underlies the reduction of the missionary project to a duplicitous effort to distract attention from a home front that was all that really mattered.

120. "Interest" is far too crude a construct to render meaningful bourgeois Nonconformists' endurance of the public humiliations and private sacrifices by which

their religious practice continued to be penalized. By not conforming to the religious ordinances of the Established Church, Congregationalists were voluntarily subjecting themselves to a plain (however prosperous) living, voluntarily sacrificing the educational opportunities and political privileges in which their established counterparts took such pride. The very architecture of their chapels paid tribute to the sacrifice on which their collective esteem and political activism would increasingly be premised. London's Fetter Lane Congregational Chapel, like many of its urban counterparts, was built at the height of the Restoration to resemble a private home. This was not, as one might think, in order to counter the theologically unsound ostentation of the establishment's physical plant but, rather, to avoid the political recriminations of the establishment's defenders. Such chapels "never had frontages to the streets, but were always at the bottom of out-of-the-way courts, where exhortation and public prayers could not be overheard by passersby . . . and there was always a secret staircase for the minister's escape if the bishop's officers broke in." John Pye Smith, 7–8.

121. This was very much the tone of the literary indictment of the early Victorian evangelicalism, particularly its Dissenting variant; see especially Dickens, *Hard Times*; see also, Valentine Cunningham, *Everywhere Spoken Against*.

122. *Evangelical Magazine* (May 1845), cited in Lovett, 2: 655.

123. See, for example, Bennett; White; and Gosse.

124. Lovett, 2: 711.

125. Arthington bequeathed a similar sum to the Baptist Missionary Society; see Chirgwin.

126. Missionaries enjoyed their greatest success—as well as their worst setback—in the twentieth century. The consolidation of European colonial rule over most of the globe was not accomplished until the opening decades of this century, and it was quickly challenged in the outbreak of colonial nationalist resistance. Here, again, missionaries were affected by imperialism in contradictory ways. On the one hand, the colonial state put a premium on the educational opportunities that missions provided, thus encouraging conversion and lesser forms of association with the missionary presence. At the same time, however, the nationalist critique of colonialism was frequently extended to the missionary project and even to Christianity itself.

127. Quoted in Driver, 15.

128. Chirgwin, 19; see also Brian Stanley, "'The Miser of Headingley.'"

129. *Edinburgh Monthly Review*, Dec. 1819; quoted in Mearns, 11, 15.

130. Horne, *The Story of the L. M. S. 1795–1895*, 12–14.

131. Inglis, 11; Pope, 105; Lovegrove, 219, n. 58.

132. Mearns, 15–16.

133. Wicks, "Bristol's Heathen Neighbors," 21.

134. The Rev. Ralph Wardlaw continued, arguing that "the claim begins with the family, and enlarges its range progressively, to kindred, and friends, and country, and mankind," 41–42.

135. Campbell, 24.

136. James, "The Conversion of Englishmen," 3.

137. Joshua Wilson.

138. Blackburn, 46.

139. Baptist Home Missionary Society, *Annual Report*, 1857, 25–26.

140. Feb 22, 1859, LMS Archives, Home, Incoming Letter, Box 11.

141. Blackburn, 27; Wardlaw, 43.

142. Blackburn, 39.

143. Congregational Union of England and Wales Home Missionary Society, *Annual Report of the Home Missionary Society* (1858), 15: "For the most part, the objects of Home Mission sympathy and the fruits of such labour are the poor of the people."

144. These are characteristic examples of a rhetoric common to home missionary reports. These particular quotes are preserved in local chapel and home missionary society histories published anywhere from 50 to 100 years after their expression; see, for example, Headingly Hill Congregational Church, "The History of Headingley Hill Congregational Church," 20; Wicks, "Bristol's Heathen Neighbors," 33; and Darwent, 128.

145. Congregational Union of England and Wales, *Annual Report of the Home Missionary Society* (1858), 9.

146. Rev. Joseph Fletcher, 3–4.

147. Wardlaw, 41.

148. Joshua Wilson, 8.

149. See Holt, *The Problem of Freedom*, 309.

150. Harris, 35.   151. Steven, 56.

152. Gray, 47.   153. Davis, *The Problem of Slavery*.

154. The missionary movement's embrace of the civilizing mission in the second half of the nineteenth century will be examined in the next chapter. On foreign missions as atonement for British involvement in the salve trade, see Andrew Porter, "Commerce and Christianity"; on the shift in antislavery discourse from European to African villains, see Austen and Smith.

155. Stuart Hall, "Race, Articulation and Societies Structured in Dominance," 325.

156. Newcastle Town Mission, *Annual Report of the Newcastle Town Mission*, 4.

157. Campbell, 8.

158. London City Mission, *An Appeal for the London City Mission*, 5.

159. These comments from several different missionary sources are reported in Griffin, 38–39.

160. Quoted in Catherine Hall, "Missionary Stories: Gender and Ethnicity in England in the 1830s and 1840s," in *White, Male and Middle Class*, 216 and 218.

161. E. P. Thompson, *The Making of the English Working Class*, 346–48; see also Gray, 52.

162. The effort to distinguish between the deserving and the undeserving poor was one of the central motivations for the reform of the Poor Law. The New Poor Law did not, however, achieve these desired results. According to Himmelfarb, "the stigma of pauperism, which was meant to differentiate the pauper from the poor, had the perverse effect of stigmatizing the entire body of the poor, thus reinforcing the very ambiguity the reformers had so strenuously tried to remove." See *The Idea of Poverty*, 525.

163. The moral and fiscal capacity for philanthropy was an important mechanism of class differentiation—separating the respectable from the residuum and the wealthy from the poor; see Mandler, "Tories and Paupers," 87.

164. LMS, *Annual Report for 1807*, cited in Lovett, 1: 3. See also Brian Stanley, "Home Support for Overseas Missions," especially chap. 6.

165. Cited in Irene Fletcher, 227. Thanks in part to the success with which middle-class evangelicals controlled these institutions and to the propaganda produced therein, few sources remain that shed light on the meaning of missions to their working-class supporters in England during this first half century of the society's existence. A fuller study at the local level than I have been able to pursue here might well bring more such material to light, however. There is more evidence for the second half of the nineteenth century in the form of the unpublished reports of the society's organizing agents, which are examined in chapter 5.

166. Clayton, 18.

167. As Peter Mandler, "Tories and Paupers," and Boyd Hilton remind us, the establishment had its own variant of Christian political economy, although evangelical influence played a primary role therein.

168. Himmelfarb, *The Idea of Poverty*, 153.

169. Or, as Stuart Hall has so evocatively put it, evangelicals became "languaged" in and through their missionary imperial involvement; see "On Postmodernism and Articulation," 55.

170. African American historians have been more successful in forcing race onto the American historiographical agenda, but race has figured therein as the antidote to class and an alternative to class analysis. Pathbreaking exceptions include David Brion Davis, *The Problem of Slavery*; Barbara J. Fields; Roediger; and Holt, *The Problem of Freedom*.

171. Benedict Anderson; see also David Brion Davis, "Constructing Race."

172. See Gibbon; see also McClintock, 52–56.

Chapter 4: Telescopic Philanthropy

1. Livingstone.

2. *Times*, Feb. 15, 1858, p. 3.

3. For perceptive commentary on literary representations of Victorian evangelicals and the figure of the missionary therein, see Pope; Comaroff and Comaroff, 50–54; and Valentine Cunningham, *Everywhere Spoken Against*.

4. Brontë.

5. Carlyle, 278.

6. Dickens, "The Niger Expedition," 134.

7. See Ibid., 117. See also Faith Lois Smith, 115–17.

8. Thackeray, 446. Lady Emily eventually marries a missionary to South Africa (789).

9. For a fuller discussion of the gendered connections between the family home and the imperial home front, see McClintock, 32–36.

10. This accords with the chronology suggested by Poovey, *Making a Social Body*.

11. Booth, 1890.

12. I thank Catherine Peyroux for pressing me on this implication.

13. Especially since, as Norris Pope reminds me, these caricatures were in circulation well before the late 1840s and 1850s, on which I focus here. See, for example, Dickens, *The Posthumous Papers of the Pickwick Club*.

14. See, for example, Essex Auxiliary of the LMS, "The Third Report of the Essex Auxiliary of the Missionary Society," July 31, 1817. This predates the establishment of the first women's antislavery society in Britain in 1825, which included as one of its goals supporting missionary labors among the slave and free black population of the colonies; see Midgley, 43–44.

15. See Carr, 8; Leeds Auxiliary Committee Minutes, Aug. 30, 1830; and the LMS's *Quarterly News of Women's Work* (Apr. 1895), 39.

16. Peter Williams, 43–69; and Payne, 1.

17. Peter Williams, 55; Brian Stanley, *The History of the Baptist Missionary Society 1792–1992*, 220; Kirkwood, 32.

18. The LMS employed only 8 women prior to 1875. Between 1890 and 1894, however, it was dispatching almost as many women (50) as men (67), and receiving more applications from women than from men. See LMS Archives, Board Minutes, Feb. 23, 1892. On similar developments within the Church Missionary Society, see Pirouet, 231–40.

19. The initiative for separate women's meetings seems to have come from women themselves and to have been resisted by male missionary activists, who saw no need for the undue multiplication of further organizations. The LMS's board of directors rejected suggestions that a separate ladies' auxiliary be formed in 1870, although it was forced to capitulate in 1875. Male missionary advocates were reluctant no doubt to lose the services that their female auxiliaries had long provided. They were also anxious about losing control over the funds raised and/or donated by female missionary supporters. LMS Archives, Board Committee Minutes, Feb. 1, 1870.

20. Prochaska, *Women and Philanthropy*, 84.

21. Patricia R. Hill makes this argument for the United States (3), where, as in Britain, statistics were not collected in ways that illuminate national levels of participation. But one can surmise from the fact that women were overrepresented in the foreign missionary movement (that was in turn the most popular of the causes sponsored by an organized religion that mobilized about half of the population on a regular basis and probably a greater percentage of women, and especially of middle-class women) that the numbers involved far exceeded that of any other movement in which women participated in this period.

22. It was also a means of creating a sedentary population, particularly in mission fields disrupted by European colonialists' land and labor policies. See Andrew Porter, "Commerce and Christianity"; Schreuder; Brian Stanley, "Commerce and Christianity"; Webster; Dachs; and Kooiman.

23. Poovey, *Uneven Developments*, especially chap. 2.

24. This argument has been developed most forcefully by Leonore Davidoff and Catherine Hall.

25. Jemima Thompson, xix.

26. Steven, 56.

27. Livingstone's agenda supports the view that imperialism and free trade were by no means incompatible in this period; see Gallagher and Robinson.

28. Brian Stanley, "Commerce and Christianity," 83.

29. *Times* Sept. 10, 1857, p. 10.   30. Ibid., Feb. 10, 1860, p. 3.

31. Lloyd, 169.   32. Jemima Thompson, lxxviii.

33. *Times*, Nov. 28, 1859, p. 3.   34. Ibid., Nov. 17, 1856, p. 12.

35. Speech given by Rev. Thomas Matheson to the Leeds Auxiliary of the LMS, recorded in the *Leeds Mercury*, Oct. 3, 1890, p. 5.

36. On the extensive missionary work that missionaries' wives undertook prior to as well as after the entry of professional single women into the foreign mission field, see Kirkwood; Valentine Cunningham, "'God and Nature Intended You for a Missionary's Wife'"; and Catherine Hall, "Missionary Stories," in *White, Male and Middle Class*, 222–23.

37. LMS *Chronicle* (June 1885), 180.   38. Jemima Thompson, xv, lxxviii–lxxix.

39. Peter Williams.   40. *Leeds Mercury*, Oct. 3, 1883, p. 7.

41. *Is It Nothing to You?*, 3–4.

42. For similar argument with respect to American women's missions, see Newman, 16.

43. Jemima Thompson, xvii–xviii.

44. Miss Helen Davies, "Day School Work in Hong Kong," LMS *Quarterly News of Women's Work* (Oct. 1892), 108–9.

45. See Davidoff and Hall, especially chap. 9.

46. Although see Vickery's caution about the extent to which women actually lived in a separate gender sphere as well as about the efforts to connect this prescriptive discourse to social and economic developments specific to the nineteenth century.

47. Vicinus.

48. I was struck in reading Jemima Thompson's *Memoirs of British Female Missionaries* by how little attention is devoted to childbirth or child rearing in the correspondence and testimonies elicited.

49. See, for example, Jemima Thompson, xxiv–xxv: "To what extent, and under what circumstances, Christian women may even now engage in personal service among the degraded of their sex in foreign lands, must be left to the consciences of individuals, and to the Providence of God to determine. 'Let every one be fully persuaded in her own mind.' There is far less ground to question whether we ought not to embrace opportunities of preparing for such employment, in contemplation of the possibility of a divine call to the work. To make His Gospel known to every creature under heaven is the great duty of the Christian church; and nothing but obstacles interposed, or pious duties appointed by God Himself, can absolve us from taking our part in the diffusion. Ought we not all, therefore, to be ready to do so, in case those obstacles be removed?"

50. Jemima Thompson, xxv–xxvi.

51. Luke, 107.

52. Many of these women were convinced that the presence of men in their organizations would deprive them of both bureaucratic control and the opportunity to speak. It was with some regret that women experienced the amalgamation of these separate organizations in the opening decades of the twentieth century. One of the first female members of the Leeds Auxiliary of the LMS, which opened its committee to women in 1906, worried about "the diffidence of lady members in joining in discussion at the meetings" and complained about "the apparent hurrying of meetings to an early conclusion without full opportunity being given to each one to express their opinion." Leeds Auxiliary Committee Minutes, Oct. 19, 1906.

53. See Valenze, *Prophetic Sons and Daughters*; Olive Anderson; and Juster.

54. Some ministers refused to allow such innovations within their chapel; see correspondence from 1889 in LMS Archives, Home, Odds, Box 9, Folder 2.

55. *Newcastle Daily Chronicle*, Sept. 26, 1883, p. 4.

56. District Secretaries Report, Dec. 31, 1899, LMS Archives, Home, Odds, Box 16, Folder 1.

57. Such as one Mrs. Halley, an Australian woman who after visiting her missionary daughter in China became so excited about the mission cause "as to enable her to overcome her nervousness in speaking; and, since her return to Melbourne, she has spent a great deal of her time in addressing ladies' meetings, and telling of China's need for more workers." "Our Australian Auxiliary," by Mrs. Hamer of New South Wales, LMS *Quarterly News of Women's Work*, Oct. 1893, 120.

58. Martindale, 24.

59. Ibid., 43. Missionary involvement did not always translate into such an explicitly feminist politics as support for women's suffrage. The political content of the meanings ascribed to gender by mission ties to foreign fields varied considerably over denominational and social space. The middle-class Congregationalists on whom this study focuses were on the left wing of the evangelical spectrum, liberals almost to a man (and woman), and probably more sympathetic to political feminism than to any of the other mainstream denominations. English Congregationalism was certainly more open to women's activism than was Irish evangelicalism; see Hempton, "Women and Evangelical Religion in Ireland."

60. Burton, *Burdens of History*; and Newman.

61. Holt, *Problems of Freedom*.

62. See again Holt, *Problem of Freedom*; and Lloyd.

63. Stepan; Pick; Searle, *Eugenics*.

64. Catherine Hall, "Competing Masculinities," in *White, Male and Middle Class*.

65. Dickens, "The Niger Expedition," 133.

66. Dickens, *Letters*, 2: 889.

67. LMS *Quarterly News of Women's Work*, Oct. 1894, 110; Oct. 1895, 107.

68. Jemima Thompson, xvii–xviii.

69. See Brownfoot; also see Kirkwood, 37.

70. LMS *Quarterly News of Women's Work*, Jan. 1893, 19.

71. *Leeds Mercury*, Sept. 30, 1897, p. 6.

72. "A Talk About Some Betsileo Girls (Whom We Are Trying to Save From Their Surroundings)," LMS *Quarterly News of Women's Work*, Jan. 1894, 15–17.

73. "Day School Work in Hong," LMS *Quarterly News of Women's Work*, 108–9.

74. Extract from a letter from Mrs. Bridle of Canton to the "Quarterly Paper of the Wesleyan Ladies' Auxiliary," reprinted in the LMS *Quarterly News of Women's Work*, Jan. 1894, 31.

75. Cynthia Herrup has suggested similarities with seventeenth-century apprenticeship schemes designed to break the cycle of vagrancy, as it were, by apprenticing children deemed to be without adequate parental supervision to Christian taskmasters. I engage this theme more directly in a forthcoming study of the social construction of the orphan in Victorian Britain and the empire.

76. For a fascinating assertion that exclusionary impulses, including those of race, are intrinsic to liberal theory, see Mehta; that racism often takes culturalist forms is argued in Gilroy, *'There Ain't No Black in the Union Jack'*, especially chap. 2.

77. Poovey, *Making a Social Body*, especially chap. 1. See also Mandler, *The Uses of Charity*, 20; and Prochaska, *Women and Philanthropy*, 29.

78. Pick.

79. Steedman, *Childhood, Culture and Class*.

80. There are interesting parallels here with the American South. Segregation was not considered necessary under slavery, and close physical contact was commonplace. It was only after abolition's elimination of the absolute legal boundaries between slave and free communities that racial segregation became the order of the day. See Woodward.

81. William Thomas, 53–54.

82. Poovey, *Making a Social Body*, 45. See also Prochaska, "Body and Soul."

83. The first quote is from the 1878 Proceedings of the Mildmay Conference; the second is from the 1882 *Report of the London Missionary Society*, both quoted in Peter Williams, 51 and 57, respectively. Williams argues that the principal proponent of women's missions, Hudson Taylor of the China Inland Mission, was an admirer of Ellen Ranyard, and wanted to employ working-class women and men in mission fields abroad as well as at home. This faith missionary initiative, however, was not a significant factor in the LMS's embrace of women's missions; and even in the Church Missionary Society the social origins of women missionaries were significantly higher than were those of their male counterparts.

84. Ladies Committee Minutes, Mar. 8, 1876, LMS Archives. This predates the racialism of the 1880s and 1890s, which accounted for the removal of a number of non-European male native agents from their posts, suggesting that this argument was peculiar, at least in this period, to the women's mission cause. See Andrew Porter, "Cambridge, Keswick, and Late-Nineteenth-Century Attitudes to Africa."

85. Annie Pearson, "Work Among the Native Women in Peking," LMS *Quarterly News of Women's Work*, July 1892, 69.

86. Cited in McIlhiney, 43. The other striking finding of this census is that about half of Britain's churchgoing population attended Nonconformist chapels. This find-

ing was so controversial that the census would not record religious information for the rest of the century. The 1851 findings remained unrevised in the Victorian public consciousness and were repeatedly dusted off whenever commentators sought to underscore the pressing nature of the domestic need for missions.

87. Although as Margot Finn reminds us, popular radicalism remained alive and well during the middle period of the nineteenth century, in self-conscious contrast to the middle-class liberalism with which it was allied.

88. See Gareth Stedman Jones, *Outcast London*.

89. Cited in Wrigley, 63.

90. R. Tudur Jones, 297. Among the characteristic organizations Jones lists are the Young Men's Mutual Improvement Society, the Book Society, the Recreation Club for Young Men, the Penny Readings Society, the Redland Field Club, the YMCA, the YWCA, the Sunday School Teachers' Preparation Class, the Evening Classes Association, the Young Men's Missionary Society, the Youth's Bible Class, the Young Men's Literary Society, the Young Men's Liberal Association, the Society for Giving Prizes to Clean and Tidy Homes, and the Durdham Down Musical Band.

91. Stephen Yeo argues that the Institutional Church was both the site of popular religious practice in late nineteenth-century Reading and a "cause" of or contribution to the churches' losing their mass base of support. Popular constituencies bound to the church by secularized leisure activities were equally bound to leave it when the mass culture industry began churning out such provisions for a lower price in money and effort; see especially 308–31.

92. R. Tudur Jones, 295–97.

93. The first settlement house, Toynbee Hall, was founded in 1884 by graduates at Cambridge, under the supervision of Anglican Rev. Samuel Augustus Barnett. See McIlhiney, especially chap. 6.

94. R. Tudur Jones, 317–18.

95. Harry Jeffs, "The Brotherhood as a Missionary Force," in LMS *Universal Brotherhood* (Jan. 1912).

96. Ibid.

97. Congregational Union of England and Wales, *Our Sunday Schools*, 136.

98. Ollerenshaw, xxv–xxxiv.

99. LMS Archives, Deputation Reports, Dec. 31, 1885, Home, Odds, Box 9, Folder 4. See also Ibid., June 30, 1886, Mar. 31, 1886, and Mar. 31, 1889.

100. Lovett, 2: 728.

101. The Forward Movement involved the appointment of some 100 new missionaries to celebrate the occasion of the society's centenary, in faith that the Lord would provide the means. Unfortunately, the means weren't forthcoming, and the society's directors were forced to revoke the policy within a year and to institute financial retrenchment instead across the board. See Ibid., 2: 727–36.

102. Stoler, "Rethinking Colonial Categories."

103. John Comaroff.

104. So proclaimed the Mayor of Leicester, Alderman Wakerley, at the annual meeting of that city's local auxiliary of the LMS in the charged atmosphere of 1898.

From an undated or identified press clipping pasted into Leicester and Rutland Auxiliary of the LMS, Minute Book, Leicester Record Office, DE 649, N/C/MB/14.

105. For an excellent discussion of the active role played by the British military in this process, see Streets. See also Dunnae's survey of the shift in characterizations of imperial heroes in popular literature during the 1880s and 1890s; foreign missionaries, who had predominated during the 1860s and 1870s, were almost completely displaced during the 1880s and 1890s by soldiers and adventurers.

106. This gendered aspect of the contest between missionary and martial imperialisms is brilliantly depicted by Catherine Hall in "The Economy of Intellectual Prestige."

107. See Trapido.

108. Langmore, 385; Stoler, "Making the Empire Respectable."

109. Albert Spicer described the LMS's work in this way at a meeting of the Society's board of directors, Jan. 23, 1906, LMS Archives.

110. From a speech given at the annual meeting of the Leicester Auxiliary; *Leicester Daily Post*, Mar. 21, 1900; pasted in Leicester and Rutland Auxiliary of the LMS, Minute Book, Leicester Record Office.

111. The bulk of scholarly attention to questions of imperial culture has been devoted to this period. Most of the "Studies in Imperialism" series (edited by John M. MacKenzie), for example, begin after 1850, and the imperial sentiments represented are usually though not always those of missions' more "martial" critics.

112. Brian Stanley, "Home Support for Overseas Missions," 56–62; and McIlhiney, 44. See also LMS *Annual Report*, 1841; W. C. Stallybrass to Prout, Aug. 24, 1854; W. Barrett to Prout, Oct. 1, 1856, and Apr. 11, 1858; LMS Archives, Incoming Letters, Home; Deputation Reports, last quarter 1887, Apr.–June 1888, Oct.–Dec. 1889, Jan.–Mar. 1890, Apr.–June 1890, LMS Archives, Home, Odds, Box 9, Folder 5.

113. Mullens, 20–21. Rev. Joseph Mullens (1820–1879) was an LMS missionary in India from 1843 until 1865, and the society's foreign secretary from 1865 to 1879.

114. *The Challenge of the Modern Situation.*

115. Matthews, "Young Congregationalists," 88.

116. Wicks, "Bristol Missionary Society," 29.

117. LMS Archives, Deputation Reports, Dec. 31, 1886, Home, Odds, Box 9, Folder 4. This agent also reported urging collectors in Burnley to collect subscriptions, "however small," from all Congregational families.

118. LMS Archives, Funds and Agency Committee Minutes, 1903, 1915, 1916; circular letters to missionaries in the field, Dec. 1916, LMS Archives, Home, Odds, Box 23, Folder 3.

119. Report submitted by the driver of the Livingstone van from Sussex, Funds and Agency Committee Minutes, Nov. 12, 1907, LMS Archives.

120. The Watchers Band was a prayer group on behalf of LMS missions.

121. LMS Archives, Board Minutes, Mar. 19, 1879.

122. LMS Archives, Literature Committee Minutes, Dec. 15, 1915, and June 27, 1916. On Nov. 28, 1916, the Literature Committee minutes note that the first such

book for the "industrial constituency" had been published by the United Council for Missionary Education: William Paton, "Jesus Christ and the World's Religions." And on December 11, 1916, it notes that Lansbury had tentatively agreed to write "Missions and Social Reform." I was not able find any reference to such a book ever being published.

123. Laqueur, xi. Patrick Joyce similarly comments on the "profound influence" of Sunday schools, whose attendants constituted 17 percent of the total population of Lancashire and 20 percent of the total population of the West Riding of Yorkshire in 1851 (246–47).

124. Ollerenshaw, xxv–xxxiv. The identification of the Sunday school as both the problem with and the solution to the churches' penetration of the working-class community was a commonplace in discussions of the "decline" of religion in the second half of the nineteenth century. In 1869, J. A. Cooper of Birmingham addressed the autumn meetings of the Congregational Union of England and Wales on the subject of "Retaining the Elder Scholars in Our Sunday Schools": "Every thoughtful Christian must be sorely grieved in heart at seeing so many of our artisans living in a state of total alienation from religious ordinances, and in entire destitution of the spiritual influence of saving truths; and surprise must mingle with our grief as we remember that a great majority of these were once scholars in our Sunday-schools, and looked up to some of us or to our fathers, as their religious advisers, teachers, and guides!" (118–23). Sunday school officers in London were still reminding denominational leaders in 1903 that "much of the effort and energy put forward in trying to reclaim the masses would be better spent in trying to keep the classes of scholars assembled under their auspices, remembering that the children of to-day are the men and women of ten years hence." See Congregational Union of England and Wales, "Our Sunday Schools," 7.

125. J. D. Jones, 60.

126. *The Leeds Congregationalist* 2 (Feb. 1903), 10, deposited with records of Trinity St. David's United Reformed Church, Acc 2119, Item 91, Leeds Archives Department, Leeds.

127. LMS Archives, Board Minutes, June 26, 1894.

128. Fison, 4–5.

129. *The Challenge of the Modern Situation*, 67.

130. Pelton, 135.

131. Fison, 4–5.

132. "In many ways," claims one LMS pamphlet aimed at Sunday school teachers, "the primitive elements in the child's nature respond to the life of the primitive people into which he enters." See Walker and Spriggs, 8.

133. *Hindu Boys*.

134. *Notes for Talks to the Sunday Schools*, 11. See also Gaunt, 50: "Is it not strange that whereas in Christian countries we show special honour and respect to our women and girls, in heathen lands it is generally just the opposite? One of the very best results of mission schools for girls is that they teach the heathen a higher idea of womanhood."

135. *The Challenge of the Modern Situation*, 10, 67.

136. Ollerenshaw, xxv–xxxiv.

137. Cooper, 118–23.

138. John Wrigley Willans, a prominent Yorkshire Congregationalists, uttered these remarks in an address to the employees of his Brighouse carpet firm, assembled appropriately enough at the Brighouse Congregational chapel. Cited in Binfield, "Asquith," 224.

139. Eddy.

140. As Benedict Anderson has reminded us, communities are always imaginatively produced rather than socially or culturally given.

141. Gareth Stedman Jones; *Outcast London*; and Himmelfarb, especially chaps. 8 and 9.

142. Mehta.

143. This literature is usefully surveyed in Eley, "Social Imperialism."

144. Harcourt, 1980: 87–109

145. Eley, "Social Imperialism."

Chapter 5: Social Relations of Missionary Philanthropy

1. This is not to say that working-class religiosity is archivally inaccessible; recent work, including in particular that of Sarah Williams and Hugh McLeod (see especially "New Perspectives"), demonstrates how much can be gleaned about the religious sensibilities of the unchurched as well as of the churched from a creative approach to noninstitutional sources, including but not limited to those of oral history. And these are certainly archival perspectives from which the findings suggested below need to be queried. In order to avoid the diffuseness of recent cultural studies of "popular imperialism," however, I have confined my inquiries for the most part to missionary archives at the local chapel as well as at the national level.

2. Laqueur.

3. See Perry, 492. Contribution lists from the Fylde Auxiliary of the LMS show Sunday school contributions to have been one-fifth of the total of that auxiliary's contribution to the LMS in 1918. See Fylde Missionary Council Papers, Minute Books, Box 2. Sunday schools were given credit in 1875 for the increase in the funds raised in Leeds: "The increased subscriptions have been largely from the Sunday schools, and your committee would take this opportunity of urging upon their friends the importance of awakening an interest in missions in early life. From our Sunday schools and the young people of our churches must come our future missionaries and supporters of the society." See *Leeds Mercury*, Sept. 28, 1875, p. 4.

4. Congregational Union of England and Wales, "Our Sunday Schools," 182.

5. Prochaska, "Little Vessels," 109.

6. Whateley, 124.

7. Rev. E. A. Wareham noted a great deal of enthusiasm among even the small and weak churches in Aberdeenshire—one of which launched a drive to sponsor native teachers that won the special support of young people. See LMS Archives, Deputation

Reports, July 17, 1891, Home, Odds, Box 9, Folder 2. The first auxiliary of the Boys Brigade was formed in 1898. The Brigades were organized primarily in Sunday schools, and their donations were earmarked for medical missions. By 1909, there were 47 companies that raised almost £120 in support of cots in LMS hospitals. See LMS Archives, Pamphlet Collection, *Annual Reports*, LMS Boys Brigades. One consequence of the organization of a Boys' Brigade at the Kirkstall Congregational Church in Leeds in 1894 was said to have been more orderly behavior in the boys' Sunday school class. See the *Headingley Hill Congregational Church Yearbook* (1894), 79, Yorkshire Congregational Union Records, Item 119.

8. *Leeds Mercury*, Sept. 19, 1910, p. 3; and Leeds Auxiliary Committee Minutes, Box 2, July 20, 1905. The use of costumes was commonplace by the turn of the century. Mention is made in the Leeds' auxiliary records of "native dress" samples being borrowed from the Mission House to be worn by participants in the annual Children's Demonstration; Leeds Auxiliary Committee Minutes, Sept. 8, 1902. Press reports on other LMS meetings in Leeds include references to children acting out missionary dramas at a 1909 children's rally, while in 1913 children dressed in native costume and, from the looks of the photo in the newspaper, in blackface makeup and performed "missionary tableaux." See the *Leeds Mercury*, Sept. 28, 1909, p. 3; and Sept. 22, 1913, p. 3.

9. LMS Archives, Deputation Reports, Mar. 31, 1885, Home, Odds, Box 9. Folder 1; see also *Leeds Mercury*, Sept. 18, 1911, p. 2.

10. See LMS Archives, Deputation Reports, Dec. 31, 1886, Home, Odds, Box 9, folder 4.

11. See the *Hunslet and Holbeck News*, Sept. 29, 1888, p. 3. See also flyers for Leeds Meetings, on the back of which are specially printed hymns; Leeds Auxiliary Committee Minute Books, Box 2.

12. See Cox, 93–95, 276.

13. See Obelkevich, "Music and Religion."

14. LMS Archives, Deputation Reports, Dec. 31, 1890, Home, Odds, Box 9, Folder 4. This comparison of missionary meeting to Sunday school meeting is important to note, as Sunday school anniversary celebrations were one of if not the most significant events of the year at the local level.

15. See Edmonton and Tottenham Chapel Records, Sunday School Teachers Meetings Minutes, Apr. 9, 1874.

16. *Headingley Hill Congregational Church Yearbook* (1894), 67–68.

17. Newcastle Auxiliary Committee Minute Books, Box 1, e.g., Apr. 15, 1905.

18. LMS Archives, Funds and Agency Committee Minutes, Mar. 27, 1906.

19. Cited in Barbara Taylor, 151–53.

20. Exeter Hall was the London site of the annual public meetings of nationally based philanthropies, prominent among which were foreign missionary societies.

21. Hollis, "Anti-Slavery," 298–99, 311.

22. Quoted in Pope, 100.

23. Hempton, "Religion in Victorian Fiction," 87.

24. Eileen Yeo, 14–15; and McLeod, *Class and Religion in the Late Victorian City*, 84.

25. Tressell, 167–68.

26. Selbie, *The Life of Charles Silvester Horne*, 46.

27. *Headingley Hill Congregational Chapel Yearbook* (1898).

28. Binfield, "The Building of a Town Centre Church," 169, 177.

29. See McLeod, *Class and Religion in the Late Victorian City*, 12.

30. "Are Ministers Ignorant of the Slums?" from B. W., *Leeds Mercury*, Sept. 26, 1893, p. 3.

31. Henry Snell, 5, 12, 15–16.

32. On the nineteenth-century "discovery" and use of the working-class child, see Steedman, *Childhood, Culture, and Class*.

33. From a description of the children at a mission chapel in Leeds. *Headingley Hill Congregational Yearbook* (1892).

34. LMS *Annual Report* (1851). The Leeds Auxiliary did come to the exceptional decision in 1878 "that in consequence of the serious depression of trade, the Subcommittee appointed to visit the Churches and Sunday Schools of the Auxiliary, had thought it best to postpone any action for the present." Leeds Auxiliary Committee Minutes, July 29, 1878.

35. LMS Archives, Deputation Reports, Mar. 31, 1887, Home, Odds, Box 9, Folder 4.

36. LMS Archives, Pamphlet Collection, *Annual Report*, LMS Boys Brigades (1919–1920).

37. LMS Archives, Deputation Reports, June 30, 1886, Home, Odds, Box 9, Folder 4. See also LMS Archives, Deputation Reports, Apr. 31, 1886: "I have been to many places in Lancashire where the Sunday Schools are large, and attended by those who are earning money from which we might reasonably look for substantial help. But in many places I have been surprised to find how little has been given to our Society as compared with the amounts given for the support of their schools and various objects connected with them. . . . In many places Chapel and School Building Debts are large; these are pleaded as an excuse for the little subscribed for Mission work. During the time of commercial prosperity these buildings were commenced, but owing to the depression of trade, money has not come in very freely, and so the Congregations finding their own expenses heavy, do not give freely to objects outside of their own communion."

38. LMS Archives, Deputation Reports, Sept. 30, 1888, Home, Odds, Box 9, Folder 4.

39. Darwent, *The Story of Fish Street Church Hull*, 176–77.

40. LMS Archives, Deputation Reports, Sept. 30, 1888, Home, Odds, Box 9, Folder 4.

41. *Headingley Hill Congregational Church Yearbook* (1882), 10.

42. St. Andrews Congregational Church Records, *Roundhay Congregational Church News* (1907), Acc 2419, Item 60. The Roundhay Sunday school was unusual in being comprised of the children of the middle-class members of this prosperous chapel.

43. See Beeston Hill Congregational Church Records, Beeston Hill Congrega-

tional Church *Manual* (May 1894), 35–36, Acc 2074, Item 41. The total was 33 pounds, 11 shillings, and 10 pence, of which 10 shillings, 15 pence came from New Years' Offering cards and 8 pounds, 12 shillings, 6 pence from Sunday school boxes.

44. LMS Archives.

45. Prout, 61.

46. Fison, 6.

47. Congregational Union of England and Wales, "Our Sunday Schools," 188–90.

48. LMS Archives, Deputation Reports, Dec. 1895, Home, Odds, Box 9, Folder 3.

49. Contra Prochaska suggests we "think of the history of philanthropy broadly as the history of kindness"; see "Philanthropy," 360.

50. LMS Archives, Funds and Agency Committee Minutes, 1905.

51. Congregational Union of England and Wales, "Our Sunday Schools."

52. See Congregational Union of England and Wales, "Our Sunday Schools," 138–62.

53. LMS Archives, Literature Committee Minutes, Dec. 16, 1902, and Dec. 31, 1909, Home, Odds, Box 16, Folder 1.

54. LMS Archives, Deputation Reports, June 30, 1886 and Sept. 30, 1888, Home, Odds, Box 9, Folder 4. I was not able to find the records of this Sunday school; this may have something to do with the school's independence, about which the chapel regularly complained. See Shipley Congregational Schools Records, Dec. 7, 1873, and June 1, 1874, 10D77/5a. The chapel itself was never admitted to membership in the Yorkshire Congregational Union because of its insistence upon the right of any and all to partake of communion, what was referred to in the records as multitudinism. See "Shipley Congregational Church 1905–1965."

55. LMS Archives, Funds and Agency Committee Minutes, 1905, and Mar. 12, 1907.

56. Thompson's address to the 1908 meetings of the Congregational Union of England and Wales is recorded in the *Leeds Mercury*, Oct. 21, 1908, p. 4; see also LMS Archives, Deputation Reports, Apr. 1897, Home, Odds, Box 9, Folder 3. In 1904, another agent confided to the Funds and Agency Committee that "in the large manufacturing towns [where socialism would presumably have been strongest] he had not felt his work to be so successful as in other places."

57. "Foreign Missions. Disgraceful Position in Leeds," *Leeds Mercury*, Sept. 19, 1912, p. 3.

58. "Readers' Opinions. Money for the Heathen," *Leeds Mercury*, Sept. 24, 1912, p. 4.

59. "Money for the Heathen. A Crime to Send It Out of the Country Now," *Leeds Mercury*, Sept. 21, 1912: p. 4. Interesting in this regard is the scrutiny to which LMS salaries were subjected by their home supporters. The society's agents reported widespread criticism of foreign missionaries earning more than those ministers in Britain who preached to poor congregations. See LMS Archives, Deputation Reports, Oct.–Dec. 1888, Home, Odds, Box 9, Folder 5. See also "Cheapness or Efficiency? The Pecuniary Needs of Missionaries"; LMS Archives, Board Minutes, Oct. 8, 1895; R. W. Thompson to Frank Lenwood, July 24, 1912, LMS Archives, Outgoing Letters,

Box 4; LMS Archives, Home, Odds, Box 23, Oct. 1917; LMS Archives, Home, Odds, Box 3, Folder 1, and Box 4, Folder 2.

60. Much more work is needed to excavate the imperial and racial coordinates of popular political culture in this period. My remarks are meant to draw attention to the temptations of racial categories structured into missionary outreach, to which at least some of the more critical members of the missionary audience succumbed. My own research base has been limited to missionary archives; I have not roamed freely into sources that illuminate popular culture more broadly. I do not mean here to suggest that working-class Britons were uniformly much less innately and inevitably disposed to racism. The possibility of transracial alliances is evidenced in Laura Tabili's recent study of the British Seamen's Union. I certainly agree with Tabili that popular racism was not an instinctive response to cross-cultural contact. That the perception of cultural distinctiveness had to be very carefully taught is an organizing theme of this book; moreover, the outcomes of campaigns to instruct or rather construct race were also, as I have tried to show, rarely those intended. However, popular agency can also, regrettably, result in more politically reactionary results than those intended from on high.

61. Prochaska, "Philanthropy," 367.

62. Rev. J. Guinness Rogers, 112.

63. *Albert Spicer*, 20.

64. Rev. Algernon Wells made these remarks in a speech to the Congregational Union in 1848; cited in R. Tudur Jones, 228.

65. On the sociological range of Victorian chapels, see McLeod, "New Perspectives."

66. Scholars were often only allowed to attend chapel services, even in the gallery, on special occasions, such as the anniversaries of the Sunday school and the LMS auxiliary; 57 percent of Sunday schools reported that scholars attended services as a school, though most withdrew before the sermon. See Congregational Union of England and Wales, "Our Sunday Schools," 101.

67. Sunday school classes at Sheffield's Cemetery Road Congregational Church, for example, were held in the kitchen or other small rooms: "psychologically this was sound, because many working people are shy, and prefer small and intimate rooms, giving a chance for the closer impact of personality, and do not like light spacious premises." See Allison, 16.

68. Cited in Binfield, "The Building of a Town Centre Church," 177.

69. Henry Snell, 20.

70. Trinity St. David's United Reformed Church Records, *Leeds Congregationalist* 4 (Apr. 1903), 1, Acc 2119, Item 91.

71. According to Bebbington, "The most important social division [within Nonconformity] was between individual congregations rather than between denominations. . . . Hence within the same denomination, if not within the same chapel, there would be people of a very different social type. Nonconformity was not simply a front organisation for the middle classes." *The Nonconformist Conscience*, 5.

72. The church rules included the following: "that in the event of any member of the Church being unable to meet his business engagements, his membership shall

thereby cease; unless upon inquiry by the officers, it be found that nothing reflecting on his Christian character has occurred in connection with such failure, in which case a vote of the Church shall be taken with a view to his reinstatement to membership." See *Headingley Hill Congregational Church Yearbook* (1890), 63, Item 119; and Headingley Hill Congregational Church, *History of Headingley Hill Congregational Church*, 3.

73. Guntrip, 135.

74. Ibid., 57.

75. Belgrave Congregational Church Records, Belgrave Congregational Church Meeting Minutes, June 29, 1904, 113 (a).

76. Three shoemakers, one joiner, three dressmakers, one tailor, one town missionary, one mechanic, one schoolmaster, one pawnbroker, one laborer, one engine driver, one hairdresser, one grocer, one bible woman, one schoolmistress, one commission agent, one gentleman (who subsequently transferred to the then more prosperous Belgrave), one designer, one draper, one painter, one machine maker, and two almshouse residents. See Beeston Hill Congregational Church Records, Roll of Church Members, Acc 2074, Item 1.

77. A. Raleigh to E. R. Conder, Sept. 23, 1865, Beeston Hill Congregational Church Records, Acc 2074, Item 41.

78. *Headingley Hill Congregational Yearbook* (1885), 8.

79. Most working-class Nonconformists, however, attended chapels that were self-supporting in however modest a fashion. The mission chapels I describe here were in the minority. Unfortunately, most of the LMS-related material that has survived to the present pertains to middle-class chapels and the urban missions they supported. This bias in the record is not necessarily evidence that independent working-class chapels were not involved in or supportive of the mission cause; their members may simply have not been in a position to take care of their chapel's archival materials, or perhaps these latter weren't deemed as important by local record collectors. I want to thank Hugh McLeod for pressing me on this point.

80. Information to this effect, e. g., lists of trustees' names, and sometimes those of deacons and school superintendents as well, is scattered throughout the chapel records I examined.

81. As late as 1912, an LMS exhibition was praised for addressing the general isolation of Congregational chapels from one another: "one of the chief benefits of the undertaking was that it had brought all the Churches closer together." See Leeds Auxiliary Committee Minutes, Oct. 25, 1912.

82. *Yorkshire Post*, Jan. 3, 1927, p. 5.

83. Leeds Obituary Notices, 3: 69.

84. See Thorne, especially 203–16.

85. Similarly, in Sheffield, the office of treasurer was held by a member of Nether Chapel for over 70 years. See Carr.

86. Cited in Binfield, "Asquith," 241.

87. Binfield, "Asquith," 241.

88. Whately, 97–99.

89. Wrigley, "What the Church Can Do For the Young People Through the Sunday School," *The Leeds Congregationalist* (Jan. 1903), 14–15, Trinity St. David's United Reformed Church Records, Acc 2119.

90. Cited in McLeod, *Class and Religion in the Late Victorian City*, 150.

91. Belgrave Congregational Church Records, Church Meetings Minutes, Feb. 24, 1903.

92. See also Guntrip, 58.

93. Newcastle Auxiliary Records, Box 1, Minute Book of the Missionary Thousand, Oct. 2, 1908.

94. Leeds Auxiliary Committee Minutes, Apr. 7, 1916.

95. Headingley Hill Church Records, "Missionary Meetings in Leeds: A Contrast," Queen Street Chapel, Leeds. *Congregational Society's Magazine* 2 (Nov. 1879), 20–21, Acc 2216, item 63.

96. Steedman, *Childhood, Culture, and Class*, 37.

97. Ibid., 63.

98. Rev. E. A. Shalders to Tidman, Apr. 10, 1866, LMS Archives, Home, Incoming Letters, Box 12.

99. Charles Phillips to Jones, June 7, 1888, LMS Archives, Home, Incoming Letters, Extra, Box 4.

100. LMS Archives, Funds and Agency Committee Minutes, Oct. 24, 1895.

101. See Beeston Hill Sunday School Teachers Meetings Minutes, Nov. 19, 1919, Beeston Hill Congregational Church Records, Acc 2074, Item 31; discussion of joint services was adjourned for time being.

102. The chapel's newsletter complained in 1904 of the "danger lest the absence of the poor in our midst should make us forgetful of their needs," and Roundhay scholars organized benefits for the "poor" children at Burmantofts, Oak Road, Salem, Marshall Street, and Belgrave. See St. Andrews Congregational Church Records, Acc 2419, Item 60, *Roundhay Congregational Church News* (Dec. 1904), and Item 14, Sunday School Teachers Meetings Minutes, e.g., Nov. 25, 1904, Dec. 14, 1906, Jan. 8, 1909, Nov. 13, 1910, and Oct. 21, 1911.

103. St. Andrews Congregational Church Records, Acc 2419, Item 14, Sunday School Teachers Meetings Minutes, May 17, 1904, and July 17, 1911.

104. "Marshall Street Congregational Church," 5.

105. Guntrip, 87–89. It may be significant that both these histories were written well after my period closes—Guntrip in 1944, the Marshall Street history in 1936. It is difficult to say whether such matters rankled in working-class Christians' hearts 40 years earlier.

106. Quoted in Paul Thompson, 147. Carolyn Steedman affirms that the aristocrats of labor who dominated the labor movement, and especially the Independent Labour Party as well as Nonconformist chapels, were almost as fearful and repulsed by the unskilled poor as their middle-class counterparts were, refusing to send their children to Board schools for fear of contaminating contact. See *Childhood, Culture and Class*, 164–68.

107. These new members were shortly given a vote, however. See New Court Congregational Church Records, Deacons Meetings Minute Books, Jan. 30, 1888, Feb. 27, 1888, and Mar. 26, 1888, N/C 69/29/1.

108. Edmonton and Tottenham Chapel records, Deacons Meetings Minutes, Oct. 29, 1875, N/C 64/20; and New Court Congregational Church records, Deacons Meetings Minutes, July 1, 1895 and Sept. 9, 1895, N/C 69/29/1.

109. See for example, LMS Archives, Deputation Reports, Jan.–Mar. 1888 and Jan.–Mar. 1890, Home, Odds, Box 9, Folder 5; see also W. Carson.

110. Smith's resolution was passed the next month by the executive committee, but victory was short-lived. In March 1905, the General Committee of the Auxiliary unanimously passed a resolution moved by treasurer George Dodgshun rescinding Smith's proposal. See Leeds Auxiliary Committee Minutes.

111. LMS, *The World For Christ*.

112. See LMS Archives, Deputation Reports, Dec. 31, 1885, Home, Odds, Box 9, Folder 4.

113. See Fylde Missionary Council Papers, Minute Book, Jan. 9, 1894.

114. See Carr, 25.

115. See Newcastle Auxiliary Committee Minutes, Sept. 21, 1905.

116. See Walton, 27.

117. Leeds Auxiliary Committee Minutes, Dec. 13, 1912.

118. Ibid., Mar. 3, 1916.

119. *Headingley Hill Congregational Yearbook* (1893), 14–15.

120. On the other hand, the women's Pleasant Sunday Afternoon at Wintoun Street Chapel in Leeds was ejected for unstated reasons, and the working men's Institute at Beeston Hill was closed in the early 1990s for "abuses" in its syllabus, after which the "numbers of young people attached to the Church quickly fell." See *Leeds Mercury*, Sept. 27, 1894, p. 3; and "Beeston Hill Congregational Church, Centenary Brochure. 1865–1965," 5, Beeston Hill Congregational Church Records, Acc 2074, Item 41. One also has to wonder if "political" considerations were not behind the Leeds Auxiliary's refusal to distribute the Brotherhood leaflets issued by the LMS Mission House in 1915, on the grounds that they were "not considered suitable." See Leeds Auxiliary Committee Minutes, Minutes of the Executive Committee, Apr. 23, 1915, Box 2.

121. Cited in Binfield, "Asquith," 239.

122. Tozer to Johnson, Sept. 23, 1892, LMS Archives, Home, Incoming Letters, Box 4.

123. District Secretaries Reports, May 4, 1898, LMS Archives, Home, Odds, Box 16, Folder 1.

124. The first factor that Agent Wilkins pointed out was that "there are large numbers of people who do not attempt to do for the support of our work what is easily within their power, mainly, I believe, because they do not realise their duty and privilege in this matter. They are so engrossed in business that they do not think seriously of their responsibility—they just give a little when a Collection is made with-

out trying to form any adequate idea of the dimension and importance of our work."
See LMS Archives, Deputation Reports, Mar. 31, 1887, Home, Odds, Box 9, Folder 4.

125. LMS Archives, Deputation Reports, Mar. 31, 1889, Home, Odds, Box 9, Folder 4. Similar complaints were voiced by the society's agent in the Midlands, Rev. Samuel Macfarlane: "The reception and cooperation I meet with everywhere is encouraging, except, perhaps where I make private calls. It is quite evident that I am much more acceptable to some of them as a pleader in the pulpit and on the platform, than in their offices and homes . . . " LMS Archives, Deputation Reports, Apr.–June 1890, Home, Odds, Box 9, Folder 5.

126. LMS Archives, Deputation Reports, Apr. 14, 1886, Home, Odds, Box 9, Folder 1.

127. LMS Archives, Deputation Reports, Apr.–June 1890, Home, Odds, Box 9, Folder 5.

128. LMS Archives, Deputation Reports, Mar. 31, 1887, Home, Odds, Box 9, Folder 4.

129. LMS Archives, Deputation Reports, Dec. 31, 1887, Home, Odds, Box 9, Folder 4.

130. Gallagher and Robinson; Catherine Hall, "The Economy of Intellectual Prestige."

131. Dunnae. The ethos of the so-called new imperial era has attracted the bulk of scholarly attention to the empire's popularization. See the now massive list of monographs and collections of essays published under the "Studies in Imperialism" (edited by John M. MacKenzie) series of Manchester University Press.

132. Mackenzie, *Popular Imperialism and the Military*, 16.

Chapter 6: The Strange Death of Missionary Imperialism

1. See Gallagher and Robinson; see also Knox.

2. That the working classes lived a culturally insulated existence, safe from bourgeois efforts to influence, was a dominant thrust of the (now old) new social history; see, for example, Meacham; See also Gareth Stedman Jones, "Working-Class Culture and Working-Class Politics."

3. Cain and Hopkins, 45–46.

4. LMS Archives, Deputation Reports, Oct.–Dec. 1890, Home, Odds, Box 9, Folder 5.

5. LMS Archives, Deputation Reports, Oct. 1885, Home, Odds, Box 9, Folder 1; and W. Carson.

6. Although as Hugh McLeod has pointed out to me, "dependent" mission chapels were only one of a range of institutions in which working-class evangelicals worshipped. Most of the latter were more independent of middle-class support, and the social relations of philanthropy therein were no doubt very different from the deference I have described. As I discuss in Chapter 5, I was not able to find records of missionary auxiliaries connected to these kinds of chapels. This bias in the record is not necessarily evidence that independent working-class chapels were not involved in or

supportive of the mission cause; their members may simply have not been in a position to take care of their chapel's archival materials, or perhaps these latter weren't deemed as important by local record collectors. In spite of being pointedly excluded from the missionary movement's district and national administration, these more independent working-class chapels supported the democratic initiatives described above; this attests to their engagement with the mission cause if not, unfortunately, to its meaning.

7. Cited in R. Tudur Jones, 229.

8. Bryan S. Turner, 152; McLeod, *Class and Religion in the Late Victorian City*, 114; McLeod, "New Perspectives," 37–38; and Burdett, 32.

9. London Female Mission, *Annual Report 1836*, 14.

10. London City Mission, West London Auxiliary, *Annual Report, 1856*. At the first tea party held by one of Ellen Ranyard's bible women in St. Giles's, "all the women present agreed on one point: 'they all had bad husbands.'" From this Norris Pope concludes that "religion was evidently a rather active consolation in the midst of an unhappy marriage" (141).

11. Paul Thompson, 296–97.

12. I am thinking here of working-class men's insistence upon their wives and children's social isolation in the film by Terrence Davies, *Distant Voices, Still Lives*; see also Carolyn Steedman, *Landscape for a Good Woman*; and Anna Clark.

13. Quoted in Haw, 54.

14. The timing and causes of organized religion in twentieth-century Britain is the subject of considerable scholarly debate, which is usefully surveyed in Green; see especially 1–21.

15. That the shift in missionary attitudes to empire after World War I was widely acknowledged is suggested by "The White Man and Coloured Races. Interview with the Rev. Frank Lenwood, Secretary of the London Missionary Society," by A. F. B., *The Labour Leader*, Feb. 29, 1920, 4. The author introduces the subject of missions by claiming that "it is an undoubted fact that many of the missionaries of the last generation approached their work in the spirit of 'masters', convinced of the superiority of the British race, sincere but still objectionable Imperialists." Citing Lenwood as his evidence, he concludes that missionaries "are becoming the champions of the native peoples against imperialism and capitalism." Even at this point, however, Lenwood, who was on the progressive end of the missionary spectrum, could be found defending the imperial project. See for example, Lenwood's "Ten Years in the South Pacific" in *International Review of Missions*, (Oct. 1922), 500: "In the Pacific there is much to show that 'the powers there are ordained of God.' The scandal of the condominium in the New Hebrides still continues, it is true, and there are individual instances in which men holding subordinate positions ignore or betray their trust, but the general trend of government in the Pacific is for righteousness." These clippings are both preserved in the Frank Lenwood Papers, LMS Archives, Home, Personal, Box 9.

16. *The LMS and School Prayers in Bangalore*, pamphlet enclosed with other material on Bangalore controversy, in LMS Archives, Home, Odds, Box 16, Folder 3.

17. This according to the Rev. William Carson; see his letter to LMS Home Secretary, Nelson Bitton, Sept. 11, 1923, LMS Archives, Home, Odds, Box 16, Folder 3.

18. Cornelius H. Patton, Home Secretary of American Board of Commissioners for Foreign Missions, to Nelson Bitton, LMS Home Secretary, Mar. 7, 1922, LMS Archives, Home, Odds, Box 16, Folder 3.

19. *The LMS and School Prayers in Bangalore*, pamphlet enclosed with other material on Bangalore controversy in LMS Archives, Home, Odds, Box 16, Folder 3.

20. Resolution passed June 27, 1923, a copy of which is enclosed in LMS Archives, Home, Odds, Box 16, Folder 3.

21. Roger Wilson.

22. Parry, 13–16.

23. Peel and Marriott, 155. Horton's support for Lloyd George's "People's Budget" of 1909 resulted in a large number of resignations from his chapel. See McLeod, *Class and Religion in the Late Victorian City*, 269.

24. R. W. Thompson to Mrs. Livingstone Bruce, May 9, 1911, LMS Archives, Home, Outgoing Letters, Box 3. One of the society's agents reported in 1910 that "a very worthy Belfast merchant, and a genuine friend of missions outside his own denomination, declared that the LMS was now run by Radicals and Socialists, and he could have no association with the enemies of his country," referring to Liberal proposals for conceding Home Rule to Ireland. See District Secretaries' Reports, Mar. 31, 1910, LMS Archives, Home, Odds, Box 16, Folder 1.

25. R. Tudur Jones, 279. Denominational loyalties remained strong across this political divide. J. Guinness Rogers recalled that when a Church of England clergyman criticized Nonconformist devotion to Gladstone at an LMS dinner, Dale defended his coreligionists. See Rev. J. Guinness Rogers, 181.

26. J. D. Jones, 225. Jones is referring here to his chapel in Bournemouth, though he also preached in Lincoln.

27. R. Tudur Jones, 335–36.

28. McKenzie and Silver, 49.

29. According to Stephen Neill, the Great Trek from the Cape to the Transvaal originated in Afrikaaner resentments of missionaries and their influence on British policy at the Cape. The LMS's John Philip's association with the cause of native rights made his name anathema to the Boers. In *Colonialism and Christian Missions*, Neill quotes an unnamed Boer farmer, who claimed that Philips "had spoiled the Hottentots, that he had got a law passed which would oblige him to marry his daughter to a Hottentot, that he would rather shoot her than see her so degraded, and that Dr. Philip had taken all his slaves from him and that he wondered at the mercy of God in suffering such a man to live" (312).

30. Moffat, *The Black Man and the War*, 9.

31. Ibid. See also Wirgman.

32. Moffat, *The Black Man and the War*, 4, 9.

33. Ibid., 11.

34. Cited in Selbie, *The Life of Andrew Martin Fairbairn*, 371–72.

35. Horne, *The Rock of Ages*, 163–64.

36. Selbie, *The Life of Charles Silvester Horne*, 112. See also Horton, 201–4, 349; and Rev. J. Guinness Rogers, 134.

37. Cited in Goodall, 246.

38. I thank David Feldman for pressing me on this point.

39. This expression is borrowed from Higginbotham.

40. Barbara J. Fields, 160.

41. Catherine Hall, "Missionary Stories," in *White, Male and Middle Class*.

42. While nationalism obviously existed prior to this period, its relevance to the working classes was limited by their exclusion from the political nation by the terms of the electoral franchise.

43. On the connections between race and nation, disputed by Benedict Anderson, see Gilroy, *There Ain't No Black in the Union Jack*, especially chap. 2.

44. Davin.

Works Cited

Ajayi, J. F. Ade. *Christian Missions in Nigeria 1841–1891*. Evanston, IL: Northwestern University Press, 1965.

Albert Spicer 1847–1934: A Man of His Time: By One of His Family. London: Simpkin Marshall, 1938, London Missionary Society (LMS; now Council for World Mission) Archives.

Alden, Dauril. *The Making of an Enterprise: The Society of Jesus in Portugal, Its Empire, and Beyond, 1540–1750*. Stanford, Calif: Stanford University Press, 1996.

Alexander, John. *Memoirs of Rev. William Alexander*. Norwich: Fletcher and Alexander, 1856.

Allison, Archibald. *Cemetery Road Congregational Church, Sheffield: 1859–1959*. Sheffield: Castle Press, 1959. Congregational Library, Dr. Williams Library, London.

Anderson, Benedict. *Imagined Communities: Reflections on the Origin and Spread of Nationalism*. London: Verso, 1983.

Anderson, Olive. "Women Preachers in Mid-Victorian Britain: Some Reflexions on Feminism, Popular Religion and Social Change." *Historical Journal* 7, no. 3 (1969), 467–84.

Anderson, Perry. "The Figures of Descent." In *English Questions*, 121–92. London: Verso, 1992.

Andrew, Donna T. *Philanthropy and Police: London Charity in the Eighteenth Century*. Princeton, N.J.: Princeton University Press, 1989.

Appeal of the Society for Promoting Female Education in China, India and the East. (1831), 4. Yale Divinity School, Special Collections, Missions Pamphlet Collection, Box 125, Folder 972.

Armstrong, Anthony. *The Church of England, the Methodists and Society, 1700–1850*. London: University of London Press, 1973.

Austen, Ralph, and Woodruff D. Smith. "Images of Africa and British Slave Trade Abolition: The Transition to an Imperialist Ideology, 1787–1807." *African Historical Studies*, 2, no. 1 (1969): 69–83.

Ayandele, E. A. *The Missionary Impact on Modern Nigeria 1842–1914: A Political and Social Analysis*. New York: Humanities Press, 1966.

Baptist Home Missionary Society. *Annual Report*. 1857. Yale Divinity School Special Collections.

Barratt, Michelle. *Women's Oppression Today*. London: Verso, 1988.

Bayly, C. A. *Imperial Meridian: The British Empire and the World 1780–1830*. London: Longman, 1989.

————. *Indian Society and the Making of the British Empire*. Cambridge: Cambridge University Press, 1988.

Bebbington, D. W. *Evangelicalism in Modern Britain: A History from the 1730s to the 1980s*. London: Unwin Hyman, 1989.

————. *The Nonconformist Conscience: Chapel and Politics, 1870–1914*: London: George Allen and Unwin, 1982.

————. "Nonconformity and Electoral Sociology, 1867–1918." *Historical Journal* 27, no. 3 (1984): 633–56.

Beeston Hill Congregational Church Records. Leeds Archives Department.

Beidelman, T. O. *Colonial Evangelism: A Socio-Historical Study of an East African Mission at the Grassroots*. Bloomington: Indiana University Press, 1982.

Belgrave Congregational Church (Leeds) Records. Yorkshire Congregational Union Records. Leeds Archives Department.

Bennett, Arnold. *Anna of the Five Towns*. 1902. Oxford: Oxford University Press, 1995.

Berg, Maxine, and Pat Hudson. "Rehabilitating the Industrial Revolution." *Economic History Review* 45, no. 1 (1992): 24–50.

Biagini, Eugene. *Liberty, Retrenchment, and Reform: Popular Liberalism in the Age of Gladstone, 1860–1880*. Cambridge: Cambridge University Press, 1992.

Binfield, Clyde. "Asquith: The Formation of a Prime Minister." *Journal of the United Reformed Church Historical Society* 2, no. 7 (Apr. 1981): 204–42.

————. "The Building of a Town Centre Church: St. James's Congregational Church, Newcastle Upon Tyne." *Northern History* 18 (1982): 153–81.

————. *George Williams and the Y. M. C. A: A Study in Victorian Social Attitudes*. London: Heinemann, 1973.

————. *So Down to Prayers: Studies in English Nonconformity, 1780–1920*. London: J. M. Dent and Sons, 1977.

————. "Thomas Binney and Congregationalism's 'Special Mission.'" *Transactions of the Congregational Historical Society* 21, no. 1 (June 1971): 1–10.

Binney, Rev. Thomas. "Opening Address." *Congregational Yearbook of 1848*. London: Congregational Union of England and Wales, 1848. 4–14.

Blackburn, Rev. John. *The Salvation of Britain Introductory to the Conversion of the*

World: A Discourse Delivered Before the London Missionary Society. London: Jackson and Walford, 1835.

Booth, William. *In Darkest England and the Way Out.* London: International Headquarters of the Salvation Army, 1890.

Borrows, Rev. William. *Salvation by Christ, the Grand Object of Christian Missions.* London: LMS, 1820. Yale Divinity School, Special Collections.

Bowie, Fiona, Deborah Kirkwood, and Shirley Ardener, eds. *Women and Missions: Past and Present. Anthropological and Historical Perceptions.* Providence/Oxford: Berg, 1993.

Boyer, George R. *An Economic History of the English Poor Law, 1750–1850.* Cambridge: Cambridge University Press, 1990.

Bradley, James E. *Religion, Revolution, and English Radicalism: Nonconformity in Eighteenth-Century Politics and Society.* Cambridge: Cambridge University Press, 1990.

Brewer, John. "English Radicalism in the Age of George III." In *Three British Revolutions,* edited by J. G. A. Pocock. Princeton, N.J.: Princeton University Press, 1980.

Briggs, Asa. "The Language of 'Class' in Early Nineteenth-Century England." Reprinted in *History and Class: Essential Readings in Theory and Interpretation,* edited by R. S. Neale, 2–39. London: Basil Blackwell, 1983. Originally published in *Essays in Labour History,* edited by Asa Briggs and John Saville. (London: Macmillan, 1967).

Brontë, Charlotte. *Jane Eyre.* 1847. New York: Bantam Classic, 1981.

Brown, Ford K. *Fathers of the Victorians: The Age of Wilberforce.* Cambridge: Cambridge University Press, 1961.

Brown, Richard. *Church and State in Modern Britain 1700–1850.* London: Routledge, 1991.

Brownfoot, Janice N. "Sisters under the Skin: Imperialism and the Emancipation of Women in Malaya, c. 1891–1941." In *Making Imperial Mentalities. Socialisation and British Imperialism,* edited by J. A. Mangan, 46–73. Manchester: University of Manchester Press, 1990.

Burdett, Jeff. "'A Strong Though Indefinite Sense of Religion': A Study of the Working Class and Religion in London's East End, 1880–1902." Senior Honor's Thesis, University of Kansas, 1992.

Burls, Robert. *A Brief Review of the Plan and Operations of the Essex Congregational Union for Promoting the Knowledge of the Gospel in the County of Essex and Its Vicinity.* Maldon: P. H. Youngman, 1848.

Burton, Antoinette. *At the Heart of the Empire: Indians and the Colonial Encounter in Late-Victorian Britain.* Berkeley: University of California Press, 1998.

———. *Burdens of History: British Feminists, Indian Women, and Imperial Culture, 1854–1914.* Chapel Hill: University of North Carolina Press, 1994.

———. "Fearful Bodies into Disciplined Subjects: Pleasure, Romance and the Family Drama of Colonial Reform in Mary Carpenter's Six Months in India." *Signs* 20, no. 3 (1995): 545–74.

————. "Rules of Thumb: British History and 'Imperial Culture' in Nineteenth- and Twentieth-Century Britain." *Women's History Review* 3, no. 4 (1994): 483–500.

————. "The White Woman's Burden: British Feminists and 'The Indian Woman,' 1865–1915." In *Western Women and Imperialism: Complicity and Resistance*, edited by Nupur Chaudhuri and Margaret Strobel, 137–57. Bloomington: Indiana University Press, 1992.

Cain, P. J., and A. G. Hopkins. *British Imperialism: Innovation and Expansion 1688–1914*. London: Longman, 1993.

Calder, James. *Scotland's March Past: The Share of the Scottish Churches in the London Missionary Society*. London: Livingstone, 1945.

Cameron, Ian. *To the Farthest Ends of the Earth: The History of the Royal Geographical Society 1830–1980*. London: Macdonald, 1980.

Campbell, John. *Jethro: A System of Lay Agency, in Connexion with Congregational Churches, for the Diffusion of the Gospel Upon Our Home Population*. London: Jackson and Walford for the Congregational Union of England and Wales, 1839.

Cannadine, David. "The Context, Performance and Meaning of Ritual: The British Monarchy and the 'Invention of Tradition,' c. 1820–1877." In *The Invention of Tradition*, edited by Eric Hobsbawm and Terrence Ranger, 101–64. Cambridge: Cambridge University Press, 1983.

Carlyle, Thomas. *Past and Present*. London: Chapman and Hall, 1843.

Carnegie, David. *Among the Matabele*. London: Religious Tract Society, 1894.

Carr, Joseph. *The Story of the Sheffield Auxiliary to the London Missionary Society*. LMS Archives, Pamphlet 78, Blue Box 22A.

Carson, Penelope. "An Imperial Dilemma: the Propagation of Christianity in Early Colonial India." *Journal of Imperial and Commonwealth History* 18, no. 2 (May 1990), 169–90.

Carson, Rev. W. "Impressions and Suggestions: A Report of Nineteen Months' Visitation Among Ministers, Churches and County Unions." 1915. LMS Archives, Home, Odds, Box 14, Folder 1.

Centre for Contemporary Cultural Studies. *The Empire Strikes Back: Race and Racism in '70s Britain*. London: Hutchinson, 1982.

Chadwick, Owen. *The Victorian Church*. London: Adam and Charles Black, 1966.

Chakrabarty, Dipesh. "Postcoloniality and the Artifice of History: Who Speaks for 'Indian' Pasts?" *Representations* 37 (winter 1992): 1–26.

The Challenge of the Modern Situation: Some Thoughts for Free Churchmen. London: John Menzies, 1911. LMS Archives, Pamphlet Collection.

Cheapness or Efficiency? The Pecuniary Needs of Missionaries. London: LMS, 1893. LMS Archives, Pamphlet Collection.

Chirgwin, A. M. *Arthington's Millions*. London: The Livingstone Press, n.d.

Christensen, Torben, and William R. Hutchison, eds. *Missionary Ideologies in the Imperialist Era: 1880–1920*. Cambridge, Mass.: *Harvard Theological Review*, 1982.

Clark, Anna. *The Struggle for the Breeches: Gender and the Making of the British Working Class*. Berkeley: University of California Press, 1995.

Clark, J. C. D. *English Society, 1688–1832.* Cambridge: Cambridge University Press, 1985.

Clayton, Rev. George. *The Recollection of the Miseries of a Pagan Condition, a Motive to Zeal in the Missionary Cause.* London: LMS, 1821. Yale Divinity School, Special Collections.

Colley, Linda. "Britishness and Otherness: An Argument." *Journal of British Studies* 31, no. 4 (Oct. 1992): 309–29.

———. *Britons: Forging the Nation 1707–1837.* New Haven, Conn.: Yale University Press, 1992.

———. "The Imperial Embrace." *Yale Review* 81, no. 4 (Oct. 1993): 92–98.

Comaroff, Jean. *Body of Power, Spirit of Resistance: The Culture and History of a South African People.* Chicago: University of Chicago Press, 1985.

Comaroff, Jean, and John Comaroff. *From Revelation to Revolution.* Chicago: University of Chicago Press, 1991.

Comaroff, John. "Images of Empire, Contests of Conscience: Models of Colonial Domination in South Africa." Reprinted in *Tensions of Empire: Colonial Cultures in a Bourgeois World,* edited by Frederick Cooper and Ann Laura Stoler, 163–97. Berkeley: University of California Press, 1997.

Congregational Union of England and Wales. *Annual Reports of the Home Missionary Society.* London: Congregational Union of England and Wales.

———. *Congregational Yearbook.* Congregational Union of England and Wales.

———. *Our Sunday Schools: As They Are, and As They May Become. Including a Review of Our Young People's Societies: Being the Report of the 'Committee for Work Amongst the Young.'* London: Congregational Union of England and Wales, 1908.

Cooper, Frederick, and Ann Laura Stoler, eds. *Tensions of Empire: Colonial Cultures in a Bourgeois World.* Berkeley: University of California Press, 1997.

Cooper, J. A. "On Retaining the Elder Scholars in Our Sunday-Schools." *Congregational Yearbook,* 118–23. London: Congregational Union of England and Wales, 1870.

Cox, Jeffrey. *The English Churches in a Secular Society: Lambeth 1870–1920.* New York: Oxford University Press, 1982.

Crafts, Nick. "The Industrial Revolution." In *The Economic History of Britain Since 1700,* edited by Roderick Floud and Donald McCloskey, 2d edition, 44–59. Cambridge: Cambridge University Press, 1994.

Cunningham, Hugh. "The Language of Patriotism, 1750–1914." *History Workshop* 12 (autumn 1981): 8–33.

Cunningham, Valentine. *Everywhere Spoken Against: Dissent in the Victorian Novel.* Oxford: Clarendon, 1975.

———. "'God and Nature Intended You for a Missionary's Wife': Mary Hill, Jane Eyre and Other Missionary Women in the 1840s." In *Women and Missions: Past and Present,* edited by Fiona Bowie, Deborah Kirkwood, and Shirley Ardener, 85–108. Providence/Oxford: Berg, 1993.

Dachs, A. J. "Missionary Imperialism—the Case of Bechuanaland." *Journal of African History* 8, no. 4 (1972): 647–58.

da Costa, Emilia Viotti. *Crowns of Glory, Tears of Blood: The Demerara Slave Rebellion of 1823*. Oxford: Oxford University Press, 1994.

Dale, R. W. *A History of English Congregationalism*. Edited and completed by A. W. W. Dale. London: Hodder & Stoughton, 1907.

Darwent, Rev. C. E. *The Story of Fish Street Church Hull*. London: Wlm Anderson, 1899.

Darwin, John. "Imperialism in Decline? Tendencies in British Imperial Policy Between the Wars." *The Historical Journal* 23, no. 3 (1980): 657–79.

Daunton, Martin. "Gentlemanly Capitalism and British Industry, 1820–1914." *Past and Present* 122 (1989): 137–40.

Davies, Terrence. *Distant Voices, Still Lives*. London: British Film Institute in association with Channel 4/ZDF, 1988. Motion picture.

Davidoff, Leonore, and Catherine Hall. *Family Fortunes: Men and Women of the English Middle Class, 1780–1850*. Chicago: University of Chicago Press, 1987.

Davin, Anna. "Imperialism and Motherhood." *History Workshop* 5 (1978): 9–65.

Davis, David Brion. "Constructing Race: Differentiating Peoples in the Early Modern World, 1400–1700." *William and Mary Quarterly*, 3rd series, 54, no. 1 (Jan. 1997).

———. *The Problem of Slavery in the Age of Revolution 1770–1823*. Ithaca, N.Y.: Cornell University Press, 1975.

Dharmarah, Jacob S. *Colonialism and Christian Mission: Postcolonial Reflections*. Delhi: ISPCK, 1993.

Dickens, Charles. *Bleak House*. 1852. London: Penguin Classics 1985.

———. *Hard Times for These Times*. 1853. Harmondsworth: Penguin, 1969.

———. *Letters*. Vol. 2. Edited by Walter Dexter. London: Nonesuch Press, 1937–38.

———. "The Niger Expedition." In *Miscellaneous Papers*, Vol. 1. London: Chapman & Hall, 1848.

———. *The Posthumous Papers of the Pickwick Club*. 1837. London: Penguin, 1972.

Drescher, Seymour. *Capitalism and Anti-Slavery: British Mobilization in Comparative Perspective*. New York: Oxford University Press, 1987.

Driver, A. H. *The London Missionary Society and the West Midlands: Notes on the Contribution of Warwickshire, North Worcestershire and South Staffordshire to LMS History, Together with a List of Missionaries from the West Midlands, Litany of Commemoration, and Provisional Programme of Triple Jubilee Celebrations*. N.p., 1945.

Drummond, James. *Charles A. Berry*. London: Cassell, 1899.

Dublin University Magazine

Dubois, W. E. B. *Souls of Black Folk*. 1903. New York: Modern Library, 1996.

Dunnae, Patrick A. "Boys' Literature and the Idea of Empire, 1870–1914." *Victorian Studies* 24, no. 1 (autumn 1980): 105–21.

Eddy, Miss. *Mrs. Pickett's Missionary Box*. The Lamp Series, no. 4. LMS Archives, Pamphlet Collection.

Edmonton and Tottenham Chapel Records. Greater London Record Office.

Ekechi, F. K. *Missionary Enterprise and Rivalry in Igboland 1857–1914*. London: Frank Cass, 1971.

Eley, Geoff. "Playing It Safe: Or How is History Represented? The new *Cambridge Social History of Britain*." *History Workshop* 35 (spring 1993): 206–20.

———. "Social Imperialism: The Use and Abuse of an Idea." *Social History* 3 (Oct. 1976): 265–90.

Eliot, George. *Middlemarch: A Study in Provincial Life.* 1872. Boston: Houghton Mifflin, 1956.

Engels, Friedrich. *The Condition of the Working Class in England*, translated by W. O. Henderson and W. H. Chaloner. Stanford, Calif.: Stanford University Press, 1968.

Essex Auxiliary of the LMS. "The Second Report of the Essex Auxiliary Missionary Society, September 12, 1816." N.p.

———. "The Third Report of the Essex Auxiliary Missionary Society, July 31, 1817." N.p.

Etherington, Norman. *Preachers, Peasants and Politics in Southeast Africa, 1835–1880: African Christian Communities in Natal, Pondoland and Zululand.* London: Royal Historical Society, 1978.

Feldman, David. *Englishmen and Jews: Social Relations and Political Culture, 1840–1914.* New Haven, Conn.: Yale University Press, 1994.

Fieldhouse, D. K. "Gentlemen, Capitalists, and the British Empire." *Journal of Imperial and Commonwealth History* 22, no. 3 (Sept. 1994): 531–41.

Fields, Barbara J. "Ideology and Race in American History." In *Region, Race, and Reconstruction*, edited by J. Morgan Kousser and James M. McPherson, 143–77. London: Oxford University Press, 1982.

Fields, Karen E. "Christian Missionaries as Anti-Colonial Militants." *Theory and Society* 2, no. 1 (Jan. 1982): 95–108.

Finn, Margo. *After Chartism: Class and Nation in English Radical Politics, 1848–1874.* Cambridge: Cambridge University Press, 1993.

Fison, Roger. *How to Promote the Missionary Interest Among Our Sunday Scholars.* 3rd edition. Revised. London: LMS, 1903. LMS Archives, Pamphlet Collection.

Fletcher, Irene. "The Fundamental Principle of the London Missionary Society." *Transactions of the Congregational Historical Society* 19, no. 3 (Oct. 1962): 138–46; no. 4 (May 1963): 192–98; no. 5 (Sept. 1963): 222–29.

Fletcher, Rev. Joseph. *An Address Delivered to the Rev. John Pyer, on his Public Designation to the Office of City Missionary in the Service of the Christian Instruction Society, on Wednesday Evening, Apr. 21, 1830, at Claremont Chapel, Pentonville.* London: R. Davis, 1830. Yale Divinity School Special Collections.

Fraser, Derek. *The Evolution of the British Welfare State.* New York: Macmillan, 1973.

Fylde Missionary Council Papers, 1894–1928. LMS Auxiliary Records. Dr. Williams Library, London.

Galbraith, John S. "Myths of the 'Little England Era.'" *American Historical Review* 67, no. 1 (Oct. 1961): 34–48.

Gallagher, John, and Ronald Robinson. "The Imperialism of Free Trade." *Economic History Review*, 2d ser., 6 (1953): 1–15.

Gaunt, Lewis Herman. *School-Mates: Pictures of School-Time and Play-Time in the Mission Field.* London: LMS, 1906.

Geographical Magazine

Gibbon, Luke. "Race Against Time: Racial Discourse and Irish History." *Oxford Literary Review* 13 (spring 1991): 95–117.

Gilbert, Alan D. *Religion and Society in Industrial England: Church, Chapel and Social Change, 1740–1914.* London: Longman, 1976.

Gilroy, Paul. *The Black Atlantic. Modernity and Double Consciousness.* Cambridge, Mass.: Harvard University Press, 1993.

———. *"There Ain't No Black in the Union Jack": The Cultural Politics of Race and Nation.* Chicago: University of Chicago Press, 1991.

Goodall, Norman. *A History of the London Missionary Society 1895–1945.* London: Oxford University Press, 1954.

Goodwyn, Lawrence. *Democratic Promise: The Populist Moment in America.* Oxford: Oxford University Press, 1976.

Gosse, Edmund. *Father and Son.* 1907. London: Penguin, 1986.

Gray, Robert. *The Factory Question and Industrial England, 1830–1860.* Cambridge: Cambridge University Press, 1996.

Green, S. J. D. *Religion in the Age of Decline: Organisation and Experience in Industrial Yorkshire, 1870–1920.* Cambridge: Cambridge University Press, 1996.

Gregg, Robert, and Madhavi Kale. "The Empire and Mr. Thompson: Making of Indian Princes and English Working Class." *Economic and Political Weekly* 32, no. 36 (Sept. 6, 1997): 2273–88.

Griffin, Rev. John. *A Retrospect of the Proceedings of the London Missionary Society, Being the Substance of a Discourse Delivered at the Instance of the Directors on the Morning of October 10, 1826, At Hoxton Chapel, on the Opening of the Mission College.* Portsea: Samuel Griffin, 1827. Yale Divinity School, Special Collections, Record Group 29, Box 69.

Guntrip, H. J. S. *Smith and Wrigley of Leeds.* Leeds: Salem Congregational Church, n.d. Dr. Williams Library, London.

Halèvy, Elie. *The Birth of Methodism in England.* Chicago: University of Chicago Press, 1971.

Hall, Catherine. "The Economy of Intellectual Prestige: Thomas Carlyle, John Stuart Mill, and the Case of Governor Eyre." *Cultural Critique* (spring 1989): 167–96. Reprinted as "Competing Masculinities: Thomas Carlyle, John Stuart Mill and the case of Governor Eyre." In *White, Male and Middle Class: Explorations in Feminism and History,* 255–295. New York: Routledge, 1988.

———. "Rethinking Imperial Histories: The Reform Act of 1867." *New Left Review* 208 (Dec. 1994): 3–29.

———. *White, Male and Middle Class: Explorations in Feminism and History.* New York: Routledge, 1992.

Hall, Catherine, Jane Lewis, Keith McClelland, and Jane Rendall, eds. Introduction to "Gender, Nationalisms and National Identities," a special issue of *Gender and History* 5, no. 2 (summer 1993): 159–63.

Hall, Stuart. "On Postmodernism and Articulation: An Interview with Stuart Hall."

Edited by Lawrence Grossberg. *Journal of Communication Inquiry* 10, no. 2 (1986): 45–60.

———. "Race, Articulation and Societies Structured in Dominance." In *Sociological Theories: Race and Colonialism*, 305–45. Paris: UNESCO, 1980.

———. "The Rise of the Representative/Interventionist State." In *State and Society in Contemporary Britain: A Critical Introduction*, edited by Gregor McLennan, David Held, and Stuart Hall, 7–49. Cambridge, England: Polity Press, 1984.

Hamid, Idris. *Troubling of the Waters: A Collection of Papers and Responses Presented at Two Conferences on Creative Theological Reflection Held in Jamaica on the 3rd–4th of May, and in Trinidad on the 28th–30th of May, 1973.* San Fernando, Trinidad, W. I.: Rahaman Printery, 1973.

Harcourt, Freda. "Disraeli's Imperialism, 1866–1868: A Question of Timing." *Historical Journal* 23, no. 1 (1980): 87–109.

Harris, Rev. William. *The Spirit of Christianity, a Missionary Spirit.* London: LMS, 1817. Yale Divinity School Special Collections.

Harrison, Brian. *Drink and the Victorians: The Temperance Question in England 1815–1872.* London: Faber and Faber, 1971.

Harrison, J. F. C. *The Early Victorians 1832–1851.* New York: Praeger, 1971.

Haw, George, ed. *Christianity and the Working Classes.* London: Macmillan, 1906.

Headingley Hill Chapel, Leeds. Records. Yorkshire Congregational Union Records. Leeds Archives Department.

Headingley Hill Congregational Church. *The History of Headingly Hill Congregational Church.* Privately printed; n.d. Leeds Archives Department.

Headingley Hill Congregational Church Yearbooks. Yorkshire Congregational Union Records: Headingley Hill Chapel Records. Leeds Archives Department, Leeds.

Heitzenrater, Richard P. *Wesley and the People Called Methodists.* Nashville, Tenn.: Abingdon Press, 1995.

Hempton, David. "Religion in Victorian Fiction." In *The Writer as Witness: Literature as Historical Evidence*, edited by Tom Dunne. Cork: Cork University Press, 1987.

———. "Women and Evangelical Religion in Ireland, 1750–1900." In *The Religion of the People: Methodism and Popular Religion c. 1750–1900*, 179–96. London and New York: Routledge, 1996.

Hennock, E. P. *Fit and Proper Persons.* London: Edward Arnold, 1973.

———. "Poverty and Social Theory in England: The Experiences of the Eighteen-Eighties." *Social History* 1 (Jan. 1976): 67–91.

Hickman, Mary J. *Religion, Class and Identity: The State, the Catholic Church and the Education of the Irish in Britain.* Avebury: Aldershot, 1995.

Higginbotham, Evelyn Brooks. *Righteous Discontent: The Women's Movement in the Black Baptist Church, 1880–1920.* Cambridge, Mass.: Harvard University Press, 1993.

Hill, Patricia R. *The World Their Household: The American Woman's Foreign Mission Movement and Cultural Transformation 1870–1920.* Ann Arbor: University of Michigan Press, 1985.

Hilton, Boyd. *The Age of Atonement: The Influence of Evangelicalism on Social and Economic Thought 1785–1865.* Oxford: Clarendon, 1988.

Himmelfarb, Gertrude. *The Idea of Poverty: England in the Early Industrial Age*. New York: Knopf, 1984.

———. *Poverty and Compassion: The Moral Imagination of the Late Victorians*. New York: Knopf, 1991.

Hindu Boys. Sunday School Leaflets, no. 2. London: LMS, n.d. LMS Archives.

Hobsbawm, E. J. *Age of Revolution, 1789–1848*. New York: New American Library, 1962.

———. *Industry and Empire*. New York: Penguin, 1969.

Hollis, Patricia. "Anti-Slavery and British Working-Class Radicalism in the Years of Reform." In *Anti-Slavery, Religion and Reform*, edited by Christine Bolt and Seymour Drescher. Folkestone, Kent: William Dawson, 1980.

———. *Pressure from Without in Early Victorian England*. London: St. Martin's Press, 1974.

Holt, Thomas C. "Marking: Race, Race Making, and the Writing of History." *American Historical Review* 100, no. 1 (Feb. 1995): 1–20.

———. *The Problem of Freedom: Race, Labor, and Politics in Jamaica and Britain, 1832–1938*. Baltimore, MD: Johns Hopkins University Press, 1992.

Horne, Rev. C. Silvester. *The Rock of Ages*. 2d edition. London: Passmore and Alabaster, 1901.

———. *The Story of the LMS, 1795–1895*. London: LMS, 1894.

Horton, Robert Forman. *An Autobiography*. London: George Allen and Unwin, 1917.

Howe, Anthony. *The Cotton Masters 1830–1860*. Oxford: Clarendon, 1984.

Howkins, Alun. *Reshaping Rural England: A Social History 1850–1925*. London: Harper Collins, 1991.

Howsam, Leslie. *Cheap Bibles: Nineteenth-Century Publishing and the British and Foreign Bible Society*. Cambridge: Cambridge University Press, 1991.

Hunslet and Holbeck News

Inglis, K. S. *Churches and the Working Classes in Victorian England*. London: Routledge and Kegan Paul, 1963.

Innes, Joanna. "Social History and England's 'Ancien Regime.'" *Past and Present* 115 (May 1987): 171–72.

Is It Nothing to You? A Record of Work Among Women in Connection with the London Missionary Society. London: LMS, 1899.

James, Rev. J. A. "The Attractions of the Cross: A Sermon Preached Before the London Missionary Society at Surrey Chapel, May 12, 1819." London: London Missionary Society, 1819. Yale Divinity School, Special Collections.

———. *The Conversion of Englishmen and the Conversion of the World Inseparable*. London: Congregational Home Missionary Society, 1835. Yale Divinity School, Special Collections.

Jeal, Tim. *Livingstone*. London: Heinemann, 1973.

Johnston, Rev. John. *The Gospel of the Kingdom to be Universally Preached*. London: LMS, 1818. Yale Divinity School Special Collections.

Jones, David. *Centenary Memorials of the Church and Congregation Assembling for Chris-*

tian Worship in Booth Chapel, Near Halifax. Halifax: 1861. West Yorkshire Archive Service, Calderdale, 285.8 JON.

Jones, Gareth Stedman. *Outcast London: A Study in the Relationship Between Classes in Victorian Society*. Middlesex: Harmondsworth, 1971.

————. "Working-Class Culture and Working-Class Politics in London, 1870–1900: Notes on the Remaking of a Working Class." *Journal of Social History* 7, no. 4 (summer 1974): 460–508. Reprinted in *Languages of Class. Studies in English Working Class History 1832–1982*, 179–238. New York: Cambridge University Press, 1983.

Jones, J. D. *Three Score Years and Ten: The Autobiography of J. D. Jones*. London: Hodder and Stoughton, 1940.

Jones, R. Tudur. *Congregationalism in England 1662–1962*. London: Independent Press, 1962.

Joyce, Patrick. *Work, Society and Politics: The Culture of the Factory in Later Victorian England*. London: Methuen, 1980.

Juster, Susan. *Disorderly Women: Sexuality, Politics and Evangelicalism in Revolutionary New England*. Ithaca, N.Y.: Cornell University Press, 1994.

Kay, Elaine. *The History of King's Weigh House Church*. London: George Allen and Unwin, 1968.

Kaye, Harvey J. *The British Marxist Historians*. New York: St. Martin's, 1995.

Kearney, Hugh. *The British Isles: A History of Four Nations*. Cambridge: Cambridge University Press, 1989.

Kidd, Alan J. "Charity Organization and the Unemployed in Manchester, c. 1870–1914." *Social History* 9, no. 1 (Jan. 1984): 45–66.

Kiernan, Victor. "Evangelicalism and the French Revolution." *Past and Present* 1 (Feb. 1952): 44–56.

————. *Imperialism and Its Contradictions*. Edited and introduced by Harvey J. Kaye. New York: Routledge, 1995.

Kirkwood, Deborah. "Protestant Missionary Women: Wives and Spinsters." In *Women and Missions: Past and Present*, edited by Fiona Bowie, Deborah Kirkwood, and Shirley Ardener, 23–42. Providence/Oxford: Berg, 1993.

Knox, B. A. "Reconsidering MidVictorian Imperialism." *Journal of Imperial and Commonwealth History* 1, no. 2 (Jan. 1973): 155–72.

Koditschek, Theodore. *Class Formation and Urban Industrial Society: Bradford 1750–1850*. Cambridge: Cambridge University Press, 1990.

Kooiman, Dick. *Conversion and Social Equality in India: The London Missionary Society in South Travancore in the 19th Century*. Amsterdam: Free University Press, 1989.

Landau, Paul Stuart. *The Realm of the Word: Language, Gender, and Christianity in a Southern African Kingdom*. Portsmouth, N.H.: Heinemann, 1995.

Langford, Paul. *A Polite and Commercial People: England, 1727–1783*. Oxford: Clarendon, 1989.

Langmore, Diane. *Missionary Lives: Papua, 1874–1914*. Honolulu: University of Hawaii Press, 1989.

Laqueur, Thomas Walter. *Religion and Respectability: Sunday Schools and Working-Class Culture 1780–1850*. New Haven, Conn.: Yale University Press, 1976.

Latourette, Kenneth Scott. *A History of the Expansion of Christianity*. Vol. 2, *The Thousand Years of Uncertainty: A. D. 500–A. D. 1500*. New York: Harper, 1937.

———. *A History of the Expansion of Christianity*. Vol. 3, *Three Centuries of Advance, 1500–1800*. New York: Harper, 1939.

Leeds Auxiliary Committee Minutes. LMS Auxiliary Records. Dr. Williams Library, London.

The Leeds Congregationalist. Deposited with records of Trinity St. David's United Reformed Church, Acc 2119, item 91. Leeds Archives Department, Leeds.

Leeds Mercury

Leeds Obituary Notices. Reference Dept. Leeds Central Library.

Leicester and Rutland Auxiliary of the LMS. Minute Book. Leicester Record Office.

Lenwood, Frank. Papers. LMS Archives, Home, Personal, Box 9.

———. *Social Problems and the East: A Point of Honour*. London: United Council for Missionary Education, 1919.

Levine, Philippa. *Victorian Feminism 1850–1900*. London: Hutchinson Education, 1987.

Livingstone, David. *Missionary Travels and Researches in South Africa: Including a Sketch of Sixteen Years' Residence in the Interior of Africa*. New York: Harper, 1858.

Lloyd, Trevor Owen. *The British Empire, 1558–1995*. 2d edition. New York: Oxford University Press, 1996.

LMS. *Annual Reports*

———. *Chronicle*

———. *Juvenile Missionary Magazine*

———. *Quarterly News of Women's Work*

———. *Universal Brotherhood*

———. *The World For Christ: A Church's Share in Winning It*. 3rd edition. London: LMS, 1905.

LMS Archives. School of Oriental and African Studies, London.

LMS Auxiliary Records. Leeds Auxiliary Committee Minutes and Newcastle Auxiliary Committee Minutes. Dr. Williams Library, London.

London City Mission. *An Appeal for the London City Mission*. London: London City Mission, 1847. Yale Divinity School Special Collections.

London City Mission, West London Auxiliary. *Annual Report, 1856*.

London Female Mission. *Annual Reports*.

Lorimer, Douglas. *Colour, Class and the Victorians*. Leicester: Leicester University Press, 1978.

Lovegrove, Deryck W. *Established Church, Sectarian People: Itinerancy and the Transformation of English Dissent, 1780–1830*. Cambridge: Cambridge University Press, 1988.

Lovett, Richard. *The History of the London Missionary Society, 1795–1895*. 2 volumes. London: Oxford University Press, 1899.

Luke, Jemima. *Early Years of My Life*. London: Hodder & Stoughton, 1900.

Macfadyen, Rev. J. A. "The Missionary Work of the Congregational Churches." *Congregational Yearbook* (1871).

Mackenzie, John M., "David Livingstone: The Construction of The Myth." In *Sermons and Battle Hymns: Protestant Popular Culture in Modern Scotland*, edited by Graham Walker and Tom Gallagher, 24–42. Edinburgh: Edinburgh University Press, 1990.

———, ed. *Imperialism and Popular Culture*. Manchester: Manchester University Press, 1986.

———, ed. *Popular Imperialism and the Military: 1850–1950*. Manchester: University of Manchester Press, 1992.

Mandler, Peter. "Tories and Paupers: Christian Political Economy and the Making of the New Poor Law." *Historical Journal* 33, no. 1 (1990): 81–103.

———, ed. *The Uses of Charity: The Poor on Relief in the Nineteenth-Century Metropolis*. Philadelphia, Penn.: University of Pennsylvania Press, 1990.

Market Harborough Congregational Church Records. Leicester Record Office.

Marks, Shula. "History, the Nation and Empire: Sniping from the Periphery." *History Workshop* 29 (1990): 111–19.

Marshall, Peter. "Imperial Britain." *Journal of Imperial and Commonwealth History* 23, no. 3 (Sept. 1995): 379–94.

Marshall, P. J. "No Fatal Impact? The Elusive History of Imperial Britain." *Times Literary Supplement*, Mar. 12, 1993, p. 8–10.

"Marshall Street Congregational Church, Holbeck, Leeds. Centenary Celebrations, 1836–1936." Typescript history. Congregational Library, Dr. Williams Library.

Martindale, Hilda. *From One Generation to Another 1839–1944: A Book of Memoirs*. London: George Allen and Unwin, 1944.

Mason, Rev. Thomas W. *One Hundred and Fifty Years in Essex: Marking the Triple Jubilee of the Essex Congregational Union: Southend-on-Sea, April 14th and 15th, 1948*.

Matthews, Basil. *Dr. Ralph Wardlaw Thompson*. London: Religious Tract Society, 1917.

———. "Young Congregationalists and the London Missionary Society." In *Congregational Workers Handbook*. London: Congregational Union of England and Wales, 1915.

Mayfield, David, and Susan Thorne. "Social History and Its Discontents." *Social History* 17, no. 2 (May 1992): 165–88.

McClintock, Anne. *Imperial Leather: Race, Gender and Sexuality in the Colonial Contest*. New York and London: Routledge, 1995.

McCord, Norman. *The Anti-Corn Law League 1838–1946*. 2d edition. London: Unwin University Books, 1968.

———. *British History 1815–1906*. Oxford: Oxford University Press, 1991.

McHugh, Paul. *Prostitution and Victorian Social Reform*. London: Croom Helm, 1980.

McIlhiney, David Brown. "A Gentleman in Every Slum: Church of England Missions in East London, 1837–1914." Ph.D. diss., Princeton University, 1976.

McKenzie, Robert, and Allan Silver. *Angels in Marble: Working Class Conservatives in Urban England*. London: Heinemann, 1968.

McLaughlin, Joseph. *Writing the Urban Jungle: Metropolis and Colonies in Conan Doyle, General Booth, Jack London, Conrad, and T. S. Eliot.* Ph.D. diss., Duke University, 1992.

McLeod, Hugh. *Class and Religion in the Late Victorian City.* London: Croom Helm, 1974.

———. "New Perspectives on Victorian Class Religion: the Oral Evidence." *Oral History Journal* 14, no. 1 (1986): 31–49.

———. *Religion and Society in England, 1850–1914.* New York: St. Martin's Press, 1996.

———. *Religion and the People of Western Europe 1789–1970.* Oxford: Oxford University Press, 1981.

———. *Religion and the Working Class in Nineteenth Century Britain.* London: Macmillan, 1984.

Meacham, Standish. *A Life Apart: The English Working Class 1890–1914.* London: Thames and Hudson, 1977.

Mearns, Andrew. *England for Christ: A Record of the Congregational Church Aid and Home Missionary Society.* London: James Clarke, 1886.

Mehta, Uday. "Liberal Strategies of Exclusion." *Politics and Society* 18, no. 4 (1990): 427–54. Reprinted in *Tensions of Empire*, edited by Frederick Cooper and Ann Laura Stoler, 59–86. Berkeley: University of California Press, 1997.

Midgley, Clare. *Women Against Slavery: The British Campaigns 1780–1870.* London: Routledge, 1992.

Mintz, Sidney. *Sweetness and Power: The Place of Sugar in Modern History.* New York: Viking, 1985.

Moffat, John S. *The Black Man and the War.* Vigilance Papers, No. 8. Cape Town: The South African Vigilance Committee, n.d. LMS Archives.

———. *The Lives of Robert and Mary Moffat.* London: T. Fisher Unwin, 1885.

Money, John. "The Masonic Moment; or, Ritual, Replica, and Credit: John Wilkes, the Macaroni Parson, and the Making of the Middle-Class Mind." *Journal of British Studies* 32, no. 4 (Oct. 1993): 358–95.

Morison, John. *The Fathers and Founders of the London Missionary Society.* London: Fisher, 1844.

Morris, Esther. Diary (1828–1845). East Sussex Record Office.

Morris, R. J. *Class, Sect and Party: The Making of the British Middle Class, Leeds 1820–1850.* Manchester and New York: Manchester University Press, 1990.

———. "Voluntary Societies and British Urban Elites." *Historical Journal* 26, no. 1 (1983): 95–118.

Mullens, Joseph. *London and Calcutta Compared in Their Heathenism, Their Privileges and Their Prospects: Showing the Great Claims of Foreign Missions upon the Christian Church.* London: James Nisbet, 1868.

Murray, Nancy Uhlar. "Nineteenth Century Kenya and the 'Imperial Race for Christ.'" Paper presented to the Historical Association of Kenya, Annual Conference, 1978.

Neill, Stephen. *Colonialism and Christian Missions*. New York: McGraw-Hill, 1966.

———. *A History of Christian Missions*. Harmondsworth, England: Penguin Books, 1964.

Nemer, Lawrence. *Anglican and Roman Catholic Attitudes on Missions: An Historical Study of Two Missionary Societies in the Late Nineteenth Century (1865–1885)*. St. Augustine: Steyler Verlag, 1981.

Newcastle Auxiliary Committee Minutes. LMS Auxiliary Records. Dr. Williams Library, London.

Newcastle Daily Chronicle

Newcastle Town Mission. *Annual Report of the Newcastle Town Mission*. 1829.

New Court Congregational Chapel (London) Records. Greater London Record Office.

Newman, Louise Michele. "Laying Claim to Difference: Ideologies of Race and Gender in the U.S. Woman's Movement, 1870–1920." Ph.D. diss., Brown University, 1992.

Nightingale, Benjamin. *The Story of the Lancashire Congregational Union 1806–1906: Centenary Memorial Volume*. London: John Heywood, 1906.

Nord, Deborah Epstein. "The Social Explorer As Anthropologist: Victorian Travellers Among the Urban Poor." In *Visions of the Modern City: Essays in History, Art, and Literature*, edited by William Sharpe and Leonard Wallock, 118–130. New York: Proceedings of the Heyman Center for the Humanities at Columbia University, 1983.

Norman, E. R. *Church and Society in England 1779–1970*. Oxford: Clarendon, 1976.

North, Eric McCoy. *Early Methodist Philanthropy*. Ph.D. diss., Columbia University, 1914.

Northrup, David. *Indentured Labor in the Age of Imperialism, 1834–1922*. Cambridge: Cambridge University Press, 1995.

Notes for Talks to the Sunday Schools. London: Baptist Missionary Society, 1916.

Obelkevich, Jim. "Music and Religion in the Nineteenth Century." In *Disciplines of Faith: Studies in Religion, Politics, and Patriarchy*, edited by Jim Obelkevich, Lyndal Roper, Raphael Samuel, 550–65. London: Routledge, 1987.

———. *Religion and Rural Society: South Lindsey, 1825–1875*. Oxford: Clarendon, 1976.

O'Connor, Maura. *A Political Romance: Italy and the Making of the English Middle Class, 1800–1864*. Forthcoming.

O'Gorman, Frank. Review of *Religion, Revolution, and English Radicalism: Nonconformity in Eighteenth-Century Politics and Society*, by James E. Bradley. *Social History* 17, no. 1 (Jan. 1992): 158–59.

Ollerenshaw, Rev. Henry. "The Best Method of Bringing Gospel Truth to Bear Upon the Working Classes of Our Land." *The Hull and East Riding Magazine* 2, no. 13 (Apr. 1868): 25–34.

Orwell, George. *The Road to Wigan Pier*. London: Victor Gollancz, 1937.

Owen, David Edward. *English Philanthropy 1660–1960*. Cambridge, Mass.: Harvard University Press, 1964.

Parker, Joseph. *The Larger Ministry*. London: Congregational Union of England and Wales, 1884.

Parry, J. P. *Democracy and Religion: Gladstone and the Liberal Party, 1867–1875*. New York: Cambridge University Press, 1986.

Paul, Kathleen. "'British Subjects' and 'British Stock': Labour's Postwar Imperialism." *Journal of British Studies* 34, no. 2 (Apr. 1995): 233–76.

Payne, Elizabeth M. *And the Women Also: A Century of Service in the Cause of Overseas Missions*. London: Baptist Missionary Society, 1967.

Peel, Albert, and J. A. R. Marriott. *Robert Forman Horton*. London: George Allen and Unwin, 1937.

Pelling, Henry. "British Labour and British Imperialism." In *Popular Politics and Society in Late Victorian Britain*, 82–100. New York: St. Martin's Press, 1968.

Pelton, M. O. "Missionary Education." In *The Mandate: A Vision of Service: Published for the Use of Ministers*, edited by Edward Shillitto, 130–141. London: LMS, 1920.

Perkin, Harold. "An Open Elite." *Journal of British Studies* 24 (October 1985): 496–501.

Perry, Alan Frederick. "The American Board of Commissioners for Foreign Missions and the London Missionary Society in the 19th Century: A Study of Ideas." Ph.D. diss., Washington University, 1974.

Phillips, John. *Electoral Behaviour in Unreformed England: Plumpers, Splitters and Straights*. Princeton, N.J.: Princeton University Press, 1982.

Philp, Mark. "Vulgar Conservatism." *English Historical Review* 110, no. 435 (Feb. 1995): 42–69.

Pick, Daniel. *Faces of Degeneration: A European Disorder, c. 1848–1918*. Cambridge: Cambridge University Press, 1989.

Piggin, Frederic Stuart. "Halèvy Revisited: the Origins of the Wesleyan Methodist Missionary Society: An Examination of Semmel's Thesis." *Journal of Imperial and Commonwealth History* 9, no. 1 (Oct. 1980): 17–37.

———. *Making Evangelical Missionaries 1789–1858: The Social Background, Motives and Training of British Protestant Missionaries to India*. Abingdon, England: Sutton Courtenay Press, 1984.

———. "The Social Background, Motivation, and Training of British Protestant Missionaries to India, 1789–1858." Ph.D. diss., University of London, 1974.

Pirouet, M. Louise. "Women Missionaries of the Church Missionary Society in Uganda 1896–1920." In *Missionary Ideologies in the Imperialist Era: 1880–1920*, edited by Torben Christensen and William R. Hutchinson, 231–40. Denmark: Aros, 1981.

Pocock, J. G. A. "The Limits and Divisions of British History: In Search of the Unknown Subject." *American Historical Review* 87, no. 2 (Apr. 1982): 311–36.

Poovey, Mary. *Making a Social Body. British Cultural Formation 1830–1864*. Chicago: University of Chicago Press, 1995.

———. *Uneven Development: The Ideological Work of Gender in Mid-Victorian England*. Chicago: University of Chicago Press, 1988.

Pope, Norris. *Dickens and Charity*. New York: Columbia University Press, 1978.

Porter, Andrew, ed. *Atlas of British Overseas Expansion*. London: Routledge, 1991.

————. "Cambridge, Keswick, and Late-Nineteenth-Century Attitudes to Africa." *Journal of Imperial and Commonwealth History* 5, no. 1 (1976): 5–34.

————. "Commerce and Christianity: The Rise and Fall of a Nineteenth-Century Missionary Slogan." *Historical Journal* 28, no. 3 (1985): 597–621.

————. "'Gentlemanly Capitalism' and Empire: The British Experience since 1750." *Journal of Imperial and Commonwealth History* 18, no. 3 (Oct. 1990): 265–95.

————. "Religion and Empire: British Expansion in the Long Nineteenth Century, 1780–1914." *Journal of Imperial and Commonwealth History* 20, no. 3 (Sept. 1992): 370–90.

Porter, Bernard. "British Foreign Policy in the Nineteenth Century." *Historical Journal* 23, no. 1 (1980): 193–202.

Prakash, Gyan. "Writing Post-Orientalist Histories of the Third World." *Comparative Studies in Society and History* (1990): 383–408.

Pratt, Mary Louise. *Imperial Eyes: Travel Writing and Transculturation*. London and New York: Routledge, 1992.

Price, Richard. *An Imperial War and the British Working Class: Working-Class Attitudes and Reactions to the Boer War 1899–1902*. London: Routledge, 1972.

————. "Languages of Revisionism: Historians and Popular Politics in Nineteenth-Century Britain." *Journal of Social History* 30, no. 1 (1996): 229–52.

Prochaska, F. K. "Body and Soul: Bible Nurses and the Poor in Victorian London." *Historical Research* 60 (1987): 336–48.

————. "Little Vessels: Children in the Nineteenth-Century English Missionary Movement." *Journal of Imperial and Commonwealth History* 6, no. 2 (Jan. 1978), 103–18.

————. "Philanthropy." In *The Cambridge Social History of Britain 1750–1950*. Vol. 3 of *Social Agencies and Institutions*, edited by F. M. L. Thompson, 357–94. Cambridge: Cambridge University Press, 1990.

————. *Women and Philanthropy in Nineteenth-Century England*. Oxford: Clarendon, 1980.

Prout, E. *Missionary Ships Connected with the London Missionary Society*. London: LMS, 1865. LMS Archives, Pamphlet Collection.

Pye-Smith, Arthur. *Memorials of Fetter Lane Congregational Church, London*. London: Warren Hall and Lovitt, 1900.

Ranger, T. O., and John Weller, eds. *Themes in the Christian History of Central Africa*. Berkeley: University of California Press, 1975.

Reddy, William M. "The Concept of Class." In *Social Orders and Social Classes in Europe Since 1500: Studies in Social Stratification*, edited by M. L. Bush, 13–25. London: Longman, 1992.

Rendall, Jane. *The Origins of British Feminism: Women in Britain, France and the United States, 1780–1860*. Chicago: Lyceum Books, 1985.

Roediger, David R. *The Wages of Whiteness: Race and the Making of the American Working Class*. London: Verso, 1991.

Rogers, Rev. J. Guinness. *An Autobiography*. London: James Clarke, 1903.

Rogers, Nicholas. "Introduction: Making the English Middle Class, ca. 1700–1850." *Journal of British Studies* 32, no. 4 (Oct. 1993): 299–304.

Rose, Sonya O. *Limited Livelihoods: Gender and Class in Nineteenth-Century England.* Berkeley, Calif.: University of California Press, 1992.

Ross, J. A. "How Missions Prevent War." *Universal Brotherhood,* July 15, 1915.

Ross, James. *A History of Congregational Independency in Scotland.* Glasgow: James MacLehose, 1900.

Rotberg, Robert. *Christian Missions and the Creation of Northern Rhodesia 1880–1914.* Princeton, N.J.: Princeton University Press, 1965.

Rupp, Gordon. *Religion in England. 1688–1791.* Oxford: Clarendon, 1986.

Said, Edward. *Culture and Imperialism.* New York: Random House, 1993.

———. *Orientalism.* New York: Vintage, 1979.

Salter, F. R. *Dissenters and Public Affairs in Mid-Victorian England.* London: Dr. Williams's Trust, 1967.

Saunders, Kay, ed. *Indentured Labour in the British Empire 1834–1920.* London: Croom Helm, 1984.

Schreuder, D. M. "The Cultural Factor in Victorian Imperialism: A Case-Study of the British 'Civilising Mission.'" *Journal of Imperial and Commonwealth History* 4, no. 3 (May 1976): 283–317.

Scott, Joan. "Women in *The Making.*" In *Gender and the Politics of History.* New York: Columbia University Press, 1988.

Searle, G. R. *The Quest for National Efficiency: A Study in British Politics and Political Thought, 1899–1914.* Berkeley: University of California Press, 1971.

———. *Eugenics and Politics in Britain, 1900–1914.* Leyden: Noordhoff International, 1976.

Seed, John. "From 'Middling Sort' to Middle Class in Late Eighteenth- and Early Nineteenth-Century England." In *Social Orders and Social Classes in Europe Since 1500: Studies in Social Stratification,* edited by M. L. Bush, 114–135. London: Longman, 1992.

———. "Gentlemen Dissenters: The Social and Political Meanings of Rational Dissent in the 1770s and 1780s." *Historical Journal* 28, no. 2 (1985): 299–325.

———. "The Role of Unitarianism in the Formation of Liberal Culture 1775–1851." Ph.D. thesis, University of Hull, 1981.

———. "Theologies of Power: Unitarianism and the Social Relations of Religious Discourse, 1800–1850." In *Class, Power and Social Structure in British Nineteenth-Century Towns,* edited by R. J. Morris, 108–56. Leicester: Leicester University Press, 1986.

———. "Unitarianism, Political Economy and the Antinomies of Liberal Culture in Manchester, 1830–1850." *Social History* 7, no. 1 (Jan. 1982): 1–25.

Selbie, W. B. *Congregationalism.* London: Methuen, 1927.

———. *The Life of Andrew Martin Fairbairn.* London: Hodder and Stoughton, 1914.

———, ed. *The Life of Charles Silvester Horne, M. A., M. P.* London: Hodder and Stoughton, 1920.

Semmel, Bernard. *Imperialism and Social Reform: English Social-Imperial Thought, 1895–1914.* London: George Allen and Unwin, 1960.

———. *The Methodist Revolution.* New York: Basic Books, 1973.

Sheffield Daily Telegraph

Shillito, Edward. "The Race Problem." *The British Congregationalist,* Jan. 16, 1908, 49–50.

Shipley Congregational Schools Records. Minutes of the Meetings of the Congregational Schools. West Yorkshire Archive Service, Bradford. "Shipley Congregational Church 1905–1965." Typescript history. Bradford Central Library.

Sibree, Rev. James. *Recollections of Hull During Half a Century.* Hull: A. Brown, 1884.

Smith, Faith Lois. "J. J. Thomas and Caribbean Intellectual Life in the Nineteenth Century." Ph.D. diss., Duke University, 1995.

Smith, John Pye. *The Connections of the Redeemer's Heavenly State with the Advancement of His Kingdom on Earth.* London: LMS, 1820. Yale Divinity School Library, Special Collections.

Smith, Mark. *Religion in Industrial Society: Oldham and Saddleworth. 1740–1865.* Oxford: Clarendon, 1994.

Snell, K. D. M. *Annals of the Labouring Poor: Social Change and Agrarian England 1660–1900.* Cambridge: Cambridge University Press, 1985.

Snell, Lord Henry. *Men, Movements and Myself.* London: J. M. Dent, 1936.

St. Andrews (formerly Roundhay) Congregational Church Records. Leeds Archives Department.

Stanley, Brian. *The Bible and the Flag: Protestant Missions and British Imperialism in the Nineteenth and Twentieth Centuries.* Leicester: Apollos, 1990.

———. "Commerce and Christianity: Providence Theory, the Missionary Movement, and the Imperialism of Free Trade, 1842–1860." *Historical Journal* 26, no. 1 (1983): 71–94.

———. *The History of the Baptist Missionary Society 1792–1992.* Edinburgh: T&T Clark, 1992.

———. "Home Support for Overseas Missions in Early Victorian England, c. 1838–1873." Ph.D., diss., Cambridge University, 1979.

———. "'The Miser of Headingley': Robert Arthington and the Baptist Missionary Society, 1877–1900." In *The Church and Wealth,* edited by W. J. Sheils and Diana Wood, 371–82. London: Basil Blackwell for the Ecclesiastical History Society, 1987.

Stanley, Henry M. *In Darkest Africa: or, The Quest, Rescue, and Retreat of Emin, Governor of Equatoria.* New York: Scribner, 1891, c. 1890.

Stead, Francis Herbert. *How Old Age Pensions Began to Be.* London: Methuen, 1909.

Steedman, Carolyn Kay. *Childhood, Culture and Class in Britain: Margaret McMillan, 1860–1931.* New Brunswick, N.J.: Rutgers University Press, 1990.

———. *Landscape for a Good Woman. A Story of Two Lives.* New Brunswick, N.J.: Rutgers University Press, 1987.

Stepan, Nancy. *The Idea of Race in Science: Great Britain, 1800–1960.* Hamden, Conn.: Archon Books, 1982.

Steven, Rev. James. "Christianity, the True Light to Illuminate the World." A Sermon Preached Before the Missionary Society in London, May 9, 1811. Yale Divinity School, Special Collections, Record Group 29, Box 29.

Stevenson, Rev. William Fleming. *The Dawn of Modern Missions*. Edinburgh, 1887.

Stoler, Ann Laura. "Making the Empire Respectable: The Politics of Race and Sexual Morality." *American Ethnologist* 16, no. 4 (Nov. 1989), 634–60.

———. *Race and the Education of Desire: Foucault's History of Sexuality and the Colonial Order of Things*. Durham, N.C.: Duke University Press, 1995.

———. "Rethinking Colonial Categories: European Communities and the Boundaries of Rule." *Comparative Studies in Society and History* 31, no. 1 (Jan. 1989), 134–61.

Stone, Lawrence, and J. F. Stone. *An Open Elite? England 1540–1880*. Oxford: Clarendon Press, 1984.

Strayer, Robert. "Mission History in Africa: New Perspectives on an Encounter." *African Studies Review* 19, no. 1 (Apr. 1976): 1–16.

Streets, Heather. "The Right Stamp of Men: Military Imperatives and Popular Imperialism in Late Victorian Britain." Ph.D. Diss., Duke University, forthcoming.

Strobel, Margaret. *European Women and the Second British Empire*. Bloomington: Indiana University Press, 1991.

Suleri, Sara. *The Rhetoric of English India*. Chicago: University of Chicago Press, 1992.

Tabili, Laura. *"We Ask for British Justice": Workers and Racial Difference in Late Imperial Britain*. Ithaca, N.Y.: Cornell University Press, 1994.

Tawney, R. H. *Religion and the Rise of Capitalism: A Historical Study*. Gloucester, Mass.: Peter Smith, 1962.

Taylor, Barbara. *Eve and the New Jerusalem: Socialism and Feminism in the Nineteenth Century*. New York: Pantheon, 1983.

Taylor, Miles. "John Bull and the Iconography of Public Opinion in England, c. 1712–1929." *Past and Present* 134 (Feb. 1992): 93–128.

———. "Patriotism, History and the Left in Twentieth Century Britain." *Historical Journal* 33, no. 4 (1990): 971–87.

Temperley, Howard. *White Dreams, Black Africa: The Antislavery Expedition to the River Niger 1841–2*. New Haven, Conn.: Yale University Press, 1991.

Thackeray, William. *Vanity Fair*. 1847. Ware, Hertfordshire: Wordsworth Classics, 1992.

Theddingworth Congregational Chapel Records. Leicester Record Office.

Thomas, Nicholas. *Colonialism's Culture. Anthropology, Travel and Government*. Princeton, N.J.: Princeton University Press, 1994.

Thomas, William, ed. *The Jubilee of Queen Street Chapel, Leeds, with Memorials of the Church and Its Pastors from the Beginning*. Leeds: Joseph Dodgson, 1875. Congregational Library, Dr. Williams Library, London.

Thompson, E. P. *Alien Homage: Edward Thompson and Rabindranath Tagore*. Oxford: Oxford University Press, 1993.

———. *Customs in Common*. New York: New Press, 1991.

————. *The Making of the English Working Class*. New York: Vintage 1966.

————. "Patrician Society, Plebian Culture." *Journal of Social History* 7 (summer 1974): 382–405.

————. "Time, Work-Discipline and Industrial Capitalism." *Past and Present* 38 (Dec. 1967): 56–97.

————. *Writing by Candlelight*. London: Merlin, 1980.

Thompson, Jemima. *Memoirs of British Female Missionaries: With a Survey of the Condition of Women in Heathen Countries and Also a Preliminary Essay on the Importance of Female Agency in Evangelizing Pagan Nations*. London: William Smith, 1841.

Thompson, Paul. *The Edwardians*. Chicago: Academy Chicago Publishers, 1975.

Thompson, Reginald. *Our Empire and the Faith*. London: Congregational Union of England and Wales, 1916.

Thorne, Susan. "Protestant Ethics and the Spirit of Imperialism: British Congregationalists and the London Missionary Society, 1795–1925." Ph.D. diss., University of Michigan, 1990.

Tilly, Louise. "Connections." *American Historical Review* 99, no. 1 (Feb. 1994): 1–20.

Times (London)

Trapido, Stanley. "'The Friends of the Natives': Merchants, Peasants and the Political and Ideological Structure of Liberalism in the Cape 1854–1910." In *Economy and Society in Pre-Industrial South Africa*, edited by Shula Marks and Anthony Atmore, 247–74. London: Longman, 1980.

Tressell, Robert. *The Ragged Trousered Philanthropists*. London: Granada, 1965 [1914].

Trigg, W. B. *History of Providence Congregational Church, Ovenden*. Halifax, John Walsh, 1937.

Trinity St. David's United Reformed Church Records, Leeds. Leeds Archives Department.

Turner, Bryan S. *Religion and Social Theory: A Materialist Perspective*. London: Heinemann Educational Books, 1983.

Turner, Mary. *Slaves and Missionaries: The Disintegration of Jamaican Slave Society, 1787–1834*. Urbana: University of Illinois Press, 1982.

Twells, Alison. "The Heathen at Home and Overseas: 'Race', Class, Gender and the Civilising Mission, 1790–1850." Ph.D. diss., University of York, forthcoming.

————. "'So Distant and Wild a Scene:' Language Domesticity and Difference in Hannah Kilham's Writing from West Africa, 1822–1832." *Women's History Review* 4, no. 3 (1995) 301–18.

Valenze, Deborah. "Charity, Custom, and Humanity: Changing Attitudes Towards the Poor in Eighteenth-Century England." In *Revival and Religion since 1700*, edited by Jane Garnett and Colin Matthew, 59–78. London: Hambledon, 1993.

————. *Prophetic Sons and Daughters: Female Preaching and Popular Religion in Industrial England*. Princeton, N.J.: Princeton University Press, 1985.

Vicinus, Martha. *Independent Women: Work and Community for Single Women 1850–1920*. Chicago: University of Chicago Press, 1985.

Vickery, Amanda. "Golden Age to Separate Spheres? A Review of the Categories and

Chronology of English Women's History." *Historical Journal* 36, no. 2 (1993): 383–414.

Viswanathan, Gauri. *Masks of Conquest: Literary Study and British Rule in India*. New York: Columbia University Press, 1989.

Walker, Vera E., and Elsie H. Spriggs. *Missionary Play Hours*. London: LMS, n.d. LMS Archives, Pamphlet Collection.

Walkowitz, Judith R. *City of Dreadful Delight: Narratives of Sexual Danger in Late-Victorian London*. Chicago: University of Chicago Press, 1992.

Walls, Andrew. "British Missions." In *Missionary Ideologies in the Imperialist Era: 1880–1920*, edited by Torben Christensen and William R. Hutchison, 159–66. Cambridge: Harvard Theological Review, 1982.

Walton, Rev. W., ed. *Other Men Laboured . . . A Grateful Tribute to the Men and Women of Nottinghamshire for Their Faithful Service to the London Missionary Society*. London: n.p., 1945. Congregational Library, Dr. Williams Library.

Wardlaw, Rev. Ralph. *The Early Success of the Gospel and Evidence to its Truth, and an Encouragement to Zeal for its Universal Diffusion*. London: [Congregational] Home Missionary Society, 1823. Yale Divinity School Special Collections.

Ware, Vron. *Beyond the Pale: White Women, Racism and History*. London: Verso, 1992.

Warne, Arthur. *Church and Society in Eighteenth-Century Devon*. Newton Abbot: David and Charles, 1969.

Watts, Michael R. *The Dissenters: From the Reformation to the French Revolution*. Oxford: Clarendon, 1978.

Weber, Max. *The Protestant Ethic and the Spirit of Capitalism*. New York: Charles Scribners, 1958.

Webster, J. B. "The Bible and the Plough." *Journal of the Historical Society of Nigeria* 2, no. 4 (Dec. 1963): 418–35.

Whateley, E. J. *Home Workers For Foreign Missions*. London: Religious Tract Society, 1878.

White, William Hale. *The Autobiography of Mark Rutherford*. With a memorial introduction by H. W. Massingham. London: T. F. Unwin, 1925.

Wicks, George Hoskings. "The Bristol Missionary Society, 1812–1912." N.p., 1912. LMS Archives.

———. "Bristol's Heathen Neighbors: The Story of the Bristol Itinerant Society, 1811–1911." Congregational Library, Dr. Williams Library.

Wilcox, Rev. John. "Jehovah's Name Magnified." London: LMS, 1811. Yale Divinity School, Special Collections. Record Group 29, Box 30.

Wilks, Rev. S. C. "Christian Missions, An Enlightened Species of Charity." London: 1819. Yale Divinity School, Special Collections.

Wille, Charles, the younger. Diaries. East Sussex Record Office.

Williams, Cecil Peter. "'Not Quite Gentlemen': An Examination of 'Middling Class' Protestant Missionaries from Britain, c. 1850–1900." *Journal of Ecclesiastical History* 31, no. 3 (July 1980): 301–15.

———. "The Recruitment and Training of Overseas Missionaries in England Between 1850 and 1900." M. L. diss., University of Bristol, 1976.

Williams, Peter. "'The Missing Link': The Recruitment of Women Missionaries in some English Evangelical Missionary Societies in the Nineteenth Century." In *Women and Missions: Past and Present*, edited by Fiona Bowie, Deborah Kirkwood, and Shirley Ardener, 43–69. Providence/Oxford: Berg, 1993.

Williams, Sarah. "Urban Popular Religion and the Rites of Passage." In *European Religion in the Age of Great Cities, 1830–1930*, edited by Hugh McLeod. London and New York: Routledge, 1995.

Wilson, Joshua. *A Plea for Home Evangelisation*. A Printed Letter To Samuel Morley, Esq., May 20, 1859. Yale Divinity School, Missions Pamphlet Collection.

Wilson, Roger C. *Frank Lenwood*. London: Student Christian Movement Press, 1936.

Wirgman, A. Theodore. "The Boers and the Native Question." *The Nineteenth Century* 278 (Apr. 1900): 593–602.

Wolf, Eric. *Europe and the People Without History*. Berkeley: University of California Press, 1982.

Woodward, C. Vann. *The Strange Career of Jim Crow*. New York: Oxford University Press, 1955.

Wrigley, Francis. *The History of the Yorkshire Congregational Union: A Story of Fifty Years. 1873–1923*. London: James Clarke, n.d.

Yeo, Eileen. "Men and Women in Robert Tressell's World." *Bulletin of the Society for the Study of Labour History* 54, no. 1 (spring 1989), 14–15.

Yeo, Stephen. *Religion and Voluntary Organizations in Crisis*. London: Croom Helm, 1976.

Yorkshire Congregational Union Records. Leeds Archives Department.

Yorkshire Post

Index

In this index an "f" after a number indicates a separate reference on the next page, and an "ff" indicates separate references on the next two pages. A continuous discussion over two or more pages is indicated by a span of page numbers, e.g., "57–59." *Passim* is used for a cluster of references in close but not consecutive sequence.

Library of Congress Cataloging-in-Publication Data

Thorne, Susan
    Congregational missions and the making of an imperial culture in
nineteenth-century England / Susan Thorne.
        p.   cm.
    Includes bibliographical references and index.
    ISBN 0-8047-3053-9 (cloth)
        1. Congregational churches—England—History—19th century.
    2. Congregational churches—Missions—History—19th century.
    3. Imperialism—Religious aspects—Christianity—History—
    19th century. I. Title.
    BX176.T46 1999
    266'.02342'009034—dc21   98-51051

    ∞ This book is printed on acid-free, recycled paper.

Original printing 1999.
Last figure below indicates date of this printing:
07   06   05   04   03   02   01   00   99